ALSO BY ANDREW VACHSS

*Flood*

*Strega*

*Blue Belle*

*Hard Candy*

*Blossom*

*Sacrifice*

# SHELLA

# SHELLA

A NOVEL BY

## Andrew Vachss

Alfred A. Knopf
NEW YORK
1993

THIS IS A BORZOI BOOK
PUBLISHED BY ALFRED A. KNOPF, INC.

Copyright © 1993 by Andrew Vachss
All rights reserved under International and Pan-American
Copyright Conventions. Published in the United States
by Alfred A. Knopf, Inc., New York, and simultaneously
in Canada by Random House of Canada Limited,
Toronto. Distributed by Random House, Inc., New York.

Library of Congress Cataloging-in-Publication Data
Vachss, Andrew H.
Shella : a novel / by Andrew Vachss.
p.   cm.
ISBN 0-679-42416-4
I. Title.
PS3572.A33S48   1993
813'.54—dc20                                             92-75207
                                                              CIP

Manufactured in the United States of America
First Edition

*for:*

Doc Pomus

and

Iceberg Slim

*truth, still shining
down*

# SHELLA

# GHOST

The first time I killed someone, I was scared. Not scared to be doing it—I did it because I was scared.

Shella told me it was like that for her the first time she had sex.

I was fifteen that first time. Shella was nine.

We bumped paths in Seattle. I was in a strip bar, looking for a guy. She was dancing there, taking off her clothes to the music, humping something that looked like a fireman's pole in the middle of the runway.

After her number, she came over to my table in the back, just a gauzy wrapper on over her G-string. I thought she was working as a B-girl between sets, but it wasn't that. Like blind dogs, we heard the same silent whistle. Recognized each other in the dark.

After that, we worked Badger together, riding the circuit. I'm not real big—Shella's as big as I am, taller in her heels. She works out regular, a real strong girl. I don't do muscle—I just talk to the marks, tell them the truth. Most of them get it then—they pay the money and go away. In L.A., a guy didn't listen. Big guy, bodybuilder. Flexed his biceps, came right at me. I stopped his heart, left him there.

♦

We kept moving. Denver, Houston, New Orleans. Shella took a mark home after work one night in Tampa. Back to the motel room just off the strip. I sat near the connecting door, waited for her signal. Nothing. Couldn't even hear her voice. When I let myself in, moving soft, the room was dark. Shella was face down on the ratty bed, lashed spread-eagle with wire coat hangers, a gag in her mouth. Her back was all bloody.

He never saw me coming. In his coat I found his works—a pair of black gloves, a wad of white cheesecloth, and a little bottle with a glass stopper. He had a plastic jar of Vaseline too. I smeared it all over Shella's back so her blouse wouldn't stick to her. Told her to get going, take the car, I'd meet her later, when I got done wiping down the rooms.

When the cops kicked in the door a few minutes later, I was still there.

They threw down on me, pistols and shotguns. Three in the room, probably had backup outside. I went easy. They'd been tracking the freak—he'd done three women in the last month. Same pattern. I told them my story. A drifter, passing through: I heard the noise, went inside—he was working on a girl. We fought, she ran away. He died.

The cops did their tests. Blood tests, DNA. I wasn't the guy who did those other girls—the dead guy was. One of the detectives said they should give me a medal. He wasn't stupid—kept asking me if I might know the girl who'd taken off. The one whose blood was all over the bed. Asked me about who might have been staying in the connecting room next door.

Shella had the car, all the money, everything. I was indigent, they said, so they got me a lawyer. He wasn't much—said the only way I could help myself was if they could find the girl who'd been in the room. I told him what I told the cops.

◆

When we finally got to court, I looked straight ahead in case Shella was dumb enough to show up. Nobody said much to me—the lawyers all talked together up at the front, where the judge was. This lawyer they got me, he came back, told me they had the death penalty in Florida, said I could plead to manslaughter, how did that sound?

I asked him how much time I'd have to do—I didn't care what they called it.

After a while, I said what the lawyer told me to say and they took me down.

◆

I did the time. Quiet time, after the first week. Some wolf thought I was a sheep. I could have killed him quick when we were alone, but then there would just be another one. I know about the other ones. I said I'd do what he wanted. He said to meet him in the showers.

He was there, waiting. I turned my back to him, dropped my towel, bent over. I felt his hands on my waist, and it happened like it always does. I whipped an elbow into his throat—crushed his Adam's apple. He went down, holding his throat, trying to scream. I got hold of his face in my hands. I could feel all the bones in his skull—I could feel them start to crack. The shower room floor was hard tile. The water was coming down on us. Blood ran out of the back of his head.

I could feel the other cons come in behind me, watching. Nobody did anything. It was a crazy, wild place, that prison—they wanted to watch me kill him. I got my thumb in his eye. Pushed it through until I felt it go all wet and sticky.

The guards pulled me off. I put my thumb in my mouth, sucked on it while I stood against the wall. I knew what they would think. That I liked the taste.

The wolf didn't die—they transferred him someplace.

◆

I got thirty days in solitary. When they opened the cage, I watched for a while. To see if the wolf had friends. Nobody came.

I was a good inmate. After what I'd done to the wolf, I couldn't fool anyone in there, but they stayed away. That's all I ever want.

The work wasn't hard. I didn't talk to anyone. Didn't have any money on the books, so I quit smoking. They came around to my cell, told me how I could get cigarettes, get anything I wanted. I looked at them until they went away.

I never got a visit, never got a letter.

In my cell, I did my exercises. Not like the weightlifters,

just stretching and breathing. Slowing down inside so I could count my heartbeats.

They let me out on a Monday.

♦

You can go a long distance in three years. I'm no good on the phone, talking to people. I reported to the Parole Officer, got a job working produce.

Soon as I drew a paycheck, I went back to the bar where Shella was dancing when it happened. Sat through all the shifts, came back a few times. She wasn't there.

I walked the strip, checked every runway in Tampa. Shella wasn't dancing there anymore. One night, in one of the bars, a man offered me a job. I don't know how he knew.

When he paid me, I bought a car. Kept looking. Couldn't find her.

I did a couple more jobs for the man, saved my money. When I had a stake, I headed north to Atlanta.

♦

I don't have a picture of Shella. Just in my mind. Big girl, white-blonde hair, gray eyes. Some things she couldn't change. The beauty mark on her left cheek, just past her lips. I put it there. She wanted one, asked me to do it. I rubbed some Xylocaine into the spot, froze it with ice cubes. Burned a hypo needle in a match flame, held two fingers inside her cheek to steady it, tipped the needle in black India ink, jabbed it in a perfect little dot—my hands are real steady. Shella said she never felt it, but

I could see little things move in her eyes while I was doing it.

Her name too. She gave it to herself. She was a runaway, she told me. When she was a kid. Some social worker in one of the shelters told her she had to come out of her shell. So they could help. A shell, that's what she needed. So she turned it around, made it her name. She told me it was all she had that was really hers.

But she didn't use it with people—it was a secret she told me. When I met her, her name was Candy. A runway dancer's name.

◆

I always thought about Shella in prison, but I thought about her strong now. Stuff she told me, signs on the track.

◆

Atlanta has a strip, they all do. Shella would be dancing someplace. She wouldn't turn tricks, wouldn't have a pimp. I asked her about that once, if she ever had one. She told me her father.

I was in Atlanta a week. Bought some stuff I needed while I was looking around. I'd never find her, the way I was working. I thought about a guy in New York. I'd done some work for him, years ago. He would maybe have something for me, for how I do it—up close. I don't use guns or bombs or anything. I could see him again, maybe make a trade.

Before I left, I got a set of ID from a guy who sent me to another guy. Driver's license, Social Security card, like that. The guy asked me if I wanted a passport, cost an extra grand. I told him no.

I bought a better car, a nice Chevy, couple of years old. I paid cash, drove it right off the lot. I mostly live in it now, keep my clothes and stuff in the trunk.

♦

In Baltimore, one of the dancers came and sat at my table after her shift, hustling drinks. Told me she wasn't allowed to date the customers, she'd get fired if the boss found out. But she'd take a chance, she said, flicking her red fingernail against one nipple, licking at her lips. Because she liked me so much.

We went to her apartment. It was Badger, like I thought. She was on her knees when the hammer came in. Big guy, said she was his wife. Going to hurt me for messing around in his patch. I told him how scared I was, took my pants off the bed, handed them over so he could have my wallet. He watched my eyes, never saw my hands. The girl didn't move to help him, didn't make a sound.

Shella wasn't like that. I had trouble with a mark once. It was in Phoenix. He took my first shot to the side of the neck—I heard a crack but he didn't go down. Pulled a straight razor out of his shirt pocket. I backed off to get room to go again when Shella hit him from behind, an icepick in her hand. She stabbed him so many times I had to pull her off.

The hammer had almost three grand in his pockets, half a dozen different credit cards, a little gun with a pearl handle. The girl talked fast, said he made her do it, she was afraid of him. Showed me a little round scar on the inside of her thigh. Cigarette, she said, a present from the hammer. So she'd remember.

He wasn't dead. I could feel the pulse in his neck. I told the girl I'd have to tie her up, give me time to get away. She said she wanted to come with me. I figured she was just scared, scared stupid—if I wanted to do her, taking her out of there would just make it easier. She lived with the hammer—let the cops think she'd done him, taken off. I told her she could take one suitcase.

◆

On the highway, she wanted to stop a couple of times, use the bathroom. I pulled off to the side of the road, walked her into the bushes. She didn't try to run.

I spotted a motel just off the Pennsylvania Turnpike, circled around, stopped at a 7-Eleven, bought enough food for a couple of days, went back and checked us in.

She told me her name was Misty. A short, chunky girl, heavy thighs, breasts too big for her body. Implants, she told me—the hammer made her do it.

I told her I'd have to tie her up. So I could get some sleep, not worry about her doing anything. She wiggled on the bed, smiled at me, said a little girl like her couldn't hurt me. That was what the hammer thought about me, I told her, and she held out her hands for the rope.

◆

She woke me early in the morning. Soft, just rubbing against me. Asked me, didn't I want to finish what we started just before her man came into the room? I thought about what Shella told me once, how it's evil to hurt someone's feelings, just to be doing it. How it's worse than a beating, makes you feel like nothing. So I didn't say anything to Misty. Never even untied her. She acted like it made her feel good, made little noises in her throat, went to sleep right after.

I didn't know what to do.

I had to find Shella.

◆

In daylight, she looked older. I untied her so she could use the bathroom—there was no window in there, nothing she could do.

She came out wrapped in a couple of towels, hair all wet. Sat down on the bed next to me.

"What are you going to do with me?" she asked.

"I don't know."

"You let me go, you're afraid I'll go back to the block?"

"Your man's not dead. He's not gonna go to the cops. You go back there, he's gonna thank you for saving his life, you tell him the right story."

"You don't know him. He likes to hurt me. He doesn't need an excuse."

"So?"

"So I can't go back."

"All right. You stay with me a few days. You got friends in Baltimore? Make some calls, find out if anything's going on?"

"Just a couple of girls at work. They'd know, maybe. But they'd rat me out in a minute, there was money in it. They're mostly junkies anyway, always getting busted. I couldn't trust them."

"You got money?"

"Yes. In my suitcase. You want me to get it for you?"
"No. It's enough, get you someplace, start over?"
"Yes.
"Okay. We'll do that, couple of days."

◆

Misty couldn't drive, said she'd never learned. Shella was a good driver, but kind of wild—I always had to watch her, especially on the highway. I took the wheel all the way past Philadelphia, found another motel near Trenton.

I didn't tie her up that night. Prison teaches you to sleep light, even with the door locked. One guy, he dropped a dime on this shakedown gang, took a PC lockup, thought he was safe. They filled a plastic bottle with gasoline, squirted it in between the bars, dropped in a match. The guards couldn't get close enough to open his cell. By the time they got a hose down the corridor, he was gone. They never got the smell out.

Misty was still asleep when I woke up in the morning.

I asked her again if she had enough money. Made her show it to me. She had a few thousand. Holdout money. Shella never did that with me. I told Misty I'd drop her at the bus station, or she could come along as far as Newark, catch a plane.

She told me she had no place to go, asked me where I was going. I told her Chicago.

She said she always wanted to try it there, said she heard it was good pickings.

I told her I was going alone. She asked me, did I have a girlfriend.

I made her stay in the bathroom while I took a shower.

I could see her through the cheesy plastic curtain. She took off her clothes and we had sex when I got out.

♦

On the road to Newark, Misty was quiet. I thought about it. I don't look like much—even if she described me, it wouldn't help the cops. But the car, the license plate . . .

I'm not a good thief, don't even know how to hotwire a car. We had to get a car once, in a hurry, me and Shella. She broke in, got it started. She thought it was funny, I didn't know how to do it.

Misty looked at me like she knew what I was thinking. "You don't like to hurt girls, do you?"

"I don't like to hurt anyone."

"I don't mean that. I mean . . . *like* to hurt them. For fun."

"It's not fun."

"Maurice liked to hurt me."

"Don't go back."

"I'm not. I'm good, you know. Real good. Everybody says so. I'm good. I look better when I'm dressed up. I could go with you."

"Why?"

"To *be* with you, okay? I can make money. Dancing, whatever you want."

"I don't want anything."

She started to cry then. Soft, to herself, not putting on a show. It reminded me of something, couldn't remember what.

◆

I drove through this long tunnel from New Jersey. It let us out in Times Square, long blocks lined with hookers. They looked used.

There's a hotel there, right near the highway. I put the car in the lot, checked us in for a week.

It didn't take long to unpack. Misty bounced around— she really liked the room. Took a real long shower. When she came out, I was lying on the bed, feeling the room.

"How come you keep it so dark in here, honey?"

"I was resting," I told her. I always rest inside myself when I'm not working, but I couldn't explain that to her.

She crawled on the bed, nuzzling between my legs. "Can I buy some clothes tomorrow, Daddy? I left most of my stuff back in Baltimore."

"I'm not your daddy."

"Yes, you are. My sweet daddy. You're gonna take care of Misty, aren't you?"

I shifted the muscles in my back, sat up. "I'm nobody's daddy," I told her. Quiet and nice. "You want to buy clothes, you got money. I'm not taking care of you."

"I know I have money, baby. I showed it to you, re-member? I was just . . . like, asking permission."

"It's yours, you use it the way you want, understand?"

"I'm sorry."

"You got nothing to be sorry about," I told her, and let her do what she thought would make me happy.

◆

She stayed up with me all that night, doing things. I listened when she talked, working my body around to a new clock. Where I had to look, I could only do it at night.

We finally fell asleep. When I opened my eyes, it was after one o'clock. Misty was sleeping on her belly next to me, my belt wrapped around her wrists, looped over the bedpost. I touched a spot in her neck and she came around.

"What's all this?" I asked her, pulling on the belt.

"I didn't want to wake you up, baby. So I tied myself up. I know it's stupid . . . I mean, I could get out of it and all . . . but I thought you'd feel better if you got up and saw me like this."

"It's okay," I told her. "You don't need to do that any-more."

She smiled. A big smile, like I just gave her something.

◆

She took another long shower. Put on black stockings with seams down the back, spike heels. Did a couple of turns in front of the mirror.

"You think my legs look longer in these?"

I told her they did. She shoved herself into a push-up bra, put on a little black jersey dress. I watched her from the bed.

She took the hotel key, went out. Came back in a half-hour or so, had a little paper bag with cigarettes and some cosmetic stuff, couple of newspapers. I read one of the newspapers while she made some calls.

I closed my eyes, listening to the purr of her voice on the phone. When she hung up, she put some stuff into a little purse, dabbed some heavy perfume between her breasts.

"I got an audition at four—I'm not sure when I'll be back, maybe I'll be working tonight . . . okay?"

"Okay. Leave the key with me. Tell the desk clerk you need another one for yourself, slip him ten bucks. It'll be all right."

She kind of posed in front of me. "Do I look sexy?"

I told her she did.

◆

I started looking that night. Not for Shella, for the man who could help me find her. He wouldn't do something for nothing, this man. I never expect that—something for nothing, that's a whore's promise.

There isn't a lot of street sex in Times Square. Come-ons, to get you inside. Movies, books, magazines, video-tapes. The places where there's real flesh, they always let you know. Live Girls, a lot of the signs say. Like there's dead girls in the other places.

In the live places, the girls are on stage, or behind glass. You put a token in a slot, the window opens up, the girl moves around, shows herself, says things. Your time runs out, the window closes, you have to put another token in to open it up again. When one of the watchers is done, they send a man into his booth, hose the place down, spray some green-smelling stuff around.

Some of the places, the girls come into your booth. Massage parlors, modeling studios, lingerie shows . . . they have all these names for the same things. They show it to you, you want to touch it, it costs you more money. The more you want the girls to do, the more it costs.

Come and Go, Shella used to call those places.

I passed them all by, not looking for her there. Shella wouldn't be in any of those places.

Little knots of hunters on the street too, looking for someone weaker than them to take down. Smash and grab. Police cars cruised around the blocks, blue and white. Right past guys selling drugs, saying "Smoke?" when you went past.

In the windows, big radios, the kind kids carry on their shoulders. Little TV sets you could carry in your pocket. Watches, electronic stuff. All kinds of knives, camera stuff. Sex stuff too: vibrators, fake cunts made out of fur, handcuffs, leather masks with zippers for mouths, dildos.

♦

I walked criss-cross through the blocks until I found the place where I used to meet the man. The club had a different name, but I figured, they do that all the time, he might still be there.

The beefy guy at the door took ten dollars from me. I sat down at the end of the bar. On the stage, a woman dressed like a little girl, short little dress with straps over a blouse . . . like a sailor suit. She had on little white socks, shoes with straps over the front. Dark hair in pigtails. Licking a lollipop, lifting up her skirt with one hand, pulling it down, teasing.

When the bartender came over, I asked him for the man, gave him the name I had. Monroe. I didn't offer him any money to tell me, that's what a hunter would do. I asked him like I was an old friend, been out of town for a while. Shella always said I didn't know how to be slick, but I could do pretty good if I had to.

The bartender went away, like he hadn't heard me. I stayed where I was. He came back, looked me over careful, like he'd have to describe me. I knew that wouldn't do any good—I don't look like anything.

I sat there, watching the woman on the stage bend over, flip up her skirt, pull down her underpants, crawl around so everyone could see. She had a roll of fat on her hips, lumps on her thighs.

The bartender came back again, leaned over.

"If I knew a guy named Monroe—*if* I knew him, understand?—who would I tell him wants to see him?"

I'm no good at that kind of stuff—I never know what to say. I told him to bring me a glass. He gave me a look, but he went and got one. I held it up to the bluish light in the bar. It was medium weight, had spots on it from the dishwasher. I took the glass in my hand, squeezed it until it popped, crushed the glass in my hand, put it back down on the bar—only the bottom of the glass was in one piece. I opened my hand so he could see there was nothing in it. No blood either.

"Tell him it's me," I said.

The bartender looked, said I could find Monroe in this poolroom on the East Side of town. Gave me the address, said Monroe would be there tomorrow night.

◆

I don't dream much. I did when I was a kid. In the institution. I'd wake up, wires in my face like I was screaming, but no sound came out, the blanket all wet from my body. I was always scared then.

Every place they put me, I was scared. All the time, scared. I ran away, a lot. Every place they put me. The foster home, the farm. I could always run away. The last time I ran, I wanted to get far away, so I stole some money from a store. Just grabbed it out of the open cash register and ran. They caught me so easy.

Where they put me, there was no place to run.

Every other place they put me, the grownups ran it. But in the institution, the kids ran the place. Not all of them, just a few.

Duke, he was the one in charge. A real big kid. I think he was seventeen. He was in other places before too. The way you could tell, he had two little blue blobs tattooed on his face. They were supposed to be tears. One for each time he was locked up before.

The first time I saw the tears, I thought, I guess I could get one myself now.

Duke had flunkies with him always. They carried his stuff. He never carried anything himself, not even his cigarettes. They always handed him whatever he wanted, even a knife, sometimes.

The first day I was there, I went in the bathroom. Duke was there, with his flunkies. He had one of the littler kids and he was slapping him. Hard. Over and over. The flunkies laughed. The little kid's face was all red and wet. Duke took the little kid back into the showers. I kept my face down, but I heard them. He made the little kid suck him.

I didn't say anything to anybody. I knew that much from the other places.

When the little kid came out of the bathroom, he laid down on his bunk with his face in the pillow. He was crying when The Man came by. When The Man asked him why he was crying, the little kid said he was homesick.

The Man laughed at him.

Every day was like that. Duke and his flunkies would take everything for themselves. If you were playing basketball when they came up, you had to get off the court. They watched whatever they wanted on the TV. If you got packages from home, they took some of it.

I never got any packages.

The nights were the worst part. The Man never checked on us at night. He stayed outside the dorm, watching his own TV. As long as it was quiet, he never came back where we were.

Fridays, we got our commissary draw. That's when we could spend our money. They held our money for us until then. Every week. On Fridays, you could buy cigarettes, candy, soda pop. It was supposed to last you all week. Duke took some from everyone.

Even the State kids, the ones with no families like me, they got something. For chores, like cleaning up the grounds outside.

One Thursday night, Duke and his flunkies came over to another kid. They woke him up. I kept my eyes closed, breathed deep like I was asleep. But I listened.

"Tomorrow, when you draw commissary, you buy me a chocolate bar," Duke told the kid.

"Please, please, Duke . . . I don't wanna . . ."

I heard a slap. "Shut up, punk," one of the flunkies said.

"Tomorrow," Duke told the kid. "Or I'll cut your fucking heart out."

Friday, the kid drew his commissary. Handed Duke a chocolate bar. Duke unwrapped it, put it on the radiator. I watched the bar get soft until it flowed down the side of the radiator.

That night, one of the flunkies picked up the gooey bar in the paper in two hands. He carried it, walking next to Duke. Duke went to the kid's bed.

"Give it up," is all he said.

The kid turned over. Duke dropped his pants. Smeared the soft chocolate all over his stiff prick and got on top of the boy.

The boy screamed, once. I heard a squishy sound and then he was quiet.

I was so scared I couldn't cry, like no air was in me.

The Man never came in.

The boy went to the Infirmary the next morning.

It was two weeks later, summer just starting, when Duke told another boy to bring him a chocolate bar the next day. We were chopping weeds on that Friday when the boy who had to bring the chocolate bar, he brought the scythe down over his foot. It went right through. I could see a piece of his toe in the tip of the sneaker.

The Man took him to the Infirmary. They know all about stab wounds there, but they don't keep you long. They took the boy to the hospital, outside the institution.

I thought the boy won then. But they brought him back a few days later, walking on crutches.

The next Friday, Duke walked by the boy's bed. One of his flunkies held up a chocolate bar. Duke smiled at the boy.

"This time, I got my own," he said.

They gang-banged the boy that night. All of them.

The next morning, The Man took him out of the dorm. He never came back.

I thought about it. Every day. Some days, it was all I thought about.

It was just after the 4th of July when Duke and his flunkies came over to me.

"This Friday," he said, "when you draw, buy me a chocolate bar, okay?"

My heart slowed down when he said that. There was a smooth, cold chill inside me. An icy feeling, but it made me warm inside.

I nodded like it was okay. My voice wouldn't work.

Thursday night. I could feel the moon, even if I couldn't see it from my bed. I walked over to it, shining through the window. Duke's bed is just below the window, the best bed in the dorm.

Everybody was asleep. The cottage was full of night sounds, night smells. The Man only looked in when there was noise.

Duke had a big portable radio, the kind with speakers on the side and a tape player and everything. One of his flunkies carried it around for him. I lifted the radio down from the shelf. Big fat batteries inside. I took them out, quiet, quiet.

Duke's sneakers were at the foot of his bed. Brand-new white leather sneakers. His socks were inside, dirty socks from yesterday. One of the boys did his laundry every week for him.

I took out one of the socks. Put the batteries inside the toe. One by one. Soft, so they wouldn't click together.

I held the ankle-part of the sock in my right hand and walked around to the head of the bed in my bare feet. Where Duke was sleeping on his back. I spread my legs apart. I could feel wetness on my face but I didn't make a sound. I swung the sock between his eyes as hard as I could. His nose splattered, red and white. He made some moaning sound and rolled over, moving his hands, but I smashed the sock into the back of his head again and again. White stuff came out of his head onto the pillow.

When I stopped, it was all pulp. The sock was sticky with hair.

I put the sock on the floor, went back to my bed.

They found Duke in the morning. Some men in white coats came later, with a stretcher. They covered his face with a sheet.

That night, Friday night, Duke's flunkies walked over to my bed. One of them was carrying his big radio. They put it on my bed and walked away.

Later, I turned it on. They'd put new batteries in it for me.

◆

It was almost five in the morning when I heard a tinkle of metal against glass. The quarter I'd put on the doorknob fell off into the ashtray I put on the carpet right under it —somebody trying the door. I slid off the bed, stood over to one side. Misty came in, closed the door behind her real quiet, walked over to the bed.

I said "Ssssh" from behind her—she gave a little jump.

"You *scared* me, honey!"

"It's okay. I didn't know it was you."

"I didn't want to wake you."

"It's okay." I sat down on the chair, watched her as she took off her clothes.

"I got a job," she said. "Dancing. First place I went to, that's good luck, right? I worked a whole shift too." She took some bills out of her purse. "Look, baby. Tips. For only one night. A new girl always does real good."

She handed me the money, the same way the flunky handed me Duke's radio.

♦

In the morning, Misty moved real soft in the bed, pulling off the little blue silk wrapper she was wearing, put her head down between my legs, licking, like she was going to wake me up that way. I shifted my body to let her know I was awake.

She looked up at me from between my legs. "I'll do whatever you want," she said, voice rough and soft.

I closed my eyes. She was a dancer now, Misty. Like the woman I saw in the bar last night, dressed in little-girl clothes. She liked me, Misty. Because I didn't get any nasty fun out of hurting her, the way the hammer did. That was enough for her.

It made me sad.

Shella came into my mind. One night, I came home later than her. She was dressed in a little-girl outfit, like that woman last night. Sat on my lap, made baby noises. I slapped her so hard she fell on the floor, started crying.

It was the first time I hit her, the only time. The only time she ever cried too.

"I only wanted to please you, Daddy," she said. "Men like little girls. I know."

I held her for a long time while she cried then. Promised I'd kill her father for her one day. So she could watch him die.

Thinking about Shella, I grew hard in Misty's mouth.

♦

New York City is a cross-hatch. The streets run east to west, the avenues north to south. The poolroom wasn't more than a couple of miles away. It was a little before ten o'clock when I started out, walking. Misty had gone to her job.

Walking downtown along Eighth Avenue, I saw everything. Cop cars drove past like they didn't.

The poolroom didn't have a sign or anything, but the number was on the door. I opened it, climbed up some metal stairs. It smelled like a housing project.

Upstairs, it was a big room, maybe forty tables. Old-style, all green felt, leather pockets. Sign on one wall. It just said NO in big letters, then little words next to it: Gambling, Foul Language, Alcoholic Beverages, like that.

The place was mostly empty, a dozen tables in use. Just like the prison yard: blacks in one piece of space, whites in another. Spanish, oriental. All separate.

The guy at the desk gave me a plastic tray of balls, pointed to an empty table over in a corner, by the windows.

I carried the tray over to the table, took the balls out one by one. I rolled them around the table with my hand, testing for drag and drift on the felt. The cloth was worn, but it ran true.

I checked the cue sticks racked along the far wall. Numbers are burned into the sticks to tell you the weight.

The highest number was 22. I looked through them until I found one with nice balance, good tip. Put some talc from a dispenser in my left palm, worked the stick through until it slid smooth. Racked the balls, rubbed the cue tip with a little cube of blue chalk I found on the table.

I broke the balls, started sending them home, one by one. It was peaceful there, the table clean and flat, the ivory balls clicking together, going where I sent them.

"You're pretty good," a guy said, coming up behind me like a surprise. I'd seen him when he first started to move. Red-haired guy, light eyes, little scar at the corner of his mouth.

"Thanks," I said.

"You . . . wanna play somebody for somethin'?"

"No thanks. I'm just practicing."

He took a seat on one of the stools, lit a cigarette like he was going to be there for a while. I like the feel of things in my hands. I like making them move, do what I want. When I look close, get locked in, I can see the weave in the felt, the grain of the ivory. The balls look big—I can see the edges where they start to curve. The cue feels like it's coming out of my arm, like a long fingertip. I ran a couple of racks, never looking up. Kiss shots, banks, getting the feel of the rails. I pocketed the last ball, racked them up again, locking the balls against the front of the wooden triangle with my thumbs to make them tight, squaring the angles, getting it perfect. I chalked my cue again, sighting down.

"You calling a shot?" the guy asked me.

"Yes."

"Out of a full rack . . . you *calling* a shot?"

"Yes."

"Which one? Corner ball?"

"Head ball in the side, two rails."

"Twenty says you don't make it."

"It goes about every five times," I told him.

"You want five to one?"

"Okay."

He put a pair of fifties on the table rail. I put down a twenty.

"The five ball?" he asked, making sure. "Five ball in the side?"

"Your side," I said, stepped to the table.

I drove the cue ball past the rack, hard against the back rail, spinning off, cracking into the rack from behind, right between the corner ball and the next one over. The five ball flew toward me, hit the left-hand long rail, banked into the short rail right where I was standing, and dropped into the side pocket like it was ducking out of sight.

"Holy shit!" the guy said. I put the money in my pocket.

He stood there, shaking his head. "You're here to see Monroe, right?"

I swept the balls off the table, put them back into the plastic tray.

"Yes," I said.

♦

He followed me over to the front desk, where I paid for my time on the table. There was a door behind the desk. The red-haired guy knocked, stood there a minute. I heard bolts being turned, and we went inside.

It was a big room, eight-sided poker table in one corner,

four men sitting there. Monroe was at the table, back to the wall.

A thick guy put his hand on my shoulder, like he was going to pat me down.

"Don't bother," Monroe said.

I walked over, stood looking at him.

"Ghost! My man! Haven't seen you in years. You haven't changed a bit, huh?"

"Neither have you," I told him. His black hair was thinner—I could see pale scalp. And his face was heavy, jowly. But I meant what I said.

"Sit down, sit down. You want a drink?"

"A glass of water," I said, sitting down. The guy to Monroe's left laughed. Nobody paid him any attention.

"Man, you should see this guy play, Monroe. Like a fucking machine," the red-haired guy said.

"I've *seen* him play," Monroe said, looking up at the redhead with his little eyes. "You wouldn't like it. Go get him his glass of water."

The redhead went away.

"So what's up, Ghost? This a social call?"

"No," I said, glancing around me. Meaning I didn't want to talk in front of a crowd. Monroe never asked my name —always calls me Ghost. I never asked why.

"Take a walk," Monroe told the others.

I waited a couple of beats. The redhead came back with a glass of water. I thanked him. He didn't say anything, just went away again.

"I'm looking for someone," I told Monroe.

He held up his hands, like he was pushing somebody away. "I don't get involved in other people's business."

"It's not for that," I said. "A woman. My woman. I lost

track of her, last time I was locked up. She's a dancer. I
figure, maybe you could ask around, reach out . . . help
me find her."

"It's not business?"

"No."

"What'd you have?"

"Her name is Candy. Big girl, late twenties, early thirties. Real light blonde hair, about my height."

He shrugged his shoulders. "A blonde named Candy,
dances topless . . . There's a thousand girls fit that description."

"She's got real light eyes, like a gray color. And a little
dot, a beauty mark, just over here," I told him, touching
the spot on my face. "And a long thin scar, like a wire-
mark, on her right thigh, all around the outside."

"What else?"

"She won't turn a trick. She'll B-drink, dry hustle, strip.
But she won't sell pussy. Not out of a bar anyway."

"They all will, the right guy comes along."

"She won't have a pimp."

"She's a lesbo?"

"No. I don't know, maybe. . . . It doesn't matter. She
won't give her money to anyone else."

"Okay. You know her righteous name?"

"No."

"She got people anywhere?"

"No."

"She could be dead, in jail, whatever. Could be married,
have a couple of kids. Those broads, they can't strut the
runways forever, you understand?"

"Yes."

He took a long aluminum tube out of his jacket pocket,
unscrewed the cap. It was a cigar, wrapped in dark paper.

He clipped off the tip with a little round knife, cracked a wooden match, got it going. "You want this as a favor?" he asked.

"No."

"Same old Ghost. Nothing for nothing, huh?"

"Right."

"So what you got?"

"Money?"

"How much?"

"How much do you want?"

"No money. I *got* money. How about you do what it is you do *for* money . . . for me. One more time."

"Okay."

"Just like that, huh? It don't matter to you?"

"No."

"I'll start tonight, looking. You come back, say, Friday night, same time, okay? Maybe I'll have something for you."

"Thanks."

"And I have your word, right, Ghost? You'll do this other thing for me?"

"Yes."

"It's a deal," he said, leaning forward to shake hands.

◆

Misty got back to the hotel just after I did. She should have been tired from working a shift, but she was all bouncing around, excited.

"I made even more money tonight, baby. It's really good here. We're doing good now, right? Could we, maybe, get an apartment or something? So we didn't have to live in this one room. It's like a prison cell."

"No, it isn't," I told her.

"I didn't mean like *actually*, honey. But, if we have a place of our own, we could have . . . stuff, you know? Our own furniture, maybe. So we could eat a meal inside once in a while, not all this take-out. Could you just *think* about it, okay?"

"I told you, I don't think I'll be staying here long."

"You're leaving?"

"I don't know what I'm doing. But I'll know soon, all right?"

"All right, baby. Whatever you say."

♦

The next couple of days, I stayed inside. Practicing. I can make myself invisible, kind of. Slow down everything inside of me, so slow I can feel the blood move in little streams through my chest. I go somewhere else in my head. Not far, I'm still me. But someplace closed off. Where I don't feel things. It just happened one day, when I was a kid— when they were hurting me. Now I can do it when I want to.

♦

One afternoon, Misty asked me to come to her club.

"I'm on television, honey."

"What?"

"Don't look at me like that—I don't mean like on *real* TV. In the window. It's a new thing. Couldn't you please do it? Just once. I'd really like you to. I mean, you've never seen me . . . work. I'm real good, everybody says so. That's why I'm in the window."

"Is anybody leaning on you?"

"It's not *that*, baby. Please?"

♦

I went the next night. It was just like she said. The club
was just a narrow doorway with a little window on one
side. They had a TV set suspended from wires hanging
there. Black-and-white, like you can rent in cheap rooms.
One long loop, the same stuff. Over and over. I stood
there and watched until Misty came on. You couldn't tell
where she was, like in a dressing room or something. She
had a regular dress on. The camera watched her pull it
over her head. She had a slip on. She took it off. Then
she was in a bra, panties, high heels, and stockings. She
kicked off the shoes, unrolled the stockings, bending over
with her back to the camera. She unhooked the bra from
behind, dropped it on the floor. She was just rolling the
panties down over her hips when the tape looped to some
other girl.

The barker was a greasy little guy in a blue jacket. He
didn't yell and scream like the other ones on the block,
just waited for someone to stop and watch the TV, whispered to them.

"They go all the way inside, pal," is what he said to me.
"No cover, no minimum."

I went through the door. Dark place, the air stung my
eyes. I ordered rum and Coke. Don't mix them, I told the
sagging topless waitress. Like I was worried about watered
drinks. She gave me a wink like I was a smart guy, knew
my way around. I drank a little bit of the Coke, poured the
shot of rum into the glass. The waitress came back a little
later.

"You don't like the Coke, huh?"

"Just for a little taste," I told her. She brought me another. I did the same thing, left her enough of a tip so she wouldn't make a fuss . . . but not so much that she'd think about working me for more.

A Puerto Rican girl with a blonde wig was on. There was music, but she wasn't really dancing. Just shaking her body parts with the music around her. People threw money on the bar. She'd kneel and pick up the bills. When she got enough, she rolled them all into a little tube, held it up so the watchers could see it, kissed the little roll, stuffed it deep inside her G-string. Every once in a while, she'd pull down the G-string real quick. The money was gone. Inside her, someplace. The men applauded, like she'd done something good.

Misty was different. She really danced, like she was moving to the music. The men didn't clap real loud for her until she got on her hands and knees, crawling the length of the bar, still moving to the music. She took a glass from in front of one man, put one hand inside her G-string, like she was playing with herself, sipped from the glass. Then she poured some of it right on the bar, put her face down, wiggled her butt real hard while she lapped it up. They really cheered for that. Men put money on the bar—Misty crawled over to the ones who put up the most, let them spill their drinks on the bar so she could lap them up again. She crawled off the stage when her number finished, looking back over her shoulder.

◆

When Misty got back, she looked tired. I was watching TV with the sound off, trying to figure out what people were saying from the way they moved. She just said a quick hello, went in the bathroom. I heard the shower.

She came out with a towel around her head, still a little wet.

"Honey?"

"What?"

"I thought you were coming tonight."

"I did."

"I didn't see you."

"I was there."

"Yeah."

"You think I'm lying?"

"I didn't say that, honey. . . . Don't be mad."

"Come here."

She came over to me slowly, her face down. Got on her knees beside the chair. "I'm sorry," she said.

"On the TV screen, in the window, it was black and white, showed you taking off your dress and all. Everything but your pants. Inside, you were dancing to some song . . . 'Fever,' I think it was called. You crawled around on the bar, licking up drinks they spilled."

"You *did* come!"

"Yes. You were very good. Dancer, I mean. Much better than the other ones. You move real nice, like a real dancer."

There were tears on her face. She took the towel off her head, held it in her hands, twisting it like she was trying to get the water out.

"What's the matter?" I asked her.

She put her head in my lap, her hands behind her back. I felt her teeth on the waistband of the pajamas I was wearing. She pulled the string loose, put her mouth on me. I patted the back of her head, sleek from the water. When I got close, I pulled gently back on her hair but she just sucked harder until I went off in her mouth.

♦

Friday night, I went back to the poolroom. They gave me a different table this time. Three tables away, a bunch of Chinese guys were playing, but not really, something else was going on. I watched them the way I watch the TV without the sound. Somebody was buying, somebody was selling. I couldn't tell what.

The red-haired guy came over to my table. "You want to try that shot again?" he asked me.

"No."

"How come? I'll give you the same odds."

"It won't go on this table. The short rail's too stiff."

"So we'll take the table you had before."

"I'm here to see Monroe."

"Yeah, so what? It'll only take a minute."

"I'm here to see Monroe," I told him.

We went through the same door. Monroe was at the table alone this time. I sat down across from him. I could feel the redhead, pushing against a cushion of air just off my left shoulder.

"What?" Monroe said, looking up at him.

"This guy has my money. He hustled me with some trick shot last time he was here. I asked him to do it again, same deal. He wouldn't do it. I should get a chance, get my money back."

"How much did you lose?" Monroe asked him.

"A yard."

Monroe took out a roll of bills, peeled off a hundred, tossed it on the table. "Get lost," he told the redhead.

"I want it from him," the redhead said, not moving.

A crackle in the air, all around me. I could feel watchers, like prison. I didn't move.

Monroe leaned forward. "Don't be stupid," he said.

The redhead was so close I could feel the air from his mouth. "I could do it," he said. "You don't need some outside shooter, do this job. Way I figure it, it's a big contract, this guy's taking my money."

"Go over there and sit down," Monroe said. "I'll talk to you later."

"Hey, come on, Monroe. This guy don't look tough to me."

"Cancer don't *look* tough either. You're out of your league. Now, do what I tell you."

"Hey, fuck you, Monroe."

Monroe looked at me. "You want to fuck this guy up, Ghost? Little favor for me?"

"No."

"You don't do favors for friends?"

"I don't fuck people up."

Monroe started to laugh then, a thin, crazy laugh. It sounded like that glass cracking in my hand. Nobody laughed with him.

"What's so motherfucking funny?" the redhead said.

"You don't get it, do you, kid?"

The redhead backed away, making a triangle out of me and Monroe with him at the tip.

"Get up," he said to me.

I didn't turn around, watching Monroe. "What's the going rate for assholes, Ghost?" he asked me.

"It's the same for anyone," I said.

He laughed again, more juice in it this time. "Okay," he said.

I got up. The redhead was right in my face. He was staring hard. I moved my eyes around his face, getting his picture. His size and shape, the set of his body.

I sat down again. "Okay," I told Monroe.

◆

We went out the back door to a fire escape, climbed metal stairs to the roof. Everybody came up there. One of the other guys brought a metal folding chair. He opened it for Monroe.

City lights all around us, but the roof was dark. Flat, just an electrical shack to one side, big skylight on the other. The door to the shack opened, a man stepped out. It must lead downstairs, be locked from the inside so nobody could burglar the place.

I took off my jacket. I was wearing a sweatshirt. Extra-large. It was baggy on me, loose and comfortable. I pulled it up to my neck, taking the T-shirt with it, holding it like that so they could see I didn't have a gun. I walked around a few feet, feeling the roof under the thin soles of my gym shoes.

The redhead took out a knife. A big one, brass knuckles around the handle, little teeth along the top edge of the blade.

One of Monroe's guys stepped forward, a short piece of rope in his hand.

"You want to rope dance?" Monroe asked the redhead.

"No, fuck that. Just give him a blade—let's get it on."

The guy stepped back. Everybody took out money, whispering in the black corners.

"Okay?" Monroe asked the redhead.

"Yeah. Do it!"

Monroe nodded. "You okay, Ghost?"

I nodded, watching the redhead. He came in like a crab, in a crouch, the knife in his right hand, holding it underhand, blade facing in. He took a swipe—I stepped to one side, watching. He was making a noise to himself, like a hum from a generator. Each time he came in, swiped, stepped back. Closing the line, coming nearer every time. I moved my left hand to my right wrist, slid back the cuff to the sweatshirt, let the car antenna slide into my hand. I snapped my wrist and it came out, telescoping to about five feet. I whipped it across his left hand before he saw what it was. He made a noise as I brought it around in a stream, slashing an X across his face. His hands came up, blood sprayed around them, and the knife fell. I kicked it away, moved in on him, giving him time, pulling the cuff off my left wrist. He grabbed for the antenna. I let him take it, raking the sharpened can opener I had taped to my left wrist across his face. I locked it in deep, pulling against the muscles. It caught near his mouth as he hit the ground, me on top. I pulled it free. He was screaming then. I chopped at the side of his neck until I felt it go.

I used the front of his shirt to wipe off the can opener and the antenna. I could smell where one of the guys had thrown up on the roof.

We all went downstairs. Some of the guys paid money to Monroe. I saw the money on the table. Monroe separated some of it, gave it to me. He saw I was looking at the money that was left.

"That's the difference between you and me, Ghost," he said. "Don't ever forget it."

I didn't say anything.

Monroe told me not to come back there. He gave me a place to meet him in two nights. Told me the car he'd be in.

♦

I went out the next afternoon, bought the papers. There was nothing about finding a body on a roof.

I don't read much. Just the papers once in a while. To see if there's trouble. Shella used to read to me, sometimes. It started when I got hurt. This guy was coming to watch Shella dance every night. He asked her for a date—she told him she didn't date the customers. So he started calling her at work. The first couple of times, she took the calls. He scared her, with those calls. That's hard to do to Shella, but he did it. Kept saying, if she wasn't going to give him a piece of ass, he was going to take one for himself. Cut it off her one night. Told her he had a razor. I told her the guy was playing with himself, talking to her like that, getting off on her being scared. I tried to tell her how I knew, from listening to guys like him the last time I was locked up. Freaks, I know them. You just listen, they'll tell you everything. He never came back to the club. I told Shella, just don't talk to him on the phone, he'll find someone else to give his terror to. She promised me. But she lied. I always knew when Shella lied.

He was waiting for her, one night. In the alley behind the club, where she walked through to get to the car. A shortcut. I was there too. Every night, I was there. Ever since I found out she was lying.

He didn't know what he was doing, the freak. When Shella came through the mouth of the alley, he was breathing so loud I could hear him from where I was waiting. You couldn't miss Shella, clicking in her high heels, white-blonde hair piled up on her head. Alone.

The freak knocked some garbage cans together when he got to his feet. Shella didn't run. Stupid bitch, Shella. She stopped, pulled something out of her purse. I could see the red neon glitter on the metal.

"Come on, cocksucker!" she yelled at the freak. "Come and get it. I got one too."

He stepped out of the shadows. It looked like he had only one arm, the sleeve of his coat dangling empty. Nothing in his other hand. He staggered like he was drunk, mumbling like he was scared Shella was a crazy woman, going to hurt him for nothing. She made a disgusted noise, snorting through her nose. She only saw a crippled drunk, trying to find a quiet place to sleep. Dropped the razor back in her purse, spun around, and started to walk out of the alley. He flew at her like a giant bat, coat flapping around him. The angle was wrong—I had too much ground to cover. He almost had her from behind when I kicked his knees from the side. He went down against the wall, came back up fast. I went at him from the empty-sleeve side—felt the flash of something heavy coming at me, threw up my hand—the lead pipe cracked across the side of my hand, right into my face. I didn't feel it until after I was done with him.

Shella got me into the car, took me to the room. My left eye was closed, my nose was all flat, pushed to one side. It bled a lot.

We couldn't go to a hospital. Shella got ice from the ice machine in the hall, wrapped it in a towel, smashed it with the lead pipe. I pushed my nose back where it should be with my fingers and Shella put the towel with the crushed ice over my face, like a mask. She gave me some Percodan she had, and I got woozy—I'm not used to drugs.

The lead pipe had tape all around one end, for a better grip. In the freak's wallet, we found the number to the pay phone at the club.

I was lying on the bed, on my back. We'd have to stay a while now. If Shella left the same night the cops found the freak in the alley, if they stopped the car somewhere and saw my face . . .

She came over to the bed, carrying a chair in one hand, sat down next to me.

"You should whip my ass," she said.

I didn't say anything.

"This is my fault. I didn't listen to you. I was talking to him on the phone, every time he called. Told him he better leave me the fuck alone, I wasn't playing. I thought he'd run away, I talked to him like that. But it made him mad. I didn't want to tell you . . . what I did . . . so I decided I'd deal with him myself. Phone freaks, they never show up in person. Like flashers. I was on the train once, in Chicago. Late at night. This guy opens his coat and it's all hanging out. He's hard and all, getting off on it. I ran over and grabbed him, right by the root. Almost yanked it off, the motherfucker. I thought . . . I'm sorry, baby."

"It's okay," I told her. Tired, not sleepy.

"You want me to . . . ?" she asked, trailing her fingers along my cock. It was soft, small.

"No."

She gave me a little kiss on my chest. Got up and went somewhere.

When she came back, I was the same way. I could feel

her sit in the chair next to the bed. "Would you like me to read to you, honey?"

I said "Sure." I don't know why I said that.

It was one of those romance books she was always reading. Paperbacks. I listened to her read, watched the story in my head. It was a stupid story, something about a princess. Her father wanted her to marry the son of some other king, make some political deal. She ran away. She got captured by some pirates. They had her tied up in a chair when the pirate captain came in. She started giving him orders when I fell asleep.

Shella fed me hot soup the next morning. Washed my face with a hot towel, gave me another Percodan, made another ice mask for me. I laid down, resting. She asked me, did I want her to read to me some more.

I told her okay.

She went to work that night. She said, if the cops took her, she wouldn't tell them where she lived. If she didn't come back, I should figure she was locked up.

She came back, though. Said the cops didn't even question the girls in the club.

Shella got a bunch of different books. She'd get them at the drugstore, off the racks. All kinds. She read to me every morning, every night when she got back to the room.

I got better every day.

One night, she asked me what was my favorite. Of all the books she read to me.

I didn't like the sex books. Or the westerns. The mysteries, like with clues, they were too complicated, too silly. I thought about it. The Sherlock Holmes stories, I told her. When she asked me why, I told her because the stories were short. When she was at work, I thought about it. Why

I liked those stories. They were so close, always together, Holmes and that doctor. Watson. Friends to the end. Real partners. Even when Watson got married, he was with Holmes. Holmes, he was ice-cold. Always did the smart thing, figured stuff out. But in one story, I forget the name, he told some guy, if anything had happened to Watson, the guy was dead.

There was lots and lots of those stories. Some were longer, like books.

Shella read to me all the time when I was getting better. Even after we left that town, when my face was healed, she would read to me sometimes. Like a treat.

There were still plenty of the Sherlock Holmes stories left when I went down in Florida.

◆

I met Monroe a little after midnight. He gave me the address: Pike Slip, off South Street. It was under a big highway on the East Side, slab of concrete like a parking lot, but no cars came there. He was in a black limo, like he was coming from a party. I saw it pull in from where I was watching. The glass in the back windows was black like the car.

I stepped out so they could see me. The back window came down. I walked over.

"Get in, Ghost," Monroe said.

Inside, it was like a living room. All leather, even a wood bar that came down from the back of the front seat. Just Monroe in the back seat. I could see two men in the front, sitting behind a screen, facing front.

"You ready to work?" he asked me.

"Yes."

"I'm a businessman, okay? I got a lot of business. There's this guy, Carlos. Carlos the Colombian, they call him. He don't know how to do things—he's a fucking animal."

I don't care why people do things. Everybody's got a reason—it doesn't change anything, why they do it. But I didn't tell Monroe that. I learned, from doing this a long time, I learned not to say anything. I just let people talk until they tell me what I need. Sometimes I nod, like I'm listening.

"We told this fucking guy, we told him he can't move weight in this town without the say-so. He's got prime stuff, I'll give him that. All we wanted was a taste, just a slice off the top. I told him nice, there's plenty for everyone, don't be greedy, you know?"

That's when I nodded. So he'd finish.

"He fucks with his own product, thinks he's Superman, nobody can take him down. Goes everywhere with this fucking army. Way I heard it, he's got himself a deal. With the *federales*. Walks around like he's got immunity. Never gets busted. Anyway, you can't get to him where he lives. Wherever the fuck *that* is, someplace out in Queens, Jackson Heights. Chapinero, they call it. Spanish for something, maybe their home town. It's all Spanish out there, wall to wall. You speak any Spanish?"

"No."

"Anyway, it ain't the money, Ghost. Everybody's got a boss. Even me, I got to answer to people. I've been paying the slice myself. For a couple a months now. You understand what I'm saying? I slice his action off the top, they slice mine. They don't care how I get it, I got to get it. They know he's moving weight, they expect me to slice it.

I tell them I can't move on this guy, they move on me. That's the way it works, right?"

I nodded again.

"Only place he goes, only place we know, is this club. Over there, in this Chapinero. Looks like a storefront on the street, but the whole cellar, they use it for this club. He goes there alone, goes downstairs alone, anyway. Leaves his boys upstairs. He likes to dance, down there. Brings a broad with him, puts on a show. I got people, watch him. He don't carry a piece.

"I send two shooters down there, couple of weeks ago. Another guy for backup. The two shooters get dead. The guy who comes out, he tells us, the place is all dark, little spotlights on the dance floor, that's all. This Carlos, he's dancing with some cunt, got his hands all over her. The shooters roll on him, bang-bang, they both get dead. The other guy, he didn't see the whole thing, but when the lights come on, Carlos, he's just standing there, nothing in his hands. Turns out they was shot in the chest, head-on. Like it happened by itself. No way Carlos does it, not like that."

Monroe's face looks at me. Just his face, not his eyes. "You got nothing to say?" he asks me.

"No."

"You understand what I'm telling you? He shoots people without a gun, okay?"

"Okay."

"This is the guy you got to do, Ghost. Here's a picture of him. You do this, I'll find this broad, Candy. I'll hunt her down for you." He looks at me with his eyes now. "We got a deal?"

"Yes," I told him.

♦

When Misty got home, I asked her, does she have to work every night.

"I don't *have* to, baby. I mean, I could have a night off anytime, I guess, I just ask the boss."

"Do you want to go someplace with me? A nightclub, like?"

"Sure! I love to party, honey. I didn't think you . . . Where would you like to go?"

"This club I heard about. In Queens. It's supposed to be nice."

"Can we go tonight?"

"Next week," I told her.

♦

I took a train to the neighborhood the next day. When I bought the token for the subway, the lady gave me a map, different-colored lines, all the stops on there. It started out underground, but then it went outside. I got out, walked around. Like Monroe said, the whole neighborhood was Spanish—the restaurants, the drugstores, even the newspapers. I walked by the storefront. It looked closed in the daytime, the window was painted over. I could read the neon sign, even when it wasn't lit. Bajo Mundo.

I couldn't see if there was a back way out. People wouldn't come to a nightclub on the subway, but I couldn't see a parking lot either.

I walked around a little bit more. I wasn't worried about people getting a look at me. Nobody sees me.

♦

I went back the next night. The elevated-train platform looks down on the club. I stood there, looking down. Cars drove up. Fancy, sleek cars. A couple of guys out front, they would take each car, drive it off somewhere. Somewhere off the block—I couldn't see where they went. Like at a country club.

I was counting the cars, trying to figure out how big the place was inside. It was about ten o'clock. The man I was looking for, I couldn't see him. Maybe he didn't come until late.

I felt them come up behind me, but I kept watching, over the railing. When they got close, one said something in Spanish. I turned around. The guy who was talking, he had a gun. They were wearing those sweatshirts with hoods on them. I was all the way at the end of the platform, dark there. Other people maybe a hundred feet away. I knew they wouldn't do anything.

I put my hands up. The guy without the gun, he reached in my jacket pocket, took out my wallet. There was maybe three hundred bucks in there. He took it. The guy with the gun made a motion like I should turn around. I did that.

I heard them move away. One of them said something. Marry-con, it sounded like.

♦

Just before midnight, three cars pulled in together. The man I was watching for got out of the back seat from the middle car. He looked just like the picture Monroe showed me. The man held out his hand, and a woman took it, came out after him. They went into the club. Men got out of the other cars, stood by the door.

When other cars pulled up, those men watched.

Just before three o'clock, the same three cars pulled up in front. The man came out, the woman just in front of him. All three cars pulled away in a line.

◆

I got my car out of the garage at the hotel the next afternoon, drove over to the neighborhood. I just drove around for a while until I found a parking space a couple of blocks away from the club. I read the signs. The car wouldn't get a ticket even if it was there for a couple of days. I left it there, took the train back.

◆

I was awake when Misty came back. I smoked a cigarette while she took her shower. She came out, wearing a pink silk thing that sort of wrapped around her.

"Do you like this?" she asked me.

"It's pretty."

She did a spin so I could see the whole thing. Sat down on the bed. Stretched like she was real tired from work.

I laid down on the bed next to her, looking at the ceiling.

"Can you get credit cards?" I asked her.

"Sure, honey. Someone's always looking to sell them at the club. What kind?"

"American Express, Mastercard, Visa . . . any big card."

"Fresh ones go for a yard. And they're only good for a couple-three days. You know . . . ?"

"Yeah." You can always get credit cards. They rough them off in purse-snatchings, slip them out of pocketbooks in the ladies' rooms . . . then they sell them. Most people use them to buy things. Then they sell the things. To the same kind of people they stole the cards from.

"You have a driver's license?"

"No, baby. I mean, I got ID, but . . ."

"It's okay."

She rolled against me, put her head on my chest, reached down, started playing with me.

"What do you need, honey? Tell Misty, I'll get it for you."

"We need a car. For when we go to this club. A fancy, nice car. We're going to rent a car, leave it there, understand? Go home in our own car."

"Why don't we just take a limo?"

"A limo?"

"Sure! We can rent one. Just for the night, okay? It doesn't cost that much. Like a taxi, only fancy. Some of the guys, the ones who come to the club, they use them. When they're ready to leave, they just make a call, the car's waiting for them out front."

"They're like cabs, right? They have a log, write down where they take people?"

"I . . . guess so."

"No good."

# SHELLA

◆

I thought about it, turned it over in my mind. I don't do things fast, except when I get right to them. Shella wasn't like that, always impatient. She was always playing, not thinking how things would come out.

We had some money ahead, once, and she wanted to rent this little house, like a cottage, right near the beach. It was okay with me. Neither of us was working then. A vacation, she said it was. Nighttime, I would go out to the beach, look at the dark water. Sometimes she came with me. One night, she didn't. When I walked back to the house, I saw the car was gone, no lights on. Figured she went into town—Shella got restless sometimes. I opened the front door, felt somebody there. I slid back out the door, closed it softly, didn't click the latch. I went around the back of the house . . . couldn't find where anybody'd got in. I found a good spot, where I could see the car when she came in. Whoever was inside, they'd have to come out sometime.

The car pulled up a couple of hours later. The door opened and I could see someone inside. Not Shella. Small, dark-haired. Whoever it was closed the door, started for the house. I stepped behind him, locked my forearm around his throat, kicked his ankles, took him down. I smelled perfume, felt long hair. A woman.

"Make a sound, I'll break your neck," I said, quiet. "Who's inside?"

"Candy," she whispered. "She lent me the car. Don't . . ."

"Who are you?"

"Bonnie. Her friend, Bonnie."

"You work at the club?" Her body was slim, slender like a boy's. Whatever she was, she was no dancer.

"Upstairs. I work the phones. Please don't hurt me."

"Where'd you get the car?"

"Candy lent it to me."

"When?"

"Nine o'clock. She brought it out to me. I told her I'd have it back by midnight—she's gonna drive me home."

"It's after midnight."

"I know. She's gonna beat my ass."

I didn't get it when she said it. I walked her over to the front door. "It's open," I told her. "Just walk in, call her name. If she's in there, by herself, there's no problem."

I touched a spot where her neck met her shoulder, felt her jump with the pain. "Don't try to run," I told her.

She opened the door. I heard her call "Candy?" I waited outside.

◆

A light came on in the house. Then another. I went around to the back, slipped in a window. I heard a sound from the front. Flesh on flesh. The girl Bonnie was on her knees. Shella was slapping her with one hand, holding the girl's hair in the other. I stepped forward, let Shella see me.

"What?" I asked her.

"It's okay. This bitch was late, that's all," Shella said to me. She turned her head, looked at the girl. "Weren't you?" she said. Slapped her again, hard.

"I thought—"

"It's okay," she said to me. Again. "I'm taking her home."

Shella was dressed all in black, like a bodysuit. Boots on her feet, face all made up like she was going out. "We'll finish this later."

I didn't know who she was talking to when she said that.

They went out together. I heard the car start up.

♦

Shella didn't come back until the next afternoon. I was in the front room, watching television.

"How come you never put the sound on?" she asked me.

"I'm trying to learn how to read lips."

She gave me a funny look, said she was going to take a shower.

When she came back inside, I was still there.

"You never ask questions, do you?"

"Sometimes."

"What you saw, last night. It's just a game, okay?"

"Sure."

"I do that, sometimes."

"All right."

"You don't care?"

"I don't know what it is."

She sat on the arm of my chair, smelling like soap and powder. "You want me to do something for you?"

I closed my eyes. Felt so tired.

"Want me to read to you, baby? Read you a book?"

I nodded, thinking about it. She gave me a little kiss, a sweet kiss.

When I woke up, it was dark. A blanket over me. Shella was gone.

◆

I knew there was something in the memory. I didn't push it, just let it pass through me. Like pain. I can see the inside of my body, sometimes. I got shot, once. A little gun. Just above the knee. It went in and out. I could see the hole in my pants when I took them off. In and out. I could see the path of the bullet. Like a tunnel, all red and clotted with white stuff. I wrapped a bandage around it, real tight. I saw inside my leg, saw the tunnel close, fill up. It got better. The scars are like dots, front and back.

Memory. Shella slapping that girl. A hotel room. In Huntsville, Alabama. Some convention. Shella said we could make some heavy scores. When we checked in, I saw the signs for the convention. Women Executives. Advertising or something. I gave Shella a look. She winked at me. Told me we wouldn't work Badger—she'd get the money herself. Just be ready if something went bad.

I was in the connecting room when I heard her come in. I heard voices, then the sound of a belt. Shella wouldn't turn hard tricks. I looked through the door. A fat woman was on the bed, face down, her wrists and ankles tied to the bedposts, a pillowcase over her head. Shella was whipping her. The back of the fat woman's thighs were red against her pale-white skin.

Shella showed me the money later. A lot of money. Why was Shella whipping that woman staying in my mind? I never remember anything for nothing. I let it run, waiting.

I got it. When Shella worked that convention, we had another room. In a motel out on the highway. Took a cab to the convention hotel when we checked in. Like we were coming from the airport. When we checked out of the hotel, we took a cab to the airport. Then we caught another one back to the motel, where we had our car.

◆

When Misty got back, I told her I knew how to do it. Told her we'd go next Friday night. She ran over, gave me a big kiss like I'd done something great.

◆

The phone rang in the hotel room. It never rings. Nobody has the number. I pointed at Misty—she picked it up.

"Oh! I'll be right down. No, wait a minute. Can you send someone up with them? Okay. Thanks." She bustled around the room, pulling on a pair of slacks.

"What?"

"You'll see, baby."

A knock at the door. Friendly knock. Misty opened it. A bellboy in a uniform, whole mess of packages on one of those carts they use in hotels to move luggage. The bellboy put the stuff where Misty pointed, on the bed. He never looked at me. Misty gave him some bills. He sort of bowed, saying thanks. It must of been too much money.

When he closed the door, Misty locked it, put on the chain. Danced around, flinging off her clothes.

She opened one of the packages, opened another. Took out a little red piece of leather, held it up.

"Isn't it beautiful?"

"What is it?"

"A *dress*, baby. Wait . . . see, it goes with these shoes, and I have stockings for it, and . . ."

"How come . . .?"

She was looking at the dress—I could see it was a dress, now that she told me—holding it up. "I'll have to use powder to get this on, but wait'll you see . . ."

She ran off into the bathroom. Closed the door. She doesn't usually do that, close the door. I heard the shower. Turned on the TV.

When she came out, she was in the red dress. It was so tight, she had to take little steps. The top of the dress pushed her breasts together so hard they were popping out over the red leather. Big zipper right down the front. The skirt was way up on her thighs. She had black stockings, red spike heels the same color as the dress. Her arms and her neck were bare, hair pulled up on top of her head, long earrings, little red balls at the end, dangling.

"What do you think?"

"It's beautiful," I told her. Shella had pranced around like that once, asked me how she looked. I told her "Good" and she threw an ashtray at me. So I knew not to say that again.

"See how it shows me off, honey? With these heels, and the dark stockings . . . ? Like I have long legs, yes?"

"Yes."

"I don't know how I'm gonna sit down in this. And I can't wear pants under it either. But it's worth it. I mean, I want you to be proud of me when we go out."

"I am proud of you. You look great, Misty."

"For real?"

"I swear."

"Wait'll you see the best part!" she said, rooting around in the other packages.

I watched her bending over the bed. The skirt rode up, white flesh above the thick black bands at the top of her stockings. I could see her sex.

"Look!" she said, holding up some black clothing.

"What is it?"

"It's a *suit*, honey. For you. You don't have clothes for a nightclub."

I let her fuss with the stuff. She was right—I never thought of it. A black suit. Smooth, shiny. A white shirt, like they wear with tuxedos, all ruffles in front. The shirt had little black buttons, black cufflinks. She even had black boots. Alligator, they looked like.

"Everything fits," I said. Surprised.

"I measured you, honey. In your sleep. Every square inch. Do you like it?"

"It's great," I said, letting her close all the little snaps and buttons on the shirt. I got into the pants. The waist was fine, but they didn't feel right. "They're too tight," I said.

"No, they're not. Here . . ." She opened the snap at the top, moved around behind me, reached inside my underwear, grabbed my cock, moved it to one side. "Try them now."

They closed fine. I gave her a look. "That means you carry left, honey. You don't . . . I mean, it's not supposed to be right in the *middle*, you understand? Once you put it where it's supposed to be, it won't move, okay?"

She looked so young then. Like something mattered, so much. I felt Shella near me, nudging me in the ribs, rolling her eyes like she did when she said I was being stupid. "It won't stay like this, I see you in that dress," I told Misty. Her face lit up.

The jacket fit real good. I looked at myself in the mirror. "The shoulders are too big," I told Misty. They stuck way out.

"They're *supposed* to be like that," she said. "It's the fashion."

◆

Later, I was on my back, Misty on top of me, breasts just brushing my face. Inside her, feeling her hard muscles inside the soft flesh. She was wet, dripping on me, pumping.

When she was done, she fell asleep like that.

◆

Later again, she woke up. Rolled off me, lit a cigarette. Put her head against her shoulder, blew smoke at the ceiling.

"How did I look in that dress, honey?"

"Beautiful."

"You *said* that. That's not what I mean. Did you think I looked like a . . . what? A college girl?"

"No."

"A whore, then?"

"No. Not that."

"But . . . what, baby?"

I took a hit off her cigarette, thinking for the truth. "What do you call those things you dance in?"

"Costumes?"

"No. The G-string, like. The little strap that goes be-tween your cheeks."

"That *is* a G-string."

"No. What do you call the thicker ones, like with a panel in front?"

"Oh!" She jumped off the bed, looked through the draw-ers in the fake-wood bureau against the wall. "This?" she asked, holding up a piece of black silk.

"I don't know. . . ."

She climbed into it, showed me. From the front, it looked like a pair of panties, but there was nothing covering the side of her legs, nothing behind but the strip that divided her butt.

"Turn around," I told her. "Bend over."

When she did, it was like she was naked, but her sex was covered by the black cloth.

"What do you call that?"

"A thong, honey."

"Can you get one the same color as the dress?"

"Sure! That's a *good* idea. I shoulda thought of it. You're so sweet. It's . . . prettier that way, huh?"

"Yes."

♦

"Are we going to dance, baby? At the club?" It was the next morning, way before she had to go to work.

"I don't know how," I told her. I hadn't thought about it.

"Didn't you ever learn?"

"No."

"Want me to teach you?"

"It wouldn't do any good," I told her. Thinking of Shella. How she tried to show me. "Just hold me, one hand on my shoulder . . . like that . . . yes . . . one hand on my waist, okay? Now just move with the music—I'll follow you." It didn't work. I tried and tried—I never get tired—but it didn't work. I kept bumping her, pushing her around, stepping on her feet. Shella finally quit. "I don't get it," she said. "I've watched you snatch flies out of the air without even hurting them. You move so beautiful when you're . . . working. But . . . it's like there's no music in you." I shook my head. Misty came over to me, smiling.

"Come on, let's just try, okay?"

I went along with it. Some song playing on the radio. It was no good. Finally, Misty just put her head against my chest, stood there close to me, swaying a little until the song was over.

◆

Friday afternoon, we took off. Misty had made a reservation at one of the motels near the airport. LaGuardia Airport, only a few miles from where we had to go later. The cab dropped us right in front, like we came in on a plane.

The room was the same as all of them. Misty took a shower for a long time. I watched TV. Then she made a call, to have the limo come for us at ten o'clock that night. She laid out everything on the bureau: makeup, nail polish, hair brushes. She said she was going to take a nap, to wake her at seven so she could get ready.

I thought it through while she was asleep. It didn't have to be tonight. Maybe he wouldn't even be there.

◆

We stood out in front of the motel, waiting so the limo driver wouldn't have to call up to the room. The parking lot was full of people making deals, standing around in little groups, talking through the windows of cars. They weren't slick about it. I saw a car pull up, three guys walk over to it. Two other guys got out of the back, opened the trunk. One guy looked through the trunk, took out a flat suitcase, opened it up, looked inside. They traded the suitcase for an airline bag, and the car drove off.

Men walked by, looked at Misty. She held on to my arm, just a light touch. Two men came up the steps, all dressed up in peacock clothes. One of them smiled at Misty, said something in Spanish. The other looked at me real hard. I dropped my eyes. I could smell their perfume as they went past us, laughing.

The limo was on time. The driver had a business suit on, wearing a cap with a little peak. He opened the back door, held it for Misty. We climbed inside.

Once we got rolling, Misty told him we changed our minds, gave him the address of the club, not someplace in Manhattan, where she'd told them at first. He looked over his shoulder, said he was sorry, but it would have to be the same price. Misty told him it was okay.

The cops ask him any questions, all he'd ever remember was Misty busting out of that dress. Me, I look like anybody.

The limo pulled right in front of the club. The driver came around the curb side. I got out first, held out my hand to Misty. Just the way he did, when I was watching him from up on the train platform.

I gave the driver a twenty. Misty told him we'd call his dispatcher when we were ready to come home.

The two bodyguards out front never looked at us.

Inside the door, a man was sitting at a white table, a gray metal box in front of him. I gave him a hundred, he handed me back a fifty. A short, muscular guy was standing next to the table. He tilted his head, and we followed the directions. There was another room straight ahead. I stood still while a skinny guy ran his hands over me. He wasn't playing around, checked my ankles, inside of my thighs, small of my back. He had a knife in a shoulder holster—I never saw one like that before.

A woman was there too—looked like a jailhouse matron, short hair, heavy forearms. She ran her hands over Misty, looked in her purse.

We kept walking, following some people in front of us. Staircase leading down. I went first, feeling Misty's hand on my shoulder.

We found a table against one wall. The place was dark, soft blue lights running in thin tubes all around the ceiling. A waitress came over, wearing a short black dress with a white apron in front. Misty ordered a frozen Daiquiri, I ordered rum and Coke, two glasses.

The room was laid out in a crooked circle, tables all around the sides. In the center, there was a dance floor. The music was slow, stringy stuff . . . guitars and piano. I couldn't see a band, the music came from everywhere. Finally, I spotted a few of the speakers—there must've been dozens of them.

A couple of tables away, a tall woman with a wild mane of black hair took out a mirror, tapped some coke onto it from a silver tube, chopped it into lines, snorted a line into each nostril through a rolled-up bill. Then she passed the mirror to the man with her.

When people went on the dance floor, baby spotlights shot down from the ceiling. Off and on, little pools of white light, big puddles of black. Like prison searchlights, just roaming around, nobody at the controls.

I drank some of the Coke, poured the shot glass of rum into what was left. When the waitress came, we ordered the same again.

After a while, we got up to dance. Just stood on the edge of the dance floor, not moving. Misty rubbed against me. I put my head down so I could hear what she was saying, but she was just singing some song to herself.

◆

He came in just before midnight. With the same woman. They took him to a table that stood off by itself. Nothing else was close to it.

I couldn't be sure it was him, this Carlos that Monroe told me about, until he got up to dance. A tall, narrow man, black hair pulled straight back from his forehead, tied in the back with a ponytail. He was wearing a long white coat, like cowboys wear, only silk. When he stood up, it was almost down to his ankles. The woman with him was wearing pants made out of that stretch stuff, like they wear for exercising, so tight her rear was two separate halves. The pants were black around the calves but they got lighter and lighter as they went up. The part covering her butt was silver. He held the coat open and she stepped inside, dancing by herself while he stood there. His hands were covered with diamonds—he held them so they framed her butt, silver wiggling inside the flash. Her hands were around his waist—I couldn't see them under the long coat.

When they sat down, a waitress brought him a silver tray, little mound of white powder on it. The woman with him had a tiny spoon on a chain around her neck. She sat on his lap, scooped some powder, held it to his nose. Did it again. She didn't take any for herself.

◆

A heavyset man came in with a blonde on his arm. The blonde was in an orange dress cut all the way down to her waist, held together with straps across the front. Misty leaned over to me. "You think I look like that?" she asked.

I wasn't sure what to say, so I shook my head.

"She looks like a cheap piece of goods," Misty said. "No class."

I nodded, watching the woman on the man's lap.

Carlos and the woman got up to dance again. The music was faster now, but Carlos still didn't move. The woman was climbing all over him, twisting like a snake, working hard.

"What's that dance, that they're doing?" I asked Misty.

"It's the Lambada . . . or, anyway, it's *supposed* to be. That skinny bitch can't shake it worth a damn. You see the way those pants are cut . . . to make her look like she's got a decent butt? She wouldn't last ten minutes on a runway."

The woman's legs were all hard muscle under the pants. I still couldn't see her hands.

◆

Misty got up to go to the ladies' room. When she came back, she told me all about it. Gold trim around the mirrors, a maid with towels, trays of perfume, coke.

The later it got, the more crowded it was. The smoke was so heavy it stung my eyes. Misty was used to it, she said it wasn't so bad.

I got up to dance with Misty again. We moved closer to Carlos. I watched him over Misty's shoulder. His eyes were closed.

In between dances with the woman, he hit the spoon again and again. The woman never got up by herself, never went to the ladies' room, never left his side.

I figured it out, finally.

◆

I pulled Misty's chair right against mine, put my arm around her, moved her close so I could whisper to her.

"I'm going to do my work soon," I told her. "Walk out, like we had a fight or something. Get them to call you a cab. Go back to the motel, check out. Take a cab back home."

"What're you . . . ?"

"Ssssh, Misty. Just do it, okay?"

"Baby, couldn't I . . . help you or something?"

Her bare shoulder was warm under my hand. I rubbed her flesh with my thumb, making a little circle.

"Is there a window in the ladies' room?"

"I don't know, honey. I mean, I didn't see one. But I could go and look. . . ."

"Yeah. Do that, okay. I'm going to take a look around myself."

She went off. I gave her a couple of minutes. Then I walked across the dance floor, found the corridor to the men's room, went inside.

It was fancy, like Misty described. But you could see it had been a corner of the basement, once. Maybe there'd been a restaurant upstairs. I went into one of the stalls, last one on the end, near the wall. Pipes running all around the base of the wall. I saw a paper tag wired to one of the pipes. Brooklyn Union Gas, it said.

I came out of the stall, washed my hands, looked in the mirror so I could see the place. In one corner, two pipes running floor-to-ceiling. On the side of the pipes, a round valve. For the kitchen that used to be upstairs?

I got back to the table before Misty did. She sat down, waited till the waitress brought us some more drinks. "There's a window, baby. But it's a real little one, with bars on the outside."

"It's okay. People watch you real close in there? Could you maybe do something before you leave?"

"Honey, I could do *anything*. . . . It's like an orgy room back there. They're all snorting up, making a mess. I saw two girls going at it in one of the stalls, right in front of everybody. This one girl was standing on the toilet with her dress up and the other one was lapping it up. They didn't even close the door."

"Yeah, they're doing it at the tables too."

"Not coke, baby, sex. This one girl was standing on the toilet with her dress all the way up and this other one was eating her. It was disgusting. . . ."

"Okay." I handed her three books of paper matches. "Put a lighted cigarette in the matches, like this." I showed her.

When the cigarette burned down, it would hit the match heads, make a little flash flame. Shella taught me that trick. "Is there a trash can, for tissues and stuff like that?"

"Yeah. There's a couple of them."

"You think you could throw a lighted cigarette in there, wrap the matchbooks around it first?"

"Sure."

We got up to dance again. The floor was so crowded now, people kept bumping into us—especially Misty. I put my lips real close to her ear, holding her tight.

"When we go back to the table, you just sit there and wait. When I come back, you go to the ladies' room, do what we said. Soon as you dump the cigarette, walk right upstairs and step out on the sidewalk. Like you need some air. Grab a cab."

"What're you . . . ?"

"I'll see you later, okay?"

She pulled my face down, gave me a deep kiss.

◆

It took me a while to work my way through the crowd to the men's room. I waited till it was pretty empty. Waited some more until I was alone. Then I stepped out of the stall. The attendant was cleaning up near the door. I stepped over to the pipes, grabbed the valve, and twisted hard. It wouldn't move. I pulled in a deep breath through my nose, got a better grip, then let it out as I twisted it again. I felt little pinpricks in the back of my neck, pain around my eyes . . . felt the valve give. I twisted it open all the way, heard a little hiss.

I went back outside. Misty got up, rubbing her head like it hurt. She went off.

I smoked two cigarettes, slow and easy. It was about fifteen minutes before I smelled it, just a faint undertrace, but I knew what it was. Couldn't move yet. Carlos was still sitting down.

Finally, he got up to dance. I got up too, started across the floor. The woman was wiggling against him, hands behind his back. I heard someone say "Gas?" I guess it's the same in Spanish. People were moving around, the music was loud. . . . Some of them could smell it.

I stepped behind the woman, hooked her as hard as I could in the kidneys. The blow knocked her into him. He spread his arms and she went down, crumpled. I could see the gun in her hand, but she was gone. His mouth was open. Somebody screamed. I shot a left into his ribs, my right hand knife-edged against his neck as his head came down. The gas smell was strong now. "Fire!" I heard someone yell. Everybody started running for the exit, a crazed crowd, stomping over each other.

I got out in the middle of the mess, running. Found the car where I left it.

♦

When I got back to the hotel, Misty was already there. Still in the red dress. She hugged me real tight, told me she got out of the club without any problem. The TV was on. She'd been watching the news. There was nothing.

I took off my clothes, took a shower. When I came out, she was still in the red dress.

"I wanted to keep it on, baby. It looks so pretty, doesn't it?"

"It looks perfect," I told her.

Early in the morning, just before she fell asleep, Misty

moved against me. "Will I ever get to wear my dress again, honey?"

"Sure," I said, holding her till she nodded off.

◆

In the papers the next morning, they just called it a gas leak in the social club. One unidentified dead man, broken neck. And a woman, broken ribs and internal injuries. They'd interviewed the woman when she came out of surgery. She said she hadn't seen anything—everybody panicked, it was a mob scene.

I thought about the gun in her hand. That woman, his bodyguard, she wouldn't say anything, ever. She wasn't his woman—it was business.

◆

I waited a couple of days, then I went to see Monroe. He was sitting where he was before. All the same people with him, except for the redheaded guy.

"Ghost! Like a fucking ghost, just like I said. How'd you do it?"

"Did you find her?" I asked him.

"I got feelers out all over the place. Don't worry about it. She's out there, I'll find her for you. Where do I . . . ?"

"I'll come back," I told him.

◆

When I came back in another week, he asked me if I had a picture of Shella. I never had a picture of Shella.

◆

Two more weeks went by. I went to see Monroe. I just stood there, looking down at him.

"You scare me sometimes, Ghost," he said. "Look, I can't come up with the girl, how about I just pay you the money instead?"

"No. That's wasn't what you said."

"Okay, okay. I'm still looking, got feelers out all over the place. Remember what I told you? Maybe she's not working. . . . She's in jail or married or something, it could take a long time to track her down. It ain't like you got any ID on her."

"I know. I'll wait."

◆

I told Misty I'd be going soon. On a trip. Somebody was looking for an old friend of mine. When they found her, I'd go out there to see her.

"In Chicago? Is that where you'll be going?"

"I don't know. Wherever she is."

"Remember when we first talked about it? In the car? I always wanted to try Chicago."

I didn't say anything.

The next morning, Misty got home from the club, took her shower, got in bed with me. I was awake.

"Honey, remember when I was telling you about the ladies' room? In the club where we went dancing? I didn't mean to give you the wrong idea."

"About what?"

"What the girls were doing in there. The lesbian stuff. When I said it was disgusting . . . ? I didn't mean doing it was disgusting . . . just, in the toilet like that, in front of everyone, you know what I mean?"

"Sure."

"I mean . . . some men, they think it's the most beautiful thing. To watch. You ever notice that? Like in porno movies . . . ? Guys'll watch two women going at it, really get turned on. But you never see women watching movies of men doing each other. How come you think that is?"

"I don't know."

"You ever . . . go to one of those movies?"

I did, once. A gay movie. The guy I was paid to do, he went there all the time. Cruising, they call it. It was the easiest one I ever did. I just sat in the back where they told me. The guy came in, sat down next to me. Didn't say a word at first. I just watched the movie, didn't answer when he started talking to me. I let him unzip my fly. When he put his head down, I broke his neck.

"No," I told her, rubbing her back.

"You think maybe you'd like to . . . someday?"

"No. I got nothing against them. I knew one. From when I was inside. Real hard guy, kept to himself."

"I don't mean *men*, honey. Girls."

"I don't go to the movies much."

"I know. But you liked that time we went, didn't you?"

"Sure." It was called *Goodfellas*. A movie about gangsters. The guy who wrote it, he knew what he was doing, how they work. It didn't seem like a movie at all, except for the music. I wished I could have watched it without the sound.

Misty put her hand between my legs, rolling onto her side, talking low against my chest.

"I could bring a girlfriend home some night. From the club, after work. Would you like that, baby?"

"Bring her here?"

"Or someplace else, if you want. There's a girl works at the club, Chantal. She goes both ways. I know she likes me, I can tell. We could put on a little show for you. I'd like that, if you would. I'm not the jealous kind, I know how to share."

"That's okay."

"You don't want me to?"

"No, it's all right."

◆

It was a Thursday night when I saw him again.

"I've been waiting for you, Ghost. Your girl's working in Cleveland, a joint off Euclid Avenue, downtown. You know it?"

"I've never been there," I told him. It wasn't true—I did some work there once. Don't know why I didn't tell Monroe.

"It's called The Chamber, this joint. Real hardcore, the way I hear it."

He was watching my face as he was talking. He doesn't usually do that. I put my eyes at the top of his nose, right between his eyebrows.

He lit a cigar. "She's using the name Roxie. She's not on

the books—the manager says she only works part-time, Friday, Saturday night, like that."

"Thanks."

"Anytime, Ghost. I'm a man of my word. Besides, I wouldn't want you getting mad at me, coming back to see me."

"I wouldn't do that."

He gave me the address of the club, asked me how I would get there. I told him I'd drive out, take a couple of days.

◆

I called Cleveland information from a pay phone. They didn't have a listing for this Chamber place. It didn't mean anything. Some of the clubs, they advertise in the Yellow Pages and all, some of them just have a pay phone in the back.

◆

I told Misty I'd be gone a couple of days, maybe a little longer. Packed some stuff in an airline bag. She sat on the bed, watching me.

"You'll be back?"

"Sure."

"You promise?"

"Why you asking me all this?"

"I'm sorry. I mean . . . I know we don't . . . just . . . I thought we could . . . keep on. . . ."

"It's okay," I told her.

◆

I took a plane into Cleveland, told the cab driver to take me to an address I remembered. On the West Side, near the water. They call it The Flats, this section.

When I got out of the cab, it had all changed. Last time I was there, it was a rough neighborhood. Waterfront bars, strip joints, whores on the street, places where you could rent a room, nobody asked your name. Now it was all fancy restaurants, little shops where you could buy expensive stuff, looked all new.

I went further along the West Side, out on Detroit Avenue. Finally, I found a place, little sign said ROOMS. I paid the man some money. Everybody had hillbilly accents. The room was small, bathroom down the hall.

◆

That night I went to the club. It was right where Monroe said it would be. No pictures of the girls on the outside. Man at the door, all dressed in black.

"Members only," he told me.

I turned to walk away. I was going to wait until the place closed, talk to Shella when she came out.

"Membership costs twenty bucks," the man said.

I gave him a twenty, went inside. It was dark, like a cave. A woman was standing next to a post, hands wrapped in leather straps high above her head. A little red ball was in her mouth, a strap around the back of her head like a gag. She had no clothes on. Another woman stood next to her, high black boots that came almost to her knees, a black corset pulled tight around her waist. When I walked past, she said "Fifty bucks." I kept walking over to the bar, asked the man for a rum and Coke like I always do.

I sipped the Coke, watched. Two women came over to the girl tied to the post. They gave some money to the woman in the corset. She picked up a leather handle with thin straps attached to it, whipped the other woman three times.

People were all in costumes. Masks, chains. It smelled like a hospital where somebody was going to die.

A stairway in one corner. Doors to rooms on the side. It felt like the ceiling was very low but I couldn't see it.

I looked around some more. No stage. No dancers.

When the bartender came back, I asked him if Roxie was on tonight.

He looked at me close, for just a second. Told me she wasn't—wait there and he'd find out for me, when she was coming back.

A man sat down next to me, another man with him, a studded collar around his neck. The first man held a leash to the collar. He asked me for a match.

I gave him a little box of wooden matches. He said thanks. Struck a match, held it against the hand of the man on the leash. I could see the flesh burn, but the man on the leash didn't say anything.

The bartender came back. Said Roxie would be coming back on Tuesday. I thanked him, left ten dollars on the bar.

I walked out. When I got on the sidewalk, I turned left, looking for a cab. A man in a raincoat came out of the alley. I was on him before he could get the sawed-off out of his coat—I heard the shotgun go off as my fingers went for his eyes, felt a stinging against my legs, twisted my body against the wall, and pulled him down with me. Shots came from in front of me, chipping the brick wall. The man's body caught a couple of them, one nipped the fleshy part of my arm.

A siren ripped out. I heard shoes slapping on the sidewalk. I bent down to make sure the shotgun man was finished. The sawed-off was on a leather strap around his neck so he could swing it free when he needed it. A photograph was taped to the inside forearm of his coat. My picture, black and white. I pulled it free.

I left the man's body there, kept moving through the alley. Came out on the next block. Started walking.

◆

I walked for a long time. A black girl came up to me, asked me if I wanted to have a party. I asked her how much. She said twenty-five, ten for the room.

I told her okay, gave her the money. She took me to this hotel, signed the book for us. We went upstairs.

Little room, one light bulb hanging from the ceiling. The sheets were yellowish, washbasin in one corner. There was no chair. I sat on the bed.

"You want some half 'n' half, honey? Get your motor started?"

"Unbutton my coat," I told her.

She did it. My shirt was red around the muscle. "Take it off," I said.

She knew what I meant. Was real careful about it. There was a slash across my arm—the bullet hadn't gone in.

"Can you get some hot water here?"

"Down the hall, honey."

"Here's what I want. You get me some hot water, okay? Real hot. I'll put my arm on the windowsill, you pour the water across it. Then you tie my shirt around it. Tight. Tight as you can. Then I'm gone. I'll give you another fifty bucks, okay?"

She nodded. I gave her the fifty. Opened the window with my left hand in case she didn't come back quick.

But she did. She poured the hot water over my arm. It ran off clean, but it was bleeding a lot.

She took some stuff out of her purse. Kotex. "It ain't much, but it'll be better than just that shirt, okay?"

I told her thanks. She put the Kotex on my arm, tied the shirt tight around it, helped me on with my jacket.

"Where's the nearest city?" I asked her.

"Big city? Akron, I guess."

"Want to make a couple of hundred bucks?"

"Doing what?"

"Can you get a car?"

"No, honey. I ain't got no car. My man, he's got a car. Nice big car. You want I should . . . ?"

"No. Just give me a hand downstairs, hail a cab for me."

She did it, standing on the sidewalk in her bright-blue dress.

I got in, told the driver to take me to the bus station.

I caught the next bus out to Chicago.

♦

In Chicago, I found a room near the middle of town. The Loop, the cab driver called it.

By the next day, my arm wasn't bleeding anymore. I changed the dressing, used my undershirt.

I went out, found an army-navy store, bought a couple of sweatshirts, a pair of pants.

I got a razor and some other stuff in a drugstore.

When I was clean, I took a cab to the airport, bought a ticket to Philadelphia.

I took a bus from there to Port Authority, then I walked to the hotel.

◆

When I let myself into the room, I could feel how empty it was. Misty's clothes were gone from the closet. There was a note on the bed.

I don't know how to say this. I hope you come back and read this, and I also hope you never come back, and then you won't read this. I don't know, I'm leaving, you don't want me anyway. I need to have a man, I guess that makes me weak. Maybe you don't need anybody. I don't think you do. I know you're looking for her, whoever she is, but I don't know why. I guess it doesn't matter. There's a man who comes in the club, he asked me did I want to move in with him. I never said I would, I never even went with him, not while I was with you, but I'm going now. I paid the room rent for three weeks, so they wouldn't put your stuff out. If you're not back by then, I guess maybe you're not coming back. I never knew your name. But I did love you, I swear.

◆

I lay down on the bed, closed my eyes. Thinking, I have to go see Monroe before I start looking for Shella again.

# JOHN

## ♣

I'm not a plotter. Shella always said the only thing that kept me from going to jail all the time was patience. Because I always know how to wait.

I tried to think it through. Monroe, he never knew where Shella was. He could never find her—it was all talk. Liar's talk. Big, boasting talk, showing off. But it worked on me. He was my hope—I made him into something and he just played it out.

He used me. Then he got scared.

Monroe would know I got away in Cleveland. He paid them for a body and he didn't get one. He'd be afraid now. I don't like it when people are afraid—it makes them smart. He didn't know where I was, but that wouldn't matter anyway. He'd know I'd be coming for him. And all I knew was the poolroom where he'd be.

So what he'd do, I thought about it, what he'd do is be afraid. Have a lot of people around him, watching for me. I didn't know where he lived. Nothing.

If I went back to the bar where I first connected with him, he'd know. They'd send me someplace and there'd be more people waiting for me.

I have to kill him. He lied to me. He made me lose time when I could have been looking for Shella. I did work for him and he didn't pay me. I have to kill him. I tried to talk

**79**

to Shella. In my head. I couldn't see her, but I knew what she'd say.

It didn't take me long to pack. In the top drawer of the dresser, where I kept my underwear and socks, there was a picture of Misty. A big picture, black and white. In her dancer's costume, smiling. On the back was a red kiss, in lipstick. Tiny little writing under it, in pencil. "In case you ever want to look for me, I'll be there." And a phone number. The area code was 904. There was a phone book in the room. In the front, it had a map of the country, with little spaces marked off. What the area code covered. 904 was the top part of Florida.

♣

Nobody paid any attention to me when I walked through the lobby—the room rent was paid. I got my car out of the garage, paid the man, and drove through the tunnel to Jersey.

♣

I followed the turnpike. Right at the speed limit. All the way through Pennsylvania into Ohio. I pulled over in Youngstown, got a motel room, slept a long time.

The next night, I drove past Cleveland, right on through to Indiana. Got off near Gary, found another room.

I slept through the day again.

That night, I found the strip, just outside of town. They all look the same, those bars. There's so many.

No sign of Shella.

♣

In the morning, I kept going west. When I saw the signs for Chicago, I pulled over by a pay phone. I dialed the number Misty had left. A woman's voice answered. Young woman.

"Could I speak to Misty?" I asked the voice.

"She's not here right now. If you'll leave me a number, I'll have her call you back."

I hung up. I guess the woman was Misty's friend. Maybe Misty would call her once in a while, check in. Everybody has a friend.

♣

Stony Island Avenue, that's what the sign said. The whole neighborhood was black, but a lot of people in the cars were white. A pass-through zone. I got back in the car, pulled in behind a white man in one of the those rich, dark boxy foreign sedans. I just followed him until we got downtown, then I peeled off and drove around until I found a place where I could park.

I bought a couple of newspapers. Then I found a room and went to sleep.

♣

At night, I went to some of the places I found in the newspapers. The more you pay, the nearer the girls get. Like bait. Table dancers, lap dancers. Some of the girls could dance, most of them couldn't. Some of them could act—it looked like they were really getting worked up doing what they did. Most of them, they just looked glazed. Nobody looked at anyone's face.

I kept spending money. Not that much money—I didn't have to get that close to know if it was Shella.

One joint had a sign in front: LIVE GIRLS. It made me think about something, but it didn't stay in my mind. I went inside. It was the same.

♣

The next night, I went north. Uptown, they called it. The first place I tried said TOPLESS, but it was full of hard drinkers, not even looking at the girls.

In another joint, I was sitting at a table near the back. A big guy in a shirt cut off to show his muscles was sitting at the next table, yelling at the girls, calling them fucking dykes, cunts, all like that. The bouncer came over, told him he had to leave. The guy kicked up a fuss and the bouncer got his arm up behind the guy's back, walked him out the door. I didn't pay attention, just watched the front so I could see the whole selection of girls before I moved on to the next place.

I felt a hand on the back of my neck. "You too, asshole." It was the bouncer, pulling me up and out of the chair. I stood up and I felt the kidney punch coming—I got my elbow into his lower ribs as I brought my heel down hard across his ankle. His hand let go—his face came over my right shoulder and I kept it going into the top of the table.

People were watching. I got up. The bouncer fell on the floor. In the front, the girls were still moving their bodies, the music was still loud.

I went out the front door. The guy in the cut-off shirt

was walking up the street toward the bar. There was a gun in his hand. His face was crazy.

♣

I didn't go far. Whatever I did in the bar, the guy with the muscles was about to do worse. The cops would be coming. I found another bar in the next block, not a strip joint. They were playing music up on a little stage in front, chicken wire all across, like they were in a cage. I tried to sit in the back, listen to the music. Country music, I guess it was. It was so loud my head hurt. One guy finished his bottle of beer and threw it at the musicians. I saw what the chicken wire was for—they kept right on playing.

After about an hour, I left. It was still early.

The last bar I went to, it was like a place where people do business. The waitresses were topless, and they had dancers and all, but they had booths in the back. I saw men talking to each other, not even watching the girls.

One booth was empty. I ordered a steak sandwich and a rum and Coke from the girl, did what I always do.

I was just going to leave when the Indian sat down across from me.

♣

He put his hands on the table, turned them over once, like it was a secret greeting I'd recognize. All I could tell was his hands were empty. I looked to my left, kept one hand under the table, measuring the distance to him in my mind.

"There's nobody else," he said, like he knew what I was thinking.

I just watched him, listening to the sounds of the joint,

feeling for a change in the rhythm. If there was anyone else, I couldn't pick them up.

Time passed. He nodded over at the pack of cigarettes I had on the tabletop. "Okay?" he asked.

I nodded back. He shook one out, lit it with the paper matches I had there.

He smoked the whole cigarette through, real calm, smoking like he was enjoying it, not nervous or anything. His right hand had a long jagged scar across the back. He ground out the smoke in the ashtray.

"You all right with this now?" he said.

"All right with what?"

"This place. Talking to me."

"Talk about what?" Thinking that maybe he had others outside—by now he'd had enough time to surround the place.

"I followed you from Morton's."

"Morton's?"

"Where you dumped that bouncer."

"I don't know what you're talking about."

"I know. I want to talk to you . . . about some work."

"I'm not looking for work."

"Not a factory, my friend. Not a car wash either. Your work. It's my work too."

"What?"

"I know what you do. I have work for you. You want it or not?"

"No."

He just sat there, the way people sit in prison. Like time doesn't matter, even the time they're doing. I was going to leave first, give him my back. The waitress came over. He didn't stare at her breasts, just ordered a hamburger and a Coke.

"Costs the same as liquor," the waitress told him.

"That's all right. And bring my friend another of whatever he's drinking over there."

The waitress took away my empty shot glass and the water glass with the Coke and melted ice in the bottom. I ate in a place once where they emptied the ashtray with you sitting right at the table—emptied it into a napkin, left a fresh one there for you. She didn't do that. In joints like the one we were in, they take away the empty drink glasses so you don't sit there sucking on the ice. And so you don't keep track of how many you had.

She brought the guy his hamburger, set up my drinks. I sipped the Coke. He nodded, like I was telling him something.

"You really an Indian?" I asked him.

"Half Chickasaw, half Apache. My name's Wolf."

"Wolf." I said it again to myself. It didn't sound right.

He saw what I was thinking. "It's really a longer name. It means something like Wolf of Long Eyes. The spotter-wolf for the pack. But it doesn't translate so good, so I go by Wolf."

"Why'd you come after me?"

"You want to know why you didn't pick me up, tracking you?" I didn't know how he could tell that. "I didn't come after you myself," he said. "I sent it out on the drums. Saw you in Morton's, got the word to my people. I just waited where I was until they got back to me. Then I came in."

"So you got a whole . . . crew out there?"

"Uptown's got the largest collection of off-reservation Indians in America. Different tribes, but it don't matter to the whites. They can't see us, can't tell us apart—it's like having yellow skin in the Orient."

"You been in the Orient?"

"Oh yes. Vietnam. Where I learned my trade. Where'd you learn?"

I didn't say anything, wondering how he knew.

"You don't use guns, do you?" he asked, like we were talking about fishing tackle or something. "We all use different things, get the work done. Is that a special style?"

"Style?"

"Like kung fu, or akido, you know what I mean. I never saw anyone do that before . . . put all their weight in one place."

"What do you want?" I asked him again. Thinking maybe this was the end of it for me. You hear about other guys in the business, how some of them like to make a ceremony out of it, talk to the target before they get it done. Telling me about his tribe and all . . . maybe he was trying to tell me I could take him out but it wouldn't help, there'd be others outside.

"I heard about you," he said. "Not your name. I heard about you for years."

"Not me."

"Oh yeah. You. I earned my name. I'm never wrong. I saw death through a little round circle of glass so many times, until it got so I could see it through concrete. You and me, we're the same. Brothers in the blood. There's men who hunt for trophies, go out into the woods in a Jeep wearing pretty clothes and blast a deer through a scope. They stalk, but they don't see. You and me, we hunt for meat. Meat to eat, meat to live. It's how we live. It's how the pack hunts."

"I don't have a pack."

"I know. But you don't do it for fun."

"Fun?"

"They call themselves professionals. You know, the greaseballs in the fancy suits, dogs on leashes, do what they're told. They don't have a pack either, they just think they do. And when the bracelets come on, they start to sing. Rats run in packs too, but they don't live for the pack, they live for themselves. There's psychos too. They like the taste. After a while, they get to need it. You're one of us, you just don't know it."

"I'm not anything."

The waitress came back, cleared off the Indian's dishes. He held up his empty glass, looked over at me.

"I'm okay," I said.

♣

The girls were circulating around the tables, getting the men to buy them watered drinks. They didn't come near the booths.

"You're looking for a woman," the Indian said. Like it wasn't a question.

"I'm not looking for anybody."

"You're not hunting," the Indian said. "You were hunting, you'd be looking for a man. It wouldn't take you that long to see if he was in a place. You go in and out, watch the dancers, make sure you see the whole shift. Then you try another place. It's a woman you're looking for."

I thought about it. I'd never find Shella the way I was going. After Monroe . . .

"If I was . . . ?"

"Nobody knows Uptown like my people do," the Indian said. "If she's here, I'll find her for you."

"For what?"

"What? For what? What's that mean?"

"What do you want? In exchange."

"Does it matter?" he asked me.

♣

I told him about Shella. I can see her better when I talk about her . . . that's why I do it in my head. He listened, that's all he did, waiting for me to finish.

"There's things you can make different," he said when I was done. "Lose weight, gain weight. Contact lenses. Cut your hair, dye it a new color. You can cover scars, change tattoos. Buy a whole new face, you got the money."

"I know."

"And things you can't." Like I hadn't said anything. "You don't have a picture, right?"

"No."

"Show me how tall she is, barefoot."

I held my hand just between my eyebrows and my hairline, like a salute.

He turned over the menu, just a blank piece of white paper on the back. "Show me the distance between the centers of her eyes."

I put my hand on the paper, spread my thumb and forefinger, closed my eyes, seeing her face. When I got it right, I opened my eyes. He took a black grease pencil out of his pocket, put a little dot at each end of the space I made. I took my hand away. He connected the dots, as straight and true as a ruler. Folded the paper, put it in his pocket.

"She ever get busted?"

"Yes."

"More than once?"

"Yes."

"Felony pops?"

I nodded.

"Ever do time?"

"Not real time. Not since she's been grown. Ten days here, a week there. Sweep arrests, a stolen car once. Nothing big."

"Maybe they'd have printed her?"

"Sure."

"We can't look past Uptown," the Indian said. "Don't come back here."

♣

I tried other places around Chicago. Music bars on Rush Street, fancy joints near the lake, dives on the South Side.

When I got back early one morning, the Indian was waiting in my room.

♣

I didn't ask him how he got in—I'm no good at it, but I know it's easy to do.

"She's not in Uptown," the Indian said.

"Thanks anyway," I told him, but he didn't get up to go like I expected.

"If she was printed, I know someone who could find her."

"Who?"

"A crazy man. He's a trader. Never pays money for work. We did something for him . . ."

I just looked at him, waiting.

". . . and he made good. Did what he said."

"Somebody told me that once . . . that they could find her."

"It'd work the same way as a job—he'd have to pay up front."

"You work for him?"

"No."

"What's in it for you?"

"There's something we have to do. Not you and me, we . . . my people and me, okay? There's places we can't go. Where you could just walk in."

"And I do this work, this work for you, and then I get to see this guy, right?"

His face was sad, like I told him somebody just died. "No," is all he said.

I waited in that room. He lit a cigarette, smoked it all the way through. I didn't move.

He ground out his cigarette butt on the windowsill, took a deep breath.

"I'll take you to him. He'll ask you some questions, make sure you're the right man. If he makes the deal, he'll find her for you. Wherever she is. Then you do it. Whatever he wants. When you finish with him, you do this thing for us. Then it's done."

"And he'll find Shella for me?"

"He'll find her. No promises what he'll find. She could be in jail, could be dead." He looked over at me. "She could be with a man," he said, like that was worse.

"I know."

"And you get it up front. But if he finds her, you owe him. Straight up."

"And you too."

"Me too."

I told him I'd do it.

♣

I didn't look around Chicago anymore. Just waited on the Indian. Stayed in my room. There was no TV, so I listened to the radio. It was mostly hillbilly music. I kept it turned down low, next to my head. They played this song once, I never heard the name of it. A man's going to be hanged in the morning, so his woman goes to the warden. She gives him her body so he'll call the hanging off. But it happens anyway. She did it for nothing. I thought of Shella—how she'd do that.

It made me sad, being cheated that way.

♣

One morning, there was a soft tap on my door. I opened it. It was one of the gay guys who lived together at the end of the hall. His partner was standing just behind him, suitcases on the floor. I didn't say anything.

The guy who knocked was wearing an orange tank top, a fat, soft-looking man, mostly bald.

"We're moving out," he said. "Just wanted to say goodbye."

"Goodbye," I told him, watching. They never spoke to me before.

"You should go too," the man said.

I didn't say anything.

"Show him," his partner said. "Hurry up." His partner was small, dark-haired. He was wearing a white silk shirt, like a woman's blouse. He had makeup on his face, eyeliner.

"You never hassled us," the fat man said. He took some slivers of steel out of a leather case, walked next door. He played with the lock for a second and the door came open. I looked over his shoulder.

The room smelled ugly. Fast-food cartons all over the place, on the floor, everywhere. In one corner there was a high stack of magazines, up to a man's waist. On the wall, there were pictures. A woman on her knees, ropes around her hands behind her back, ropes around her ankles. She was wearing a blindfold. All the pictures were like that. Most of them were slashed, like with a razor. One woman's face had a black X across it. The windows were sealed shut with duct tape. Everything smelled like rot.

"The cops'll be here soon," the fat man said. "Don't open the closet."

I turned around to leave. The little guy with the eyeliner on his face was standing in the door, facing out. He had a pistol in his hand, held close by his leg.

♣

I walked down the stairs to check out, my duffel bag over my shoulder. The clerk didn't say anything, didn't even look up.

When I hit the street, I saw an Indian working under the hood of an old car. I moved slow, so he could see me.

I found another hotel a few blocks away. The window looked out into an alley. The same Indian was out there, working on the same car.

♣

About a week went by. I went for a walk one day, had something to eat. When I opened the door to my room, the Indian was sitting there.

"It's time," he said. "Time to meet the man."

"Okay."

"Not now. Sunday. We have to go to his office. When there's nobody around to watch. Be downstairs, five in the morning. I'll pick you up."

♣

I was there, waiting like he said. It was a cab that pulled up. The Indian was in the back seat. He didn't say anything to the driver. The cab took off. Still dark out.

I couldn't see the driver's face through the partition— he was wearing one of those chauffeur's caps. His hair was long, black.

The cab was quiet inside, moving steady, stopping for all the lights. I saw the meter in the front—it was running, like we were a fare.

We got on the highway, headed downtown.

"You're not asking any questions?" the Indian said.

"I don't have any questions," I told him.

♣

The cab pulled over. The Indian took a little black box from his pocket, pushed a button. I heard a beep from the front seat. The driver held the palm of his hand flat against the plastic partition. The Indian held his hand against it, like the way you shake hands in prison when they don't let you touch.

The Indian got out. I followed him. He had a red rose in his right hand. The building was the tallest one I ever saw—I couldn't see the top from the ground.

♣

The security guard was sitting in front of a whole bunch of little TV sets. Each one had a different picture, black and white. One looked like an underground garage.

The Indian held up the red rose. The security guard hit a switch. One of the little TV screens went blank.

We walked over to the elevators. When the door closed, the Indian pushed 88.

When we stepped off the elevator, the floor was empty.

I followed the Indian down a long corridor, all windows to our left. The doors on the right were all open, nobody inside the rooms. Clicking, beeping sounds, like machines talking to each other. The Indian moved quiet, but he moved fast. The corridor made a right-angle turn at the end, and then we started down another hallway. This was down the middle of the building, no more windows.

The Indian held up his hand. I stopped behind him. He pointed to the carpet in front of us. I looked close. There was a thin line across the hall, side to side. Another one a few feet away. I stared at it until it came clear . . . a bunch of little X's covering about four feet, longer than any man's stride. The Indian held his finger to his lips, pointed to the spot on the carpet where the X's started. He stepped back, took a short run, and jumped over that section. He walked off a few feet to give me room—then I did the same thing he did.

We made one more turn and the Indian walked into an office. A man was at a desk, typing something. He was facing away from us, next to a big window. The Indian tapped on the door frame. The man spun around, like he was surprised to see us.

The Indian walked in, took a seat in front of the desk. I sat down next to him. On the man's computer screen I saw what looked like the floor plan of a building.

The man turned to face us. He had a long neck, a small head. Like a weasel. There was a big lump over one eye, bulging. The lump was pale, even whiter than his face. His eyes were bright blue, like the neon signs they use to get you inside the strip joints.

"You don't make much noise, Chief," the man said.

The Indian didn't say anything.

"Is this him?" the man asked.

The Indian nodded.

The man looked at me like he expected someone else. He turned away from us, tapped keys on his computer. Stuff came up on the screen, black on a white background. Too far away for me to read.

"You ever been in Houston?" he asked me.

I didn't answer him.

"Ever been in the Four Seasons Hotel on Lamar? In Houston?"

I watched him. The Indian didn't move.

"Ramon del Vega was found in a room there. With his neck broken. Looked like a robbery. Except he had a gold-and-diamond Rolex still on his wrist. Almost nine thousand cash in his pockets."

I didn't say anything. I remembered the guy. The people who set it up, they had me registered in that hotel. I got a call. The voice just said "Now" and hung up. I went to the top floor, taking the stairs. Saw the room-service waiter outside the door with a tray. I stood there against the wall. As the waiter was bowing his way out, his hand full of cash, I stepped inside through the open door. The guy inside started to say something. I broke his neck. Then I went back to my room. Two men came to my room, gave me the money I was promised. I checked out before they found the body.

I never knew the guy's name before this.

The man with the lump on his head kept tapping the keys, asking me more questions. I sat there, listening. The man rubbed the lump on his head.

"You're sure this is him?" he asked the Indian again.

The Indian got up, walked over to the side of the room. There was a postage meter, one of those electronic scales. The Indian made a gesture for me to come over, stand by him. The man got up from his desk, came over with us. He walked twisted. Standing next to me, he was much shorter. One leg was in a big crooked boot that laced up the front, like the foot was too big for a shoe. The Indian took something out of his pocket. Flicked his wrist, a long blade shot out. He put the knife on the postal scale. The dial on its face lit up. It said:

0    4.3       1.21.

Then he put his hand on the scale, just barely touching it with his fingertips. The numbers flashed, kept changing. Only the first 0 stayed the same. The middle numbers jumped: 1.1, 0.9, 1.3, 0.7. The end numbers jumped too, only not as much: 0.29, 0.52.

"It reads in tenths of an ounce," the Indian said to the man. "You can't hold your hand steady enough to stop the numbers jumping. It's too sensitive."

"So?" the man said.

"Try it," the Indian told him.

The man put his hand on the scale. I could see him lock up his face, concentrating. He couldn't stop the numbers from jumping. He pushed down hard—it didn't make any difference.

"Pick a number," the Indian told the man.

The man looked at the Indian. Rubbed the lump on his head again. "Zero point six," he said.

The Indian nodded at me. I put my fingers on the scale, getting the feel, letting my fingertips go right inside my head, no wrist or arm between them. I thought about the numbers the man wanted until they came up on the face of the scale. It fluttered a little bit, then it locked in. I held it there.

"Pick another," the Indian said.

"One point eight," the man said.

I let my fingertips go heavier until the number he wanted came up. I locked it in again.

The Indian lit a cigarette. I held the numbers while he smoked it through. The man watched the scale. Then he limped over to his desk and sat down.

♣

We were sitting back across from him. Time passed. I didn't keep track of it. The man looked over at the Indian.

"So what's that prove?"

"You know what it proves," the Indian told him. "You want him to bend a crowbar in his bare hands, break some boards, crap like that?"

"I have to be sure."

"You know how to do that. What you told me. About Raiford."

"He'll sit for it?" The crazy man talked. Talking like I wasn't there.

"You got Wants and Warrants?" the Indian asked.

"No."

"You told me he jumped parole."

The man rubbed his lump again. "You trust me? I could get him pulled in, he's the same guy."

"You won't."

The man sat there for a few minutes. Then he got up, limped over to something that looked like a Xerox machine. He lifted up the cover, turned it on. It made a whining noise. Then he went back to the computer, tapped some more keys. "Okay," he said to the Indian, "let's run him."

The Indian got up, gestured to me to follow. He spread his hand out, palm down, pointed to the glass plate on the Xerox machine. I put my whole palm against it. Left it there for a minute.

"Okay," the man said from his desk.

The Indian took a spray can from next to the Xerox, wiped off the glass.

We sat down again. Waited.

In a few minutes, there was a beep from the computer screen. The man hit the keys again, read the screen.

"It's you," he said.

♣

The Indian and I smoked a couple of cigarettes apiece while the man played with his computer. He spun around in his chair to face us.

"The PVW is off," he said.

"Parole Violation Warrant," the Indian said. Looking at the man, explaining it to me.

"Yes. You're dead," he said to me. "Killed in a train wreck in South Carolina. Amtrak out of D.C., heading for Florida. Unidentified white man, mangled pretty bad. We just ran his prints, got a match with yours. You're off the computers. Dead."

I didn't say anything.

"You know what I want?" the man asked, looking right into my eyes.

I nodded.

"I find your girl, you do this for me . . . that's our deal?"

I nodded again.

"Show us," the Indian said.

"What?"

"You know *he* can do it. . . . Show us *you* can."

The man smiled. His teeth were yellow, crooked, all mashed together in his mouth. He went back to his computer.

♣

"Huntsville, Alabama," the man said.

I watched him.

"Room 907. Marilyn Hammond. Executive VP for an options-trading firm on the coast. Declared an income of one hundred and eighty-eight thousand dollars last year. She's a white female, five foot four, a hundred and fifty-one pounds. Brown hair, brown eyes. Divorced, no kids. That's what she's doing now."

"That's not Shella," I told him.

"No, that's not her, that's what she *does*. This Marilyn, she's heavy into S&M. That's the way she gets off. Your Shella, she's a hardcore top, you understand? After you went down in Florida, she took off. But she didn't go back to dancing . . . she disappeared into the fem-dom underground."

"Disappeared?"

"She can't hide," the man said. "It's easy to find fetish

players. All they think about is their games. It's perfect for your girl . . . she doesn't even have to be an outlaw. She's not even selling sex now. They advertise in the magazines. Role-playing. Discipline sessions. All that stuff. I can find her."

I thought about that cottage we'd rented a long time ago. That girl, Bonnie. Shella slapping her.

♣

"We have a deal?" the man asked me.

"We're changing the deal," the Indian said.

The man rubbed the lump on his head, not saying anything.

"We want to do your work first," the Indian said. "Then, when you find his woman, he doesn't have to come back and see you."

The man smiled his smile again. "So what I promised you for bringing him to me, for getting him to do the work . . . you don't want to wait for that either?"

"No," the Indian said.

"You're worried he's going to find his girl and take off . . . not come back and do the work?"

"No."

"What if he does the work and I don't find the girl for him?"

"You will."

"You threatening me?"

"Yes."

The man turned to me. "You okay with this? You do the work for me first, then I find the girl?"

"You look while I'm working," I told him.

"The Chief here will tell you what I need done, okay?"
"Yes."
"When it's done, you get your girl."
I nodded.
"I can find her," the man said. "I can find anyone."
I just looked at him—this part was over.
"I found you," the man said.

♣

As we stepped outside, a cab pulled up. A different one. We got in the back. The Indian didn't say anything to the driver.

When we turned into the block near where I was staying, the Indian turned to me.

"Get your stuff, check out, okay?"

I did what he told me. The cab was still waiting out front. I put my duffel bag in the trunk.

"You got a car around here?" he asked me.

"Yes."

"Give me the keys." I did it. "Show me where it is."

The cab pulled up next to my car.

"I'll follow in your car, okay?" the Indian said.

♣

The cab went along Broadway, turned into a block lined with apartment buildings on both sides. The sign said Carmen Avenue. The cab came to a stop. The driver didn't say anything.

I smoked a cigarette. After a while, the Indian opened the back door. I got out. We took my duffel bag from the trunk. I followed the Indian inside the building. It was a big apartment, long. It went all the way through: windows on the street, windows out back, into an alley. My car was parked back there.

The Indian opened the refrigerator, showed me there was food inside. Furniture in the apartment, like somebody lived there. He gave me two keys. "One's the front door downstairs, one's for this place. The rent's paid, nobody'll bother you. There's a phone in the living room. When you hear it ring, pick it up, don't say anything. If it's me, I'll talk. If you don't hear my voice, just hang up." He gave me back my car keys too.

"I'll be back tomorrow morning," the Indian said. "I'll call first. Anybody rings the bell downstairs, don't pay attention."

"I got it."

He turned like he was going to go. Then he spun around and faced me. Stuck out his hand, open. I didn't know. . . . I put out my own hand. He grabbed it, squeezed, hard. I squeezed back, careful not to hurt him.

Then he went out the door.

♣

I opened my duffel bag, laid out my stuff. Took a shower. Turned on the TV set. I left the sound off, watching the pictures in the front room. The curtains were closed—it was like night.

A nature show came on. A snake caught a big fat furry animal. It swallowed the furry animal, a big bulge all through its body.

The snake was a monster. Dangerous to anybody. But

when it was all stuffed with food, it could hardly move. And it couldn't bite.

♣

I made a sandwich, took some cold water from the refrigerator. When I finished, I smoked a cigarette. The telephone was one of those old black ones, with a dial instead of push buttons. I looked at it for a while.

I don't know one single phone number. Not one.

I tried to think about what happened. It's hard for me. I asked Shella if I was stupid, once. A long time ago. Her face got sad.

"You're not stupid, baby. Not like dumb-stupid. You don't get things because you don't feel them, that's all. Like your brain is all scar tissue."

"I never got hit in the head. Not real hard, anyway."

"You just do it different than most people. There's things we don't want to remember. I worked with a girl once. She was a real racehorse, a sleek girl with legs that went on forever. Everybody called her Rose . . . 'cause she had such long stems, get it?"

"I guess. . . ."

"Oh, shut up. Just listen for a minute. Rose was hooking big-time. Worked out-call, never less than five yards a night. She didn't draw lines, a three-way girl, she'd take it anyplace you wanted to put it. You get *that*, right?"

"Yes."

"She killed a trick. Stabbed him to death with a letter opener. The papers said he didn't have a drop of blood left in him when she was done. She didn't even try and run for it—the cops found her right there. I went to visit her in the jailhouse. At first, it was like she didn't recognize me. I held her hand. Then her eyes snapped and she knew who I was. I asked her what happened. She just said . . . 'Flashback.' That's all she said. Flashback.

"At her trial, the doctor said something happened to her when she was a kid. He didn't know what it was. Rose wouldn't tell him. Rose looked like a million bucks at the trial, flashing those long legs, smiling. The doctor said it was more important to her not to go back where she was —it would cost her too much.

"They found her guilty. Got a life sentence. I kissed her goodbye. She was still smiling.

"It wasn't even a year later that I read about it in the papers. She escaped. With a guard that was working her section of the prison. He was married, had two kids. They never found either of them."

"What do you think happened?" I asked her.

"I don't know. Something ugly."

"No, I mean . . ."

"Oh. I figure Rose got the guard's nose open. Some men, they'll give up everything for a taste."

"You think I'm like that?"

"You? No, honey. I don't think you're like anything. Whatever you buried, you put it down deep."

♣

I tried to think about it. The chocolate bar, when I was a kid. How it felt when I broke Duke's face open with that sock full of batteries. Swinging that sock, I knew if I didn't finish him I'd be gone. There'd be nothing left of me, I'd just disappear. Like every part of my body was in my arm

. . . it felt like a feather when I moved it, but it weighed a ton when it came down. Little explosions in my head, like light bulbs breaking. Pop. Pop. Pop. A thousand of them.

They still go off in my head when I work. But only a couple of them now.

I tried to think about what Shella said that time. But all I could think about was that she went to Rose's trial. Said goodbye to her before she went down.

♣

The phone rang in the morning. I picked it up, didn't say anything.

"I'm on my way up." The Indian's voice.

The front door to the apartment opened. The Indian stepped in, a key in his hand. We sat down in the front room.

"What do you want to know?" he asked me.

"Just where it is."

"The work?"

"Yes."

"It's not that simple. *You're* not that simple. You think that crazy little man in that high office can't make somebody dead if he wants them gone? He's a rogue. Some kind of genius, I guess. I don't know the name of the agency he plays for. Every time I have to meet him, he's in a different place. Always with his machines, like a guy with bad kidneys—he has to be hooked up every day or he dies. One of our brothers is in the basement at Marion. You know what that is?"

I nodded to tell him I did. Marion's the max-max federal

joint, the hardest one they have. And the basement is for the men who are monsters even in there.

"He can fix it. Get our brother out of there. He can't spring him free, not put him on the street. But he can get him transferred to another place. Where we can work something out later."

"What did he do, your brother?"

"What he did was, he took the weight. They got him down as a big-time serial killer. Ten, twelve bodies, all over the country. They dropped him for one. Cold and clean, no way around it. It was a setup. He came out of the room holding an empty shotgun. They let him do the work, then they took him. The crazy man sent for him—he had his machines hooked up right inside the jail where they were holding him. He told our brother he knew about the tribe, made him an offer. Our brother, he pleaded guilty to all the hits we did going back a few years. The cops cleared the books, the heat's off us. And our brother's down for forever."

"And he springs him for what?"

"For finding you, which we did. For bringing you to him. Which we did. And for you doing that piece of work."

"He'll do it?"

"Sure. He knows about our tribe. He knows me. But he doesn't know all of us. He goes back on it, any of it, we'll take him out. Whatever it costs. He knows that much about us, about our honor."

He saw me looking at him. Shook his head, lit a cigarette.

"That's our legend, that's who we are. When we say we'll do something, that's what you get. Or we die. Any one of us gives his word, he has to do it or die. And if he dies, the word goes to the next one. If we all die, the legend still lives. We're not cheats, or liars. We're not thieves. We're assassins."

"I . . ."

"Assassins, my friend. Hunters, feeding our families. Only we hunt humans, not animals. We were driven off our land. Some of us imitated the conquerors. Some of us turned to liquor. But the warriors among us, they have always stood in the mountains, watching the white man's fires. We are their children. You can hire us, but you can't own us."

"How many men . . . ?"

He waved his hand, like a mosquito was near his face. "Men? It's all of us. Our women are more dangerous than we are. They do our work too. And we raise our children to follow."

"Kids?"

"The white man raises his children to rule. We raise ours to hunt."

"Why don't you just do it yourselves? What the man wants?"

"We can't get close enough to the target. And we never could."

I lit a smoke of my own. He wasn't saying anything now, waiting on me.

"Your brother, the one who's in prison?"

"Yes?"

"You send him letters and stuff? Go to see him on visiting day?"

He nodded his head. Slow, the way you talk to a dope. So he'll understand. "Sure," he said.

♣

He took a picture out of his bag. A black-and-white photograph. A man, maybe fifty years old. He had a round, fat
face, short blond hair. More pictures. A mug shot, front
and side. The man was smiling in the mug shot—I never
saw that before. Close-up pictures of his arms. Tattoo of
an eagle. The eagle was holding a black man in his claws.
On the other arm was a hangman's noose. The words Aryan
Justice were underneath it. Another picture: the man was
standing in front of a crowd, waving his arms. Some of the
crowd had shaved heads, some had real long hair, mus-
taches. They all had weapons: rifles, pistols. The Indian
turned the picture over. On the back: 7/5/39, 6′1″, 235,
blond/blue.

"That's him," the Indian said.

♣

"It don't seem so hard to me," I told the Indian. "This guy,
he speaks in front of crowds and all."

"He doesn't go on the street. Doesn't go out at all. He
lives inside a compound . . . like a fort, understand? The
only way to get inside, you have to be one of them."

"So why can't you . . . ?"

"You have to be white to be one of them."

"Don't they have . . . ? I mean, the crazy man, he has
guys work for him."

"Undercovers? Forget it. They could never get inside.
This guy, he's the boss of a crew. And they've got an acid
test. You know what that is?"

"No."

"Like an initiation. Something you got to do before you even get to meet the man."

"What's the test?"

"You got to kill a black man. See? That's why they can't go inside. He's got too many buffers, too many layers. By the time you get inside, you're already outside, see? Outside the world."

"How do you know all this?"

"The crazy man explained it to me. See, sometimes, one of the followers, he turns. Rolls over. He gets dropped for something, he makes a deal. So we know how they work. Anyway, the crazy man tried it. Tried to put someone inside. Set up a phony hit on paper, made this black guy disappear, like the undercover killed him. Turned out that wasn't the test . . . you got to do a kill right in front of them. So they can see it. This guy, he thought he was inside, but he was in the ground."

"They killed him?"

"That's what the crazy man says. Says he can't prove it either. They never even found the body. Now the head man, he's more careful than he ever was. They'll never make a case against him."

"So the crazy man, he wants . . ."

"Revenge. He lost a man, he has to make it right. It's not like for us, not like loyalty. It's like . . . I can't explain it, it's like someone fucked with his machines or something. He was telling me about it, he kept saying he just needed a better plan, that's all. Just a better plan."

"And that's me?"

"That's all of us. You're just the end-piece."

"He could find my Shella?"

"Dead or alive, my friend. Guaranteed."

"If she was . . . dead, how would I know it was really her that died? He just made *me* dead, on paper, right? Couldn't he do it for her?"

"Yeah. We thought of that. So we told him, she turns up dead, he'll have to prove it. She's been busted, they probably have her prints. Or a picture. Something. He said, you wanted it, he could find some of her relatives, prove it to you that way. Okay?"

"Yes."

"You know any of her relatives? You'd know them if you meet them?"

"Yeah. I'll do it. But if Shella turns up dead, tell him I want to meet her father. I'll know him."

"It's a deal," the Indian said.

♣

I'm not like Shella. Sometimes, when we had to stay in a room for a few days, she would get all jumpy. Make up excuses why she needed to go out. Try on different outfits, do her hair different ways, take a dozen showers. There was nothing she wanted to watch on television once—she smacked the set so hard she broke it.

If I didn't have to work, maybe I'd never go out.

The Indian told me he'd need some time to scope things out, find the best way to get me inside, close to the man I had to fix.

I waited for the Indian to come back.

♣

He came one morning, told me we were going to take a ride. It was a big car. I sat in the back seat with the Indian. There were two more of them in the front.

We drove for a while. The signs kept saying North. Different routes. The Indians didn't say much. Even when they did, I couldn't understand most of it. They were speaking English and all, but the words were funny.

The roads got smaller and smaller. Concrete to blacktop to dirt. We turned onto a little path. The car had to go slow. There was a big house and a barn. A couple of dogs ran out to meet the car. They didn't bark or anything, just watched.

We drove into the barn. Everybody got out. The two in the front seat went off.

"There's a bathroom over there," the Indian pointed for me. I didn't have to use it, but I figured this was something he was telling me, so I went in. When I came out, a few of them were standing around.

They all had guns.

I wondered if Monroe knew any Indians.

♣

We walked back in the woods. There was a pond. Quiet.

"It's our land," the Indian said. "We own it. We bought it. Paid for it. Nobody comes on our land. Not now."

We kept walking. Something moved in the woods next to us. One of the dogs.

We came to a clearing. The Indian walked away from

the others. They kind of squatted on the ground, watching everything except us.

"You ever shoot a gun?" the Indian asked me.

"No."

"I didn't think so. We have to work this out, be real careful. We only get this one chance. Understand?"

"Yes." I didn't, but I knew he'd say more.

"Remember the acid test I told you about? You have to do someone. Like, just to be doing it. That should get you close enough. But you can't do it your way. If they know you work with your hands, they won't let you get close to the head man. Searching you wouldn't do any good, see? So the first job, you got to do it like a shooter. That's what we're going to show you."

"I never . . ."

"I know. You don't have to be any marksman, just know how it works."

He took a gun out of his coat. A silver gun. He squatted down. I got down next to him. He turned the gun sideways so I could see what he was doing. He pushed a piece of metal with his thumb and the round part fell sideways out of the gun. He tilted the gun in his hand and the bullets spilled out.

"There's two ways to fire this, okay? Single-action and double-action, it's called. You can cock it first, like this. . . ." He pulled back the hammer. I heard a click. "Then just pull the trigger." The gun clicked again. He slid something forward with his thumb, opened it up, held it sideways. "See? The hammer has this little spur on it. The spur comes forward, it hits the cartridge right in the center. . . ." He showed me a bullet. It had a little round dot on the back, right in the center. "That's the primer. It kicks off the powder inside, and the bullet shoots out the front. You see?"

"Yes."

"Or you can just pull the trigger without cocking it." He did it. Click, click, click. The round part turned every time he pulled the trigger.

"See how it works?"

"Yes."

He opened the gun again, handed it to me. "Look down the barrel," he said.

I did it. He made a grunting noise, took the gun out of my hand. "No. Not like that. Here, watch me." He let the light come over his shoulder, held his thumbnail where the bullet would come out, looked down the barrel from the back end. He handed it to me. I did what he did.

"What do you see?"

"It's all cut up inside. Twisted cuts."

"Those are lands and grooves. When the bullet comes through, they make it spin." He twirled his finger in the air, like a corkscrew. "It makes the bullet go straight."

"Okay."

"Hold it in your hand. Get the feel."

I took the gun. It had a heavy, solid weight. Like it was all one piece, not a bunch of parts. The grip was black rubber. I closed my eyes, getting the sense. Like a pool cue. Swinging it in little circles. I ran my fingers all over it.

I felt the Indian tap me on the shoulder.

"You go away someplace?"

"What?"

"You've been holding that piece for half a damn hour, man."

"Oh. Yeah, I guess . . ."

"You ready to learn now? Learn how to kill somebody with that thing?"

"I already know how," I told him.

He gave me a funny look. Took the gun from me, opened it up, put the bullets in. Stood there with it in his hand.

"With a pistol, you don't really aim it. You point it, just like your finger. Like it's growing out of your hand. Get a balance. . . ." He spread his legs, crouched a little bit, held the gun in two hands, one hand wrapped around the other. "Keep your weight low, raise the pistol, sight along the line, okay? Keep the sight just below what you're aiming at. Take a deep breath, let it out. Then *squeeze* the trigger, don't jerk it. Squeeze it so slow you won't even know when it's pulled back far enough to go off. It makes a loud noise—you're not used to it, it can spook you. So . . . put these on." He handed me earmuffs, it looked like. Only the round parts were red. Red plastic, I think. There was foam all around the inside. I fit it over my head. He put one on too, only his earpieces were blue.

I watched the gun in his hands. He walked over, took out a knife, scratched a big X in a tree that was lying on its side. "It's dead," he said. Like he wouldn't shoot a tree that was alive. Then we stepped off about twenty-five feet.

"Watch," he said. He took his stance. I watched his finger move back. There was a crack. It was loud, even with the earmuffs. We walked back over to the tree. You could see the bullet hole just to the right of the X.

"When you use this, you crank them all off. Six shots. Shoot fast. *Empty* the gun. This is a Ruger, Speed Six. Nice, simple piece. It won't jam on you, like an automatic does sometimes. Thirty-eight Special. It'll kill a man, but the more bullets you put into him, the more certain you make it."

He pulled the trigger again. Five times. It sounded like the cracks ran into each other, one loud boom. I saw wood chips fly from the dead tree. We walked back over. The center of the X was all eaten out.

The Indian opened the gun, tipped it back, put the empty bullets in his pocket. "Another thing," he said, "with a revolver, you don't leave cartridges behind at the scene. You use this, you do just what I did, okay? Save the cartridges, dump them someplace else."

"Okay."

"You ready to try it?"

"Yes."

He handed me the gun, six bullets. I did what he did, put them inside. Then I took the same stance he did, crouched there, focusing in on the tree. I took a deep breath, let it out. I could feel my heart beat slower. Slower. I pulled the trigger.

"What are you doing?"

I stopped, turned to him. "What you told me. Pulling it slow."

"Not *that* slow, goddamn it! That trigger was actually moving, that's what you're telling me?"

"Sure."

"How could you tell?"

"I could feel it."

"Damn! Okay, I'm sorry. You got to do it a *little* quicker, okay? You'll be shooting a person, not a damn target. People move."

"You said . . ."

"*Forget* what I said. Try it again, okay?"

I did it again. The first shot made the gun jump in my hands. I fired as it came back down, did it again, picking up the rhythm. Then the gun was empty.

We walked back over. There were more rips in the tree, all around the X.

♣

"He's a natural," a voice said. Another one of the Indians. They must of walked into the clearing while I was shooting.

"I told you," the Indian said.

I practiced some more with the gun. They had all kinds of guns. Rifles, shotguns, a big black pistol that spit bullets out so fast it was like a hose squirting. They worked with the different guns, trading them back and forth. I tried the silver gun in one hand. Then in the other. After a while, it didn't make a difference. It sounded like a war.

Later, one of them brought some sandwiches and cold lemonade. It tasted good. Fresh and clean.

♣

In the afternoon, a woman came into the clearing. An Indian woman, with her hair in braids. She had a bow in her hand. We all sat around while she practiced with the bow and arrows. She was good.

She came over to where I was sitting. Bent down and looked at me. Her eyes were black. Not just the little round part in the center. All black.

"You're the one," she said.

The Indian was next to me. "That's him," he said.

She kept looking at me. "My brother is in their prison," she said. "My own brother. Hiram. From the white man's

Bible, they named him. They separated us, but Hiram came for me. He brought me to my people. Now you will help bring him to me."

Nobody said anything. She held out her hand to me. I took it. Came to my feet, not letting my weight pull against her, but she felt strong enough to do it.

She handed me the bow. "Shall I show you?"

"Yes," I told her. I don't know why I said that.

We walked away from the others. She handed me an arrow. I held it in my hands. It didn't feel right. I shook my head. She smiled, handed me another.

I put it in the bow. I could see how to do it from watching her. She walked away. Pulled a leaf from one of the trees. She licked the back of the leaf, pasted it right over the X the Indian had cut into the dead tree. Then she came back to where I was.

I pulled back the string. I made my left fist into a stone. I pulled all the weight out of my body, put it into my right hand. I could see down the length of the arrow. It was straight. I saw the tip of the arrow, saw the leaf, brought them together. In between my heartbeats, I let the string go.

It went through the middle of the leaf.

The woman bowed her head, like she was in church.

"My name is Ruth," she said.

Then she took the bow from me and walked out of the clearing.

♣

On the drive back to Chicago, the Indian told me how it would work.

"You keep the pistol," he said. "It's ice-cold. Came right off the production line at the factory, never been registered. The way they'll work it, they'll take it from you after the hit. Tell you they're going to get rid of it for you. But they'll keep it. Just in case. It'll have your prints all over it, so they'll always have something on you. You can't wear surgeon's gloves, can't act like a pro around them. You're supposed to be this white-trash nigger-hater, okay? Those kind, they never think things through. You're joining the group 'cause you like to kill niggers, see? Hate's their game. At least that's the game for the troops. The generals, they always have something going on the side."

"What do I do?"

"Do? You don't do nothing. Not for them. You hit one of *our* contracts, see? That's if it works. If they let you go cruising around, tell you to pick a target at random, we can make that work. But if they just *bring* one to you, you got to do it. Just do it. They'll have your prints, so what? Fingerprints don't have a clock on them. You're dead, right? If they threaten you with the prints on the gun, just act scared." He looked at me, watching close. "Can you do that?"

I thought back to the juvenile institution. The training school, they called it. "I think so," I told him.

"From now on, you carry the gun. Don't bother with a holster—just find a comfortable place to carry it. Walk around with it, so the weight goes inside your space, understand? So it don't show . . ."

"Okay."

"They have a joint in Uptown. Not far from us. Just a storefront. They hand out their leaflets, make speeches through bullhorns, crap like that. That's gonna be the hard part for you."

"What?"

"Talking. You watch television?"

"Sometimes."

"Read books?"

"No."

"Okay, no problem. We got a VCR over at the apartment. I'll bring you some tapes. You watch the tapes, you'll see how they talk, what they say. You don't have to be no undercover expert for these boys . . . they got that acid test, like I told you."

"How do I . . . ?"

"You do the *work*. Probably on the street, it all goes down right. Sooner or later, probably sooner, they'll take you inside. To the compound. Take some time, get you alone with the head man. Then you do him. We know where the compound is, but the head man never goes out on the grounds. We watched for a week, once. You get in, we'll be watching. They got all these boys in their camouflage gear on the perimeter. We can go past them anytime we want—they'll never see us. Soon as you do the work, you just step outside. Tie a rag around your head, like this. . . ." He took a red scarf out of his pocket, flipped it into a long, thin piece, tied it around his head. He looked even more like an Indian, the kind you see on TV. "You step out with something around your head, we start shooting. Just run for the perimeter . . . run out of the compound. We'll be there, take you away."

I nodded. I guessed they could just shoot me at the same time, but it didn't feel like that.

"You got any questions for now?" He lit a cigarette, gave me one. I smoked it, thinking.

"That woman, Ruth. The guy who's in Marion, she says that's her brother. Is that her brother like he's *your* brother, or . . ."

"You mean, did they have the same mother and father?"

"Yes."

"They did. But we're all . . . together. The same as blood. Okay?"

"Okay."

We drove for a long time. It got dark out. They never stopped for gas—there was a pump on their farm. The driver kept right around the speed limit, staying with traffic.

"You need ID," the Indian said to me.

"All right."

"The crazy man, he can fix you up with a whole set. And you need a legend too."

"Legend?"

"A history. Like where you came from. I figure, you were in prison, right?"

"Yeah. In Florida."

"What for?"

"Manslaughter."

"Good. Okay, tell them you killed a nigger down there. They'll like that. Tell them as much truth as you can. Whatever name you were under, tell them it was a phony. Your new ID, that'll be the real you. You never said your name."

"My name?"

"What do people call you, friend?"

Monroe called me Ghost. Shella always called me John. Like a joke, her joke. Said I was the only john she ever had. Like I was a trick.

"John," I told him. Thinking about something I saw on TV once. A man signing a motel register. "John Smith," I told him.

One of the Indians in the front seat laughed. It was the first time I realized he'd been listening.

I didn't know what he was laughing at, but it didn't feel like it was me.

♣

The Indian brought me a whole stack of cassettes for the VCR the next day. I watched them over and over again. With the sound on. It was mostly news stories, long ones sometimes. "The Face of Hate," stuff like that. People showing off for cameras, wearing costumes. I'd heard all this stuff before. In prison, there were a couple of guys, in there for killing an old black man. Stomping him to death. Just to be doing it. They had a lot of tattoos. The only one I remember was a spider web on one guy's elbow. When he made a muscle pose, you could see it.

They even had a tape of the head man—the one I was supposed to do my work on. He was giving a speech. Kept talking about race like it was everything. He used dog words. Mongrels, mutts. White people were pure and other people made them dirty, he said. Just being around them would make you dirty.

I heard all that before. Niggers will only fight if they're in a crowd. One-on-one, they're cowards. That's what they told me, the first time I was locked up. I didn't know if it was true. I didn't want to fight anyone—I was afraid of them all. Never hit a nigger in the head—you can't hurt them there. I found out that was a lie. Maybe it was all lies.

"Try and find something in there that's you," the Indian told me.

♣

The Indian brought some more stuff one day, watched the tapes with me for a while. A bunch of college kids raped a black girl. They took turns, and they did it together too. They called her names while they were doing it. One of them made a videotape of it, and the cops found it when they searched the fraternity house. They showed some of it on the news, with pieces of it covered up with black patches, but you could tell what was going on. The girl was all messed up. Drunk, or high. Just sort of laying there.

The college boys said it was a party.

"They say they hate niggers so much, why would they want to have sex with them?" the Indian said. The way people say things when they don't expect you to answer them.

Anyone who's ever been in prison could have told him.

♣

I kept watching the tapes. Watching and listening. One of the shows had interviews with kids. Skinheads. I watched the tape a lot. The older guys, the ones in the organizations, they talked about the skinheads like they were an army.

But the skinheads seemed wild. They were mad at everybody, not just blacks.

Like nobody wanted them, and they knew it.

♣

"What do you see? Just before you go to work on someone, you see anything?"

Nobody had ever asked me that before, not even Shella. I looked at the picture of the head man. The mug shot they gave me. I didn't see anything.

"Not from a picture," the Indian said. "When you're right there."

I closed my eyes, slowed everything down so I could see it. When it happens, it's so fast. I slowed it down. Back to that first time. Duke. He was lying on his back. It was dark in there, but I could see him. I could see . . . his skeleton. Bones underneath his skin. His skull inside his head. "Little dots," I told the Indian.

"Red dots? In front of your eyes? Like when you're mad?"

"Black dots. Not in my eyes. On the body. Not like . . . measles. Just in different spots. All over."

I closed my eyes again. Saw Duke. Touched my face. Between the eyes, the bridge of my nose, a spot on the neck.

"Laser dots," the Indian said.

♣

"You ready to go?" he asked me a few days later.

"Yes."

"Tonight?"

"Sure."

"Okay. I talked to the crazy man. Anybody checks, the guy who did time in Florida was John Smith. It'll all match. We got a room for you. Once you move in, you're on your own—you won't see us again until you finish the work."

♣

He came back that night. I had everything in my duffel bag.

"Let me see the piece," he said.

I handed him the gun. He opened the cylinder, looked down the barrel. "Dusty," he said. He sounded disgusted. He took out a handkerchief, twisted up the corner, poked it through the barrel with a pencil, then pulled it back and forth. "Do that every day, okay?"

I said I would.

They drove me to the Greyhound station. I gave him my car keys. He gave me a ticket stub.

"You came from Atlanta," he told me. "You left around eight in the morning. The trip took about eighteen hours, stopped once in Cincinnati. The ticket cost ninety-eight bucks and change. You got in around two in the morning —just about now. Tonight you stay at this place on Madison. Don't hang around the station—you get picked up with the piece, it's gonna waste a lot of time. Tomorrow, you start out for Uptown. Take the A Train to Sheridan and walk from there. Get a room on Wilson, just off Broadway. It's a wood-frame house, blue front. Then you're on your own."

I stepped out of their car, the duffel bag in one hand. The Indian stepped out with me, watching my face.

"You have money?" he asked me.

I said I did. He held out his hand. I saw, people do that. I held his hand, squeezed when he squeezed.

The Indian shook his head. Sad, like he knew I wasn't going to believe him. "We'll be there when you come out," he said.

♣

I walked through the bus station once, then I came out on Randolph and walked over to the flophouse on Madison. The guy at the front desk looked at me too long—it was good I wouldn't be there past tonight.

Before I went to sleep, I put my handkerchief through the gun barrel a few times.

♣

The next morning, I found the train station, where the Indian said it would be. I took the A Train—it ran outside, above the street. I got off at Sheridan. It was a short walk to the blue house on Wilson. They gave me a room on the top floor. Seventy-five dollars a week.

The room was clean. Even the glass in the window. I looked out. There was an alley back there. An Indian was working on a car with the hood up.

♣

"It's better if you don't just walk in," the Indian had told me. "We'll save that if nothing else works."

When I tried to concentrate on all I had to say, my head hurt. I slept most of the day.

When I woke up, there was a note under my door. The

name of a car wash was printed on it. Underneath it said:
TOMORROW MORNING, GET A JOB.

♣

First thing in the morning, I walked over to the car wash.
An Indian was running it. I asked him for a job. He didn't
ask me anything, not even my name. He pointed to a black
guy, said he was the foreman. I went over to him. He gave
me some towels, told me to wipe down the cars when they
came out of the chute.

I worked all morning. The foreman told me it was lunch-
time. The black guys had a place for themselves in the
back. They all sat down and started to play cards. They
slapped the cards down hard, yelling at each other. They
were playing for money—I saw it on the table. One of them
had a long razor scar down the side of his face. He saw me
looking at him. He looked back—a prison yard stare.

I walked away.

The white guys were by themselves too. Just talking and
eating their food. They had a bottle of wine they were
passing around.

I walked across the street to a deli, got a sandwich and
a bottle of cold water. I sat down next to the car wash.

The Indian boss came by, squatted down next to me. He
spoke without moving his lips.

"Bad enough working with niggers, huh? Having one for
a fucking foreman, that's real hard for a white man to
swallow."

He got up and walked away.

♣

That afternoon, I was wiping down a red Thunderbird. When I finished, the woman got in her car, handed me something. It was two quarters. I put them in my pocket. One of the white guys shook his head, pointed toward a big barrel right next to where the cars came out, a sign on it said TIPS FOR THE MEN.

"We all throw in, split it up at the end of the day," he said.

I threw my two quarters in there.

I finished the shift. We all walked around the back. The Indian came out, gave everyone their pay, in cash. I got twenty-five dollars. Then the black guy, the foreman, he dumped the barrel over. There were a few bills, mostly coins. The black guy counted it up. He split it into two piles, put one pile in his pocket. Then he dealt it out, one coin at a time. He dealt to everyone, all sitting around in a circle. A quarter for one guy, a quarter for the next guy. He started with the first guy to his left. When he came back around to himself, he dealt himself a quarter too. The black guy with the razor scar on his face watched. When he saw the foreman deal himself a share, he put his right hand in his pocket.

I knew what was going to happen. I just didn't know when.

♣

That night, I went to the bar they told me about. It was like all the others, except there was two different flags over the mirror behind the bartender. One was red, with a flat blue X, white stars inside the blue stripes. I saw this flag before, plenty of times, in the South. The Confederate flag, Shella told me it was. The other flag was green on the ends, with white in the middle. The white had a design with horses or something on each side and some other stuff too. I never saw that one before.

I drank the way I always do. Watched the girls. Smoked a few cigarettes. "If nobody comes up to you after a couple of nights, you have to start a talk," the Indian said.

Nobody came near me.

♣

The next night, I was there for a couple of hours when a guy sat next to me. The barmaid came right over, like she knew him, brought him a beer.

He tipped the glass of beer toward me, nodded his head. "Haven't seen you in here before," he said.

"I just got in," I said.

"Where you from?" His accent was like most of the white men in Uptown. Not South, exactly. Harder.

"Florida."

"Looking for work?"

"I got a job."

"Around here?"

"Yeah. In a car wash." I could see the guy didn't know what I was. He wasn't looking for somebody to do work. "Bad enough working with niggers," I said. "Having one for a fucking foreman, that's real hard for a white man to swallow."

"Yeah, that's the way it is now. The fucking apes don't

respect nothing. They're out of control. It's hard to be a white man today. They got all that Affirmative Action shit."

"Yeah." I didn't know what he was talking about. But I felt good inside—I must of gotten it right. I wished the Indian could see me.

"They don't come in here," he said. "They know better."

"Good."

"See that flag?" he said, pointing to the green and white one over the bar. "It's the Rhodesian flag—the true Rhodesian flag, after they kicked out the British. When it used to be a white man's country. Before the nigger-loving UN gave it to the apes. It was a fucking jungle when they started. White men came from England, took it over. Cleared the land. It was a beautiful place. No race mixing, no fucking integration. It was a place for a white man to go, if he had the balls. No matter what your trouble was over here, that was the place to go. Paradise."

"I wish I had known about it," I said.

"You'd go there?"

"It would be better than prison." Telling the truth as much as I could, the way the Indian said.

"You was in prison?"

I gave him a funny look, like you do in there when somebody's close to pushing you.

"Hey, no offense, friend. I been there myself. Armed robbery," he said. Like it was something special. "What'd you go for?"

"I killed a nigger," I told him.

"Is that right? Hey, Katie, bring me another beer. And give my friend here whatever he's drinking. Bring them over to my booth."

# SHELLA

♣

The booth was in the back. They're always in the back. A fat guy in a red T-shirt watched us. The way the guy talking to me looked at the fat guy, I could see they were together.

The armed robbery guy did the talking. Nigger this, spic that. "They're really monkeys, you know what I'm saying? You leave them alone, they'd kill each other. Animals. All they want to do is fight and fuck."

I looked at him. He thought I was saying something—his face got a little red. "Hey! Don't get me wrong, pal. I like a good piece of ass better than the next guy. Fucking queers, they're just as bad as niggers, in my book. My point, see, my point is that animals, they need *control*. Like dogs. Dogs are good, they learn to obey, right? Now, niggers, they ain't the real problem. Some people think they're the big problem, they don't know what's going on. You know what the big problem is?"

"What?"

"The Jews, man. The Jews, they're the ones trying to bring the race down. They ain't really white either. I mean, where's Israel? In Africa, am I right? The Jews ain't nothing but Arabs themselves. But you got to give this to the Jews, they're smart. It's in their blood, the way they're bred. A Jew bitch has a retarded kid, you know what they do?" He made a slitting move across his throat.

I looked at him. Every time I did that, he talked more.

"I'm telling you the truth. See, the difference between the Jews and these other beasts, the Jews got a *plan*. Hitler, now he knew what was going on. There's a man who knew the truth. He had the right fucking idea, you know? The ovens."

"The . . . ?"

"Yeah! Exterminate them. That's what has to be done. But the white man in this country, he's lost his balls. This ain't a white man's country anymore—it belongs to the niggers and the Jews."

He talked like that for a long time, until I told him I had to get up in the morning to go to work. "See you tomorrow night?" he said. I told him sure.

When I walked out the door, I could feel somebody behind me. All the way to the house where I had a room.

♣

I went to the car wash the next morning. Just before the lunch break, a car came through. An old Ford station wagon. The guy driving it was the guy from last night, the fat guy. Only he didn't have a red T-shirt.

I didn't show I knew who he was. He didn't leave a tip when we finished wiping down his car.

♣

I went back to the bar that night. This time, I had something to eat. A hamburger and fries. In a booth.

The armed robbery guy came in around nine o'clock. He saw me and came over. Stuck out his hand.

"Hey, partner! Good to see you."

I didn't know what to say so I tried to smile, but I could see that was making him nervous so I said, "Sit down. I'll buy you a beer."

I must of done it right, because he sat down, smiling at me.

While we were waiting for the waitress, he said, "My

name is Mack. Mack Wayne." He stuck out his hand. I took it, squeezed a little softer than he did. He liked that.

"I'm John Smith," I told him.

"Hey, that's funny. I mean, if we took your name and mine, we'd get John Wayne."

I looked at him.

"John Wayne, get it? Like . . . The Duke, right?"

Something moved in me, but I couldn't feel it in my face. "Yeah," I said. "Good."

He drank his beer, talked some more about niggers, queers, and Jews. He said the Jews owned all the newspapers and all the television stations, so the white man never got to hear the truth. Then he said he had to make a phone call.

When he came back, he talked some more about the same stuff. A woman came by our table. A chubby woman with dark hair. She was about thirty-five, in a tight black skirt and high heels, wearing a white sweater with a low neck so you could see the top of her breasts where the bra pushed them together.

"Hey, Ginger!" he said. "Come over here and meet a friend of mine."

He introduced us. Just said my name was John, and we were pals. She sat down, next to me in the booth. Mack ordered some more drinks. Ginger pressed her thigh against me. She had long nails, red. She talked about niggers too—how they all wanted to rape white women and they should be castrated. She had heavy perfume and she stuck her chest out a lot.

After a while, she got up. "I have to go to the little girls' room," she said. She ground her hips hard walking away —she didn't know how to do it the way a dancer does.

Mack leaned over to me. "Hey, pal, I know all the signs. Ginger goes for you. You play your cards right, you could have yourself a nice date tonight."

"Yeah?"

"I guarantee it. I know these girls. I'm gonna take off now, leave you two alone."

I said okay, like it was a good idea.

When she came back, she didn't ask where Mack had gone. She sat across from me. I bought her a couple more beers. She asked a lot of questions, but she wasn't listening much. She was like him—if I looked at her, she got nervous, but if I was quiet, she went ahead and talked.

It was almost eleven when she said she had to be going. "I got to get up early in the morning—I work in a beauty parlor, over on Lawrence."

"I work near there too," I told her.

"You live around here?"

"Just over on Wilson."

"Is it nice?"

"Yeah. I mean, I guess so. It's clean."

"Is it like an apartment or . . . ?"

"Just a room."

"Oh. Well, you know, I was thinking about moving from where I am, finding someplace closer to work. Do you know if they have rooms available?"

"I think so."

"Maybe I could take a look at yours sometime, see how it looks."

"Sure. Anytime you want."

# SHELLA

♣

She walked back with me. We went upstairs. She looked all around the room, looked out the window into the alley. I stepped behind her, held her breasts from the underside. She wiggled her butt back against me. She tried to turn around, but I held her there. She didn't fight or anything.

I undressed her, holding her like that. Her breasts were floppy out of the bra. Her thighs were like orange peel when the panty hose rolled down.

I fucked her on her back, her face in my shoulder. When we were done, she lit a cigarette. I laid down next to her and she talked some, asked some questions.

"You don't say much, do you, honey?"

I thought I was making her nervous, so I turned her over on her stomach and fucked her again. It took me longer the second time. She made a little grunting noise just before I finished. Then we fell asleep.

She got up a couple of hours later, moving quiet. I was lying with my head turned to the wall, my face on my arm. I can see good in the dark. She looked through the chest of drawers, at my clothes. Then she went in the closet where I keep the duffel bag. She found the gun. I could see her hold it, looking back at where I was sleeping.

She put the gun back.

Then she got dressed and went out.

♣

The room felt thick in the morning. I opened the window. They still hadn't got that car fixed in the alley.

On my lunch break, the Indian boss walked by. He asked me for a light for his little cigar. When he bent close, he said, "She's with them."

I wanted to tell him I knew that. I'm not stupid because I don't talk. Not stupid like they think. But I didn't say anything.

♣

A couple of nights later, Mack asked me, "You really killed a nigger?"

"Why?"

"No offense, pal. Just, would you mind if we checked you out? I mean, there's a reason, okay? There's people I want you to meet. Important people. Big people. We've got something going, something I know you'd like. But the people in charge, they have to be careful, you understand?"

"I guess."

"Look, what's done is done, right? I mean, you didn't escape or anything . . . ?"

"I got paroled. But . . ."

"Hey, no problem. I know what you're going to say. I'm not a cop. Cops, they're no better than anyone else. Nigger-lovers too, most of them. Even the righteous ones, you got to remember who they work for. . . ."

"The Jews?"

"Yeah! You're getting with the program, John. All right. Listen, all I need is some . . . details. Like where you did time. And when . . . Okay?"

So I told him.

♣

I kept going to the bar. Every night. That woman Ginger didn't come back into the place.

I kept going to the car wash too.

The Indian boss came by one day. When he leaned over to get his light, he said, "There's a basement in your house, where you stay. Go there tonight when you get back from the bar."

♣

There was a guy with Mack that night. A younger guy, a skinhead. He had an earring in one ear, a metal loop, with a little hand grenade dangling from it. Tattoos all over his forearms. He was wearing a leather jacket, jeans, big stomping boots on his feet.

"This is Rusty," Mack said to me.

The skinhead looked hard at me, smiling all across his face so I could see his teeth. "But I ain't rusty, friend. I keep in practice, you get what I mean?"

"No," I told him.

"Johnny ain't no big talker, Rusty. Like I told you. He's a man *does* things."

"Yeah?"

"Yeah!" It was Mack answering the skinhead, not me. We had hamburgers, like always. Mack started talking about the niggers and the Jews. The skinhead, Rusty, he wasn't really listening. He didn't settle in his chair, all bristly, jumpy. He kept staring at me. I looked back sometimes, so he wouldn't think I was afraid. I know his kind —they think you're afraid, they try and hurt you.

"You like to go hunting, man?" he finally asked me.

"I never been," I said.

"*Nigger*-hunting, man. You up for that?"

"Sure."

The skinhead looked over at Mack. He was smiling again.

"Just like that?" he asked me.

"Like what?"

"Go out cruising, spot a nigger, shoot him?"

"Okay."

"*Okay?* Okay, huh? You got any particular . . . preference . . . what kind a nigger you want to shoot?"

I thought about it a minute, trying to get it right. "A fat one," I told him.

Mack laughed so hard he spit up some of his beer.

♣

I could feel him in the basement when I went downstairs that night.

"They're about ready to break," the Indian said.

"They asked me tonight," I told him.

"You know when they want to do it?"

"No."

The glow from his cigarette tip lit his face for a minute. I waited for him to tell me.

"I don't think they got the heart to cruise the South Side, do a drive-by on some gang-banger. But they might. . . . They go that route, you got to do it. Just stick the piece out the window and crank some off. Try to hit some buck flying the colors, okay?"

"I don't . . ."

"One of them in a gang jacket, okay? You've seen them, right?"

"Right."

"Don't spray the stuff around. Make 'em get you close, you understand. You start firing wild, you're liable to take down some kid. . . . Even late at night, they're all over the street."

"Okay."

"I got a better idea. Don't know if we can pull this one off, but it'd be worth it. Come on, let's take a ride."

♣

It was a black four-door Ford. We got in the back seat. A couple of Indians were in the front. I looked close—they were the same ones.

They didn't say anything to me.

"We got a job order," the Indian said. "On a pimp. He works close by, just past Belmont. Runs a string of street girls. He does the gorilla thing, works *little* girls too, understand?"

"Yes." It felt funny to understand what he was saying. I did understand, this time.

"His name is Lamont James, but he goes by Steel. That's what he calls himself, Steel. He's going anyway. You get a chance, do him, it'd be perfect."

I didn't say anything. The Ford turned a corner, doubled back, went around again.

A few minutes later, one of the Indians in the front seat said something I didn't get.

"There he is," the Indian next to me said. "Look at him. Right out of the fifties. Thinks he's Iceberg fucking Slim."

I saw him. A tall, thin man, leaning against the fender of a big pink car with a white padded top. He was wearing a long black coat. He had a white hat too, a big one with a thick pink band.

"You have him?" the Indian asked.

"Yes."

♣

It didn't happen until a couple of nights later. A Thursday night it was. I was talking to Mack in the booth when the skinhead walked in. He had a little baseball bat in one hand.

"Come on out back," he said to me.

When I stepped out into the alley it didn't feel like it had so many times before. I got asked to step out into alleys a lot, and I was always alone when I did. There was a bunch of guys there, all with shaved heads.

"I'll let you know," the skinhead said to Mack. Then he told me, "Come on," and we all walked over to a car. An old white Chrysler.

They showed me where to sit. Next to the window in the back, on the passenger side.

The car started moving, heading south.

The skinhead reached in his jacket, took out a pistol. A big one. He handed it to me.

"I got one," I said, showed it to him.

He slapped hands with the guy in the front seat.

"Let's do it!" he said.

♣

I saw the pink car at the end of the block. A lot of people on the street. I couldn't see him. The Chrysler was moving good—like they had a long way to go.

"There's one," I said.

The guy driving slowed down. "What?"

"A perfect nigger," I told him.

"Where?" Rusty said.

He was just stepping out of the pink car. "There," I told him.

"A pimp," Rusty said. "You wanna do him? It's pretty close to home. . . ."

"Go around the block again," I said.

Rusty rubbed the top of his head. "Do it," he said to the driver.

We came back around, moving slow. "I don't know about this," the guy in the passenger seat said.

I was afraid they'd go someplace else. I wished I could think of something. Then I said, "Stop the car."

They pulled over to the curb.

"Let me out. Keep driving. I'll catch up with you at the end of the block."

Rusty looked at me. Like he never saw me before. Then he nodded. I took out the gun, held it next to my leg— the way the guy with the eyeliner did in the hall when they told me to get out of the rooming house. I opened the door, stepped out. The car moved away.

I walked up the block. The pimp was back against his car, talking to a fat little white girl. He had his hand on the back of her neck. She was wearing a pair of red shorts and a halter top, looked about fifteen.

I walked up real close, people all around. I held the gun up, pointed it at his chest. He saw it. "Hey, man! Don't . . ."

The girl put her hands over her mouth, like trying to stop a scream. I pulled the trigger. It made a loud bang. The pimp grabbed his chest. I put the gun real close to him and kept pulling the trigger. I heard a click, the gun was empty. The pimp was on the ground. People were running around, yelling. I walked away. I can move faster than it looks.

The white Chrysler was at the end of the block. I started running when I saw it. The back door was standing open. I jumped inside.

"Go!" Rusty yelled.

♣

We didn't hear the sirens until we were a couple of blocks away. The Chrysler pulled over to the curb. We all got out, got into another car, a small red one. It was a tight fit in there.

The driver went down by the lake, then he came back, driving slow. They stopped right in front of my house.

"You think you got him?" Rusty asked. "We didn't see nothing, just heard the shots."

"I got him."

"Better give me the gun. We'll get rid of it for you."

"Okay."

"We got one!" the guy in the front said. Like he was surprised. Scared too.

♣

When I walked in the bar Saturday night, Mack had a newspaper in the booth. I sat down next to him. He pointed to something in it.

"Lamont. Ain't that a perfect nigger name?"

"What?"

"The nigger who got it last night. That was his name, Lamont." He was smiling, a big smile, looking at me.

"I didn't know," I told him.

"Oh, man, how *would* you know? Listen, John, you showed me something last night. A lot of guys, they're just talk. Like those boys who took you around . . . ? They're pretty good with baseball bats, doing little 'actions,' they call them, you understand?"

"No."

"Like nigger-stomping, get it? Strike a blow for the race. I mean, lotsa people talk about they going to kill this or kill that, you know what I'm saying? But *doing* it, that's what separates the men from the boys. Like going to prison. You see a lot of guys can't hold themselves together in there, right?"

I nodded.

"Well, it's the same thing. You can't really tell about a man until he has to *do* something. The people I'm with, they do things."

"I thought you said . . ."

"Not those *kids*, Johnny. Men. Men like us. The kids, they're with us all right, but they're not really down for race war. They're like a . . . gang, or something. Not an army. Not professional. They're too wild. You can't count on them. Like the leader says, the niggers got us outnumbered. For now, anyway, until the white race wakes up. So discipline, that's what we need."

He stopped what he was saying when a waitress came close. Ordered some beers. He never did that before, stopped talking.

When the waitress went away, he leaned over close to me. "You like killing niggers, John? Let me tell you something, there's lotsa people feel the way you do. But killing them one at a time, they ain't never gonna get it. The leader says, we kill them one at a time, the fucking monkeys could *breed* faster than we could kill 'em. What we need, what this country needs, is race war. Race *war*. And we got the start of it. Not so far from here. We want you with us, John. And you know what the best part is? You'll be with your *brothers*. Men who'll give their lives for you, go with you to the end. What do you say?"

"I don't get it."

"Look, how'd you like to quit working for niggers over at that car wash? Make some real money?"

"Sure."

"Okay. I got the word. Got it this morning. You got a car?"

"No. All I got . . ."

"That's okay. You had a car, you couldn't bring it anyway. Security don't allow it. Tomorrow night, I'll pick you up myself. Take you to our camp. Then you'll hear what we're about, okay? Make up your own mind. You decide you don't want to be with us, no hard feelings. And I'll guarantee you a month's pay, tide you over until you get another job, if that's what you want. Okay?"

"Okay."

He handed me a bunch of bills. I put them in my pocket.

"Tomorrow night. Ten o'clock. You be out in front of your house."

"Okay, it's over on . . ." I stopped, like I just figured out he must know where I lived. Where they dropped me off last night.

"See, John. We know what we're doing." He winked at me. "See you tomorrow night, brother."

♣

There was a note on my bed. BASEMENT, is all it said. I left the lights on in my room for a while. Then I turned them off like I was going to sleep.

He was there. "Was that enough for them?" he asked me.

"Tomorrow night, they're coming to take me someplace. He gave me some money too."

"I guess that did it. They took the gun from you?"

"Yes."

"Good. Listen to me now. I got to tell you a couple of things. First, don't go to the car wash tomorrow. A guy like you, like you're supposed to be, he wouldn't go to work a car wash job, he had money. What time he's supposed to pick you up?"

"Ten."

"Okay. Stay in tomorrow, like you were sleeping late. Then go out, spend some of that money. Over on Sheridan, they got daytime whores working. Get one of them, spend some money. That's what you'd do."

"All right."

"You have to . . . practice? What you do . . . with your hands?"

"No."

"Good. Now listen. We know where their camp is. We'll be there before you. And we'll be there from then on. Until you come out, okay?"

"Yes."

"I don't know how they work it. Could take weeks before you even see the head man. Or they could take you right to him, I don't know. We don't know what they do, inside. Waiting don't bother you, right?"

"No."

"You talk like this when you're around them?"

"Like what?"

"Yes. No. Okay."

"I guess."

"They don't look at you funny?"

"They do all the talking. They like to talk."

His teeth were real white in the basement. "Kill the niggers, huh?"

"And the others."

"What others?"

"Jews. Spics. Queers."

"No Indians?"

"They never said."

"You understand what they're saying?"

"The niggers are apes. All they want to do is fight and fuck. Especially fuck white women. Rape them. So the races get mixed. The white man don't know his true place in America. This is a white man's country. Like Rhodesia."

He gave me a look.

"Rhodesia's in Africa," I told him. "White men, they built it right out of the jungle. A long time ago. But the niggers took it for themselves. And the UN, they didn't do nothing. What we need is race war. But the white man, he's too beaten down here. The white man needs to see the light. So what we need is to start the fighting. Then the white man will show his true colors."

"Damn! You *listen*, huh?"

It made me feel good, what he said. "I always listen," I told him.

"So they're going to wipe out all the niggers?"

"That wouldn't do any good," I told him. "They're not the real enemy. They're like dogs—it all depends on who their masters are. The Jews—they're the ones in control. All this stuff, it's part of their plan."

"The Jews, huh?"

"Yes."

"You ever think about that stuff?"

"No."

"Ever kill a Jew?"

"I don't know. . . . how could I tell?"

He made a sound that was like laughing, but kind of strangled. He lit a cigarette, cupping the tip in his hand. Walked around in a little circle.

"You get a chance, ask one of them how it got its name. Rhodesia, okay?"

I nodded, waiting for him to say more.

"You know my name?" he asked.

"Wolf."

"Yes. Listen, now. You get a chance, do him. Don't wait around for the perfect moment—it might not come, okay? You need to be alone with him to do it?"

"It would be better. . . . depends on how many others."

"Yeah. That's what I figured. You remember how to come out?"

"Tie something around my head and run."

"Yeah. You got it."

He didn't say anything for a long time. I waited. He came over, stood real close to me.

"If you think they're on to you . . . if it looks bad . . . just . . . run for it. Don't wait to do him. Run for it. We'll get him some other way."

♣

I stayed in my room the next morning. Lying on my bed
with my eyes closed. Like you do in prison. I was watching
television. In my head. There's no sound in my head either.
I like to watch the nature shows. I look at the ones I saw
before.

There was one. A caterpillar. It crawls over a plant, like
a bright worm. Eating and eating. Then, one day, it stops.
Stuff comes out of it until it's all covered. Then the stuff
gets hard. It looks like a jewel, hanging there. A long time
passes, and the shell cracks. The shell cracks, and a butterfly
comes out.

Then it flies away. I don't know what happens to it after
that. When I was a kid, I saw something like that, but I
don't remember it so good.

♣

When I got up, it was almost twelve o'clock. I walked over
to Sheridan. The whores were out. I saw one, a short blonde
in red shorts. For a minute, I thought she was the same
one that was with the pimp I killed, but it wasn't her. This
one was older.

It was twenty dollars for her, ten for the room. The room
was much smaller than mine. A long, narrow room with a
bed. There was a paper shade on the window. The sunlight
came in. The sheets were gray.

She asked me if I wanted something special. Everybody
wants something special. It costs more.

It didn't take long. She cleaned herself off, squatting over
a basin on the floor.

# SHELLA

She asked me my name, said to come back and see her. I told her John, and said I would.

♣

I had something to eat in a restaurant. I thought about the car wash for a minute—it's open on Sundays. You could work seven days a week if you wanted to, but you had to work at least five, they said. Walking back to my room, I saw a blue-and-white police car go by. The cop on the passenger side gave me a cop look. I looked down—I never looked back.

I wondered if Shella knew I was coming.

♣

My rent was paid till Monday, so Sunday night was the right time to go anyway. Maybe they knew that, the people Mack was with.

I packed my duffel bag. There was plenty of time, so I watched some more television in my head.

A show about white tigers.

♣

A little black car pulled to the curb. A low, smooth-looking car. A Firebird, I think. Mack got out of the front seat. He shook hands with me, opened the trunk, put my duffel bag in there.

"All set?"

"Sure," I told him.

There was nobody else in the car. He drove on the highway by the lake, heading back downtown.

"We got a ways to go," he said. "Make yourself comfortable. . . . That seat goes all the way back, like an airplane."

I pushed the buttons on the side of the seat until I got it right. I wanted to close my eyes but I thought it would make him nervous.

"How come they call it Rhodesia?" I asked him. "I mean . . . where'd that name come from?"

"From Cecil Rhodes, John. Cecil Rhodes, the Builder of the Empire. He started that country with his own bare hands. You get there first, you're entitled to stamp your name on a country, right?"

"Right."

Two black guys on motorcycles went past us real fast, cutting in and out of traffic. I expected him to say something, but he didn't.

We went back downtown and kept going. We stopped to pay a toll. The signs said we were heading to Indiana.

He was smoking a lot. I felt like I should say something, but I didn't know how.

We turned off the highway. There was a sign, but all I could see on it was South and some number.

He drove careful, not too fast.

"Could you use a beer, Johnny?"

I told him sure.

♣

When we got back on the road, the clock on the dashboard said 12:45.

"You have any questions?"

"When does it start?"

"What?"

"The race war?"

He turned sideways to look at me. His face was a little sad. I never saw him look like that before.

"This is a military operation, John. We're a guerrilla force. . . . You know what that is?"

"No."

"Like . . . we hide in the jungle, then we sneak out and zap them and sneak back. See what I mean? We don't have enough manpower to just march in and take over. It's our job to start the fire. First it gets going strong enough by itself, then we provide the leadership. When the white man rises up angry, he's not going to know what to do. The Jews, they've been running the government so long, the white man's forgot how to do it. That's where we come in."

"Where?"

"We all got our jobs. Those boys you went out with, we got people who work with them. They're the shock troops. They keep the action going. Heighten the contradictions, that's what the leader taught us. I don't work with them myself. Me, I'm in recruitment."

"Recruitment?"

"Sure. That's one of the most delicate jobs of all. I have to, like . . . screen the applicants. My judgment is very important. I started out just bringing guys in. At the plant where I worked. I put in a long time doing that. When I'd find a right guy, I'd turn him over to one of the coordinators—the guys who run the individual groups. And I worked my way up. What I do now, I recruit for the cells."

"The cells? Like in . . . ?"

"No. A cell is a small group. It operates all by itself. With specific targets. We got procurement cells . . . they raise money for our treasury. I recruited for them. You're my first recruit for the Lightning Squadron."

"What's that?"

"Doing what you did Friday night."

"Killing niggers?"

"Killing whoever. Like I told you, it's not niggers we're worried about."

"Killing Jews?"

"Whoever. Any enemy of the race. There's plenty of white men who're enemies of the race too. Traitors."

"That's what I'll do?"

"Yeah. I seen other guys from the Lightning Squadron, but I never brought one in myself before. I'm supposed to look for guys. For different things we need. But as soon as I met you, I said to myself, there's a man for the squad. It's a real honor, Johnny. For me too, I want you to know. I passed your name on to HQ, and they checked you out."

"HQ?"

"Headquarters. They got an Intelligence Unit. You wouldn't believe the places we got people. See, the Jews are clever, Johnny. They're always trying to infiltrate our operations. So we got to be sure who we're dealing with. They checked your record. We got other ways too. Remember Ginger?"

"Sure."

"She's one of us."

"Ginger?"

He smiled, looking out the windshield. "Yeah, sure. It's not just men in with us. Women. Kids too."

"The skinheads, right?"

"No, I mean *little* kids. We raise them right, in the white man's way. The leader says they're the hope of the future, the kids. We got kids eight years old, know more about their true heritage than the average grown man could ever imagine. Anyway, a man's gonna be considered for the squad, we got to test him. The acid test, we call it. Mostly, unless the man has got a name for himself, like if he was with us inside, we bring him out, give him the test. This time, the leader told me, test this guy outside. We got to be careful, can't be bringing too many guys inside. In case they don't pass the test, see?"

"I guess so."

"Johnny, listen to me a minute. These are serious people I'm taking you to. You can't fuck with them. These men will be your brothers. And that's forever. This ain't something you can get tired of, go on to something else. Your brothers, you know what that means?"

"They're all white?"

"Yeah, of *course* they're all white, for Christ's sake. That's not what I mean. Brothers. Like *blood* brothers. This is for a cause, Johnny. A holy cause. You'll see, inside. When they show you right in the Bible. This is bigger than any of us. No matter where you go, your brothers will be around. Even in prison. You'll never be alone."

I guess he meant it to be a threat, but it sounded like it was a good thing, the way he said it.

"It's on me, I bring a man in. You do good, it'll be on me. You fuck up, it'll be on me too."

"I won't fuck up," I told him.

He put his hand on my shoulder, squeezed it hard.

♣

We drove for a long time. The roads kept getting smaller. He never checked directions or anything. We were outside the cities. Just a farmhouse once in a while. The clock said 2:12.

It was still dark when he turned off onto a dirt road.

"We have to go slow from here," he said. "The first checkpoints won't stop us—they're just watchers."

I didn't say anything.

There was a telephone between the two front seats. He picked it up, pushed in a number.

"It's me," he said. "I just passed checkpoint three. I've got him with me."

He listened for a minute, then he put the phone back.

♣

We came around a bend in the road and there was a log lying across it on an angle. We couldn't drive past. Mack stopped the car. Spotlights came out of the night—little ones, slicing across each other.

Men came out of the woods. They were dressed like soldiers, in those suits that look like the woods, green and brown. They all had guns.

Mack told me to get out of the car. He did too. One of the soldiers patted my clothes. Then he told me to take my jacket off and my shirt too. Mack said it was okay. They didn't ask him to do it.

"No wire," one of the soldiers said.

"All the way," another said to him.

The first soldier told me to take all my clothes off, even my shoes and socks. I did it. It was cold out there.

Another soldier stepped over to me. He was putting a rubber glove on his hand. "Bend over and spread 'em," he said. "Just like in the joint."

I did it. He was rough with his finger. When he took it out, he pulled off the rubber glove, threw it away in the woods.

"Okay, get dressed," the first soldier said to me.

Another one had my duffel bag on the ground. They took everything out, piece by piece, going over it.

"It's clean," one of them said.

Mack came over to me, held out his hand. "They'll take you the rest of the way, Johnny. You're gonna see things you never dreamed of. I know you're gonna make me proud of you. Proud that I brought you in."

"You're not coming?" I asked him.

"No. I won't see you again, not for a while. Maybe never. It depends."

"Goodbye, Mack," I said.

"Goodbye, brother," he said, turning away.

♣

On the other side of the log, they had a pickup truck and a couple of Jeeps. They had those bars that run over the top of the cabs, all with lights on them. I got in where they told me, and they chased each other going back. It made a lot of noise.

From the way they were dressed, I thought they would live in tents. But it was all buildings, like a little town. I couldn't see much—it was still dark. They put me in a big room with bunks in rows. Like the juvenile institution they put me in once. Only there was no bars on the windows.

♣

I got up when it turned light in the morning. There was only two other guys sleeping in the dorm where I was. Neither one moved when I got up.

My duffel bag was at the foot of my bunk. I took it into the shower room, got cleaned up, changed my clothes. Still nobody came around.

I went outside and sat down on the steps. I had a cigarette. It was quiet, like being around a bunch of drunks sleeping it off.

I wondered if everybody was sleeping. If the smiling man in the mug shot was sleeping real close to me, someplace.

I didn't try and figure out what to do. Shella told me once she danced because she was good at it. I told her she was good at a lot of things, she could do them too. She said that was sweet, for me to say it. And she gave me a kiss. Like a kid does, maybe. On the cheek. She told me I was good at different things too. I knew the one thing I was good at, so I asked her, "What else?" She looked at me a long time. I didn't move, just watched her watch me. Finally, she came over, sat next to me. "Waiting," she said. "That's what you're good at, honey. Waiting."

♣

A guy with a beard and a watermelon belly walked past where I was sitting. "They serving breakfast yet?" he asked me. I told him I didn't know. "Come on, let's take a look," he said. I got up and walked with him.

It was the next building. Like a cafeteria, except that the tables were all scattered around and the food wasn't already cooked.

The woman behind the little counter was skinny. She looked real tired. The place was almost empty—I only saw a couple of guys, eating in one corner.

"You got pancakes this morning, Flo?" the fat man asked her.

"I didn't make up the batter yet," she said. "How about some bacon and eggs?"

"Suits me," he told her. "What about you, friend?"

I said that would be good. I didn't see any cash register and I couldn't tell what things cost. We sat down at one of the tables. When the food was cooked, the woman behind the counter said it was ready and we went over and got it.

In the middle of eating, the fat man told me his name was Bobby. I told him my name and we shook hands. The other guys who were there, at the other table, when they got finished eating, they picked up their plates and brought them over to the counter. The waitress took them and put them in a big rubber bin.

Bobby took out a pack of cigarettes, asked me if I wanted one. I said thanks.

"When'd you get in?" he said.

"Last night."

"Yeah, I heard a new man was coming. Who brought you in?"

"They didn't tell me their names," I said. "A bunch of guys."

"Oh, you mean the transport team. No, I mean, who was your recruiter?"

I looked at him.

"Your recruiter, man . . . the guy who talked to you about—"

"He knows what you mean." A voice behind me. I didn't recognize it. When he stepped around, I could see it was one of the soldiers from last night. A short man wearing a black T-shirt. His arms were big, like he lifted a lot of weights. "See, Bobby, this man, he just got here. And he already knows more than some of the veterans. Like how to keep his mouth shut, see?"

"Hey, don't get your balls in an uproar, all right, Murray? I was just being friendly, a new man and all."

Murray introduced himself, sticking out his hand. He put a lot of pressure into the grip. "Flo take care of you all right?" he asked me.

"Sure."

"Okay. You all finished? Good. I'm gonna take you to meet some people."

I took my plates over to the counter. When the woman came over, I told her, "It was good. Thanks." She gave me a funny look.

♣

It was wide daylight now, and I could see everything as I walked across the compound with Murray. It wasn't all that much, not as big as it looked at night. Most of the buildings were like houses; only one was higher than the first floor.

You could walk to anyplace they had. The front was open. Across the back, there was this high fence, but it didn't connect to anything. Like they started it and never got it done. Murray saw me looking at it.

"When it's finished, the whole compound'll be behind a

wall. That's just the preliminary work you see there. This is all our land. We own it. Free and clear, and all legal. Five thousand acres . . . a lot more than you see here. All the woods around here, even the road you came in on, it's all ours. That's one thing the leader taught us, to own our own. Own our own. There's no welfare in here, no government, no IRS, no nothing. On our land, we make all the rules. You want to live pure, you want your kids to be raised pure, you got to own your own to do it."

I nodded the way I always do when I don't understand something. He kept showing me things, saying how they owned it all.

We came to this house at the back, near that fence they were building. Murray knocked on the door. The guy who answered it was wearing a shoulder holster like he was used to it. He turned his back and we followed him. It looked like a regular house, living room and kitchen and all. We walked past, to the back, where the bedrooms would be. It was a much bigger room than I thought, bigger than the living room. A man was sitting behind this desk they made out of a door laid flat across a pair of sawhorses. The walls were covered with maps, colored pins stuck in them.

The guy behind the desk was wearing a white shirt and a dark tie. He had glasses, and he looked older than the others, but maybe that was because he was losing his hair in front and he combed it over from the side. That always makes you look older.

The guy with the shoulder holster said, "Thanks, Murray," and Murray got a look on his face like he wasn't happy about the way the guy said it, but he didn't say anything himself before he walked out.

The guy in the shoulder holster told me to have a seat,

pointing with his finger for me to sit on the other side of the desk from the guy in the white shirt.

I sat there and waited.

♣

The guy in the white shirt studied me. I couldn't figure out if I was supposed to be nervous, so I lit a cigarette like I needed something to do. I guess it was a good idea, because the guy in the shoulder holster lit one too.

The guy in the white shirt was looking at his fingernails. "What'd you kill the nigger with?" he asked me.

"I shot him," I said.

"Not *that* nigger, the one in Florida."

I remembered the Indian, telling me to stay right next to the truth as much as I could. The lawyer they got to throw me away in Florida, I remember him asking me where the weapon was . . . what I had killed the guy with. They just had "blunt object" on the police report, the lawyer said, and it would be better if I told them where the weapon was. So I knew the answer. "A tire iron," I told the man in the white shirt.

"Why?"

" 'Cause it was right there."

"Not why you used a tire iron," he said. He was using that tone people use when they talk to me sometimes— like I'm stupid and they're being nice about it but it's hard work. "Why did you kill him in the first place?"

"I was in this motel," I told him. "He had a white woman in his room with him. I saw her leave. I said something to him and he said something back. The next thing I know, it was done."

"You lost your temper?"

"I guess. . . ."

"You hate niggers?"

"Yes."

"How come?"

"How come?"

"Yeah. How come. How come you hate them?"

" 'Cause . . ." I tried to think of all the stuff Mack told me—it all got mixed in my head. I knew they'd think I was stupid. "'Cause . . . if it wasn't for them, this would be a good place."

"What place?"

"America. Our country. It would be a good place without the niggers. They're dirty animals. And all the government wants to do is make them happy."

"The Jew government," the guy in the shoulder holster said.

I nodded. The guy in the white shirt gave the other one a look, like he shouldn't help me with the answers.

"You want a pure race?" he asked me. "A pure white race?"

"Yes."

"Are you willing to do battle for your race?"

"Yes."

He leaned back in his chair, rubbing his chin like he was considering something.

"You a pretty good shot?" he asked me.

"If I get close enough."

They both laughed, but it sounded like they thought I said the right answer.

**161**

♣

They gave me a lot of stuff to read. Piles of it. Books and magazines and little thin things with covers. I took it all back to the dorm.

I tried to read the stuff. I don't read so good, but I know how.

They had a television in the dorm. I was watching it one day when the guy in the white shirt came in. He asked me why I had it on with the sound off. I told him I was trying to read the books he gave me. He looked at me for a minute, then he said "Good," and walked out.

♣

There were always people around, but I was by myself. Like prison. Like being out of prison too, when I thought about it. I thought about it. I thought about what people say in prison, how you have to kill time. They would do all these things . . . basketball, dominos, read magazines. To make time pass. They thought I was stupid because I didn't do anything. To make time pass. I'm not stupid. Not like they think, anyway. Time passes by itself—you don't have to do anything.

It is different, though, prison. Being inside, you don't work. When I was outside, before Tampa, I was with Shella. I didn't think about her—she was there. When I was inside, I would think about her. Like studying. But all I ever figured out was that Shella had the answers, not me.

I thought about her a lot in the compound. No dreaming—I wasn't asleep when I did it. Shella had bad dreams sometimes. She woke up once, making noises like she couldn't breathe. I grabbed her—she was strong. When it was over, my shoulder was bleeding. From where she bit me. She was sorry, sad about that. She poured some stuff on where she bit me.

She wanted to tell me what was in her bad dream, but when she started to tell me about the broomstick, I got sick and she stopped.

"Don't you ever have dreams, honey?" she asked me.

I never thought about it before that. I guess I don't.

♣

Shella liked to dress up. She had all kinds of clothes. She even had eyeglasses she wore sometimes. I put them on once—they were just plain glass. She wore them when she put her hair on top of her head, when she went out sometimes, all dressed up like an older lady.

She didn't wear the glasses for reading. Shella read all the time. I asked her to read some of it to me once, but I couldn't understand the words. It wasn't like the stories. After a while, I fell asleep.

♣

One time when Shella got her period, she had terrible cramps. They hurt so bad she cried. I didn't know what to do. I got a cold washcloth, tried to put it on her head. She threw the washcloth at me. "It's my guts that hurt, not my head, you stupid bastard!" she yelled. But when I put on some of the music she liked, she said it gave her a headache.

I asked her if she wanted a cigarette. A drink, maybe?

She was curled up in a little ball then, holding her stomach. When I touched her back, it was like iron.

It hurt me to hear her cry like that. I filled the bathtub with hot water. The bathroom got all steamy. I put some of the green bubble stuff she liked in there. I pulled her robe off. Then I picked her up in that ball she was wrapped in and carried her inside. I lowered her into the tub. She tried to bite me, but I held her face hard against my chest until I got her in.

"It's too hot," she said, but I kept her there.

She came out of the ball and laid back. I held the back of her neck so she wouldn't go under.

"The water's all turning red," she said, real quiet.

After a while, she started to cry again. But it was different, the crying. I let the water out of the tub. Then I stood her up against me and showered her off. All the bubbles and the blood ran down the drain.

She was still crying when I dried her off. I took her into the bedroom and put her on the bed.

"Could I have powder?" she said.

I knew the powder. Baby powder. Shella always puts it on under her pants. I spilled some on her. "That's too much," she laughed. A little laugh, like a giggle. But she wasn't crying by then. I rubbed it all over her. Then she rolled over and I did it on her back too. On her bottom and legs too. Then I covered her with some sheets and she fell asleep.

It was dark when she woke up. I was in the chair, next to the bed. I patted her. She took my hand and kissed it. "I'll make it up to you, baby," she said. Then she went back to sleep.

# SHELLA

♣

I don't dream, but I can see things, like on a screen if I close my eyes. I did that in the compound. A lot, sometimes for a whole day. I would think about why I was there, and then it would start. Shella.

A couple of nights after she had the cramps, Shella came in and took a shower. She was in there a long time. When she came out, she was naked. I was on the bed, watching TV. Shella turned it off. It was dark in the room, but I could see good. The neon sign outside the motel flashed off and on against Shella's body. She was red, then she was blue.

"Do you want a cigarette?" she said.

I told her okay, and she lit one for me. Then she crawled onto the bed on her hands and knees, watching me. She licked me a couple of times and I got hard.

"You want something special?" she asked me.

"What?"

"*Special*," she whispered. "Like you haven't had before."

I knew she meant sex. I closed my eyes, thinking. I dragged on the cigarette until it was done.

"You can't think of anything, can you?" Shella was still whispering. "Nothing you want you didn't already have, huh, baby?"

"Anything is . . . I mean, anything you . . ."

"Ssssh, baby. I know. I was thinking too. Special. Like something I never did with anyone else, you know?"

"Yes."

"But I couldn't think of anything I haven't done," she said. She lay down on my chest. Her body was shaking.

Her hands dug into me. I could feel wet on my chest but I couldn't hear her cry.

♣

Nothing much happened where I was. People came in and out all the time, and you could tell some things were going on in other parts of the place. There was a lot of practice with guns. I did that too. I didn't know anything about the guns, but they showed me. The guy who showed me, he liked to do that. He was glad I didn't know anything so he could teach me. He was a good teacher— he wanted to make people smart, not tell them they were stupid.

The targets were pictures of people. Some were famous people. Some were just different kinds of people. Black people were their favorite.

Gunfire was always going on.

♣

They had classes in other things. Political classes. And fighting too. One teacher, he was dressed all in black, even with a hood over his face. He said he was a ninja. He mostly talked.

Every time he would ask for a volunteer, I would sit very still. I was scared to do this. But one day he made me. He told me to come up behind him and get him in a choke hold, try and pull him down.

I was so afraid I'd break his neck that I grabbed him around the jaw instead of the throat. He hit me hard in the ribs with an elbow and then chopped me in the neck. It hurt, where he hit me.

He told me to stick with guns. Some of them laughed.

♣

I was there about two weeks when Murray told me the leader was going to talk the next morning.

Everybody in the whole camp was there. In a big hall in the back, with the doors open.

He was the man in the mug shots. The same man. He was a good talker. There must have been a couple of hundred people in the room, but he didn't use a microphone and he didn't shout.

It was a good speech. He said we were the warriors. The warriors of the right. Not the right wing, he said, the right way. Mostly he talked about race. Pure races. How they got all mixed together. Like dogs. Mongrel dogs. He said our race was like snow on the ground, covering the dirt underneath. When the snow melts, it could wash all the dirt away. But if you mix stuff in with the snow, it gets all filthy. It's not beautiful anymore. Not pure.

He said niggers weren't the real enemy. It was the Jews. It's the Jews who gave us the niggers. The Jews needed animals to work the land around Israel—that's where Israel is, Africa. So they started experimenting with different animals. They are real fine scientists. And that's how they ended up with niggers, like a cross between apes and people. The niggers are just animals—they were being used by the Jews. He said even the stupidest niggers were waking up to this. Niggers in the big cities hate the Jews too. He said they were getting smarter to be feeling that way.

That's what comes of educating niggers. He said the Jews hate themselves because they really want to be white. He said the big Jews are born smart, but the regular Jews, they're always trying to be friends with the niggers.

The leader said that our race was dying. The niggers and the Jews breed faster than we do. Soon there would be more of them than us. And that would be the end. He said white men have always known this, but we always got ruined by fighting among ourselves. That's what he said. He said there were a lot of white-power movements, but they always fought each other.

He said he would give examples. He said that Europe was all white men. Nothing but white men. If white men fight white men, white men have got to lose. He said that over and over again.

He had a Bible with him, and he talked about what was in it. He talked about resources—he said that a lot, resources. How if we had enough resources we could have our homeland.

"Partition!" he yelled. And everybody cheered.

He said Partition was our own land. A couple of states for white people only. Our own schools, our own churches, everything our own.

The Promised Land, he said it like it was holy. He said it was promised to us, right from the Bible. The truth of God.

God was a white man, everybody knows that. Even the niggers know that. That's why they hate us.

He talked for a long time. When he was done, everybody yelled. Some of them waved guns in the air.

# SHELLA

♣

Everybody talked like the leader, but he was the best at it. I practiced with the guns they had. I read the stuff they gave me. They watched TV a lot—they never watched the nature shows. They played cards a lot. Mostly, they just worked, like anyplace else. Cooking, cleaning, fixing. Some of them, they would just come and go.

Everybody called everybody brother in there. Everybody did it. I never heard white people do that before I went to prison the first time.

They never seemed to go out in the woods, but they were always dressed for it.

Murray came by the dorm one morning. He walked over to my bunk, sat down on the next one. I was glad I had some of the reading in front of me.

"How come you don't put up no pictures?" he asked me.

I didn't know what to say. I used to hate that, before I figured out I didn't have to say anything. But that was for other places. I looked around the big room. Guys had pictures on the walls near where they slept. Mostly women. From magazines. Their favorites were women wearing soldier stuff, like a naked girl with a rifle. I don't understand pictures, why people have them. I mean, maybe a picture of a real person, to remember them. But men who buy magazines, they don't know those women. Shella tried to explain it to me once, but I stopped listening once she got crazy. When Shella talks about why men do things with women, she gets twisted up inside and scary. I couldn't think of anything to say to Murray so I just shrugged. He gave me a look, like he knew something about me. I saw

the muscles flex hard across his arm as he looked at me.
I seen that kind of look all my life.

♣

Murray came by where I was a lot. I got used to seeing
him. One night, he just looked in the door. "Come on,"
he said. "Cadre meeting."

I got up and went outside with him. I followed him,
walking across the compound. He was almost bouncing, he
was so pumped up, humming to himself, clenching his fists.

Inside the room where he took us there was maybe eight,
ten guys. Nobody was saying much, just smoking and standing around.

The guy in the white shirt came in the back door, turned
an easy chair so it was facing us, and then he went and
stood in the corner.

The leader came in and sat down. He had a suit on with
a white shirt but no tie. He looked like the mug shot, just
like it. Everybody stood up when he walked in. Then he
made some gesture with his hand, like waving, and everybody sat down. I was the last one to sit, because I didn't
know what to do. And the guy in the white shirt, he never
sat down.

"I just wanted to walk in here and tell you, again, how
much the Nation values your sacrifices. I know it's no fun,
giving up what you did, making those sacrifices. Like the
good book says, if there's a reason, there's a season. There's
a time for everything. Soldiers make sacrifices . . . that's
the way of the warrior. But tonight, you're getting a little
break. Not the whole camp, now, just this cadre. What
we're going to have is a little training exercise, a full-dress

rehearsal. Some of you have already been blooded, some of you haven't gone the distance. Tonight isn't that. Tonight's just a way of spreading our message. Any questions?"

Nobody said anything. I was toward the back of the room, but I could feel people behind me.

The leader looked all around the room. He had a way of looking you in the face that didn't challenge you. Not trying to stare you down, just making sure you was listening to him. You could look back at him and it wasn't the signal to fight.

"Being a Christian doesn't mean you don't have anything to do with sex," he said to us. "A man is going to want sex, that's the way nature intended it. But in these times, a man has to be careful. There's a lot of traps out there."

He took a pipe out of his shirt pocket. A white pipe with a yellow stem. He pushed down the tobacco with his thumb, fired a wooden match, and took his time getting it going. Nobody else lit up. When he got it going, he took a puff. Then he held the pipe in his hand, looking at it, just settling down.

"You men are going to have a little party tonight. Just down the road, about an hour's drive from here, there's a little prostitution ring operating. They've got three trailers parked side-by-side in this spot out behind a tavern, back in the woods, where you can't see them from the road. Billy knows where it is—he'll be leading the convoy.

"Now let me tell you a little bit about this operation. It's run by white men, but they don't act like it. They don't serve niggers in the roadhouse, but out back, they get the same rights as white men. You understand what I'm saying to you, boys? You fuck one of those trailer whores, and you may be going in right behind a nigger. You may be pulling sloppy seconds after a jungle bunny. Now, we *told* the guy who runs the operation we wouldn't stand for this. Explained it to him real clear. He said he was gonna set up a separate trailer for them, and we went along. But we sent our own people in, and you know what they told us . . . ? The niggers can only go in the trailer on the left, but the girls, they go to all of them. They're on rotation, you see what I'm saying?"

Some of the men nodded. I just watched him. He was too smart—there had to be more.

"Anybody here know how to make a good fire?" The leader looked around the room.

One guy raised his hand. I could see from his face that he knew all about fires. The leader looked across at the guy in the white shirt. They kind of nodded to each other.

"Okay," the leader said. "We got a rifleman here too?"

Three of the guys put their hands up. The leader looked at the closest one, a guy with long blond hair and a mustache. "Where'd you learn?"

"I was in the 'Nam," the blond guy said.

"Good enough, brother. What about you?" He was asking another guy, a guy with a shaved head.

"Prison guard," the man said.

The leader moved his eyes to the third man. He was bigger than the others, with his hair combed forward over his eyes, like bangs. "Hunting . . ." he said. Like he was ashamed of it.

The leader kept asking questions. He had a soft, friendly voice. Everybody liked him, you could see it.

"No reason why you can't have a little taste before you get to work. Thing is, with whores, you got to be careful. A whore is a liar, always remember that, men. A whore is a liar. Lying is their trade. Lying on their backs, lying with their mouths. So you have to watch yourselves at all times, be careful you don't get something you didn't bargain for. Everybody know what I mean?"

Everybody nodded. Somebody said "Yeah," but so soft I couldn't tell who it was.

"Is that right?" the leader said. "You all know what I mean, huh? Well, okay, how about *you* tell me what I mean." He pointed at a guy right across from me. A bloaty-looking guy with real hairy arms.

"Don't go out without your rubbers. . . . I mean, don't go in without them," the fat guy said. On his face was a look like he got the right answer.

A couple of men laughed, but they stopped when the leader looked at them.

"Yes, that's certainly true," he said. "But I'm thinking of something else. Some of these little girls, well, they're not girls at all. Understand?" He looked around the room. "Now, who knows how you tell whether you're looking at a real woman, or one of those transvestites . . . a homo-sex-ual dressed up like a woman?"

Nobody said anything. Nobody knew the answer.

I knew.

I knew the right answer.

I raised my hand. The leader nodded at me. I touched my Adam's apple. The leader smiled. "Now, where'd you learn that, son?"

I didn't know what to say. I didn't know why I raised my hand. I was stupid, that's why I did it. I couldn't tell him about Shella, how I learned those things, where I'd been. I felt myself being pushed in, like the air was too heavy. I didn't know what to say.

"In prison," I said.

The leader sort of chuckled. "Yes, that's been the graduate education for many of us, hasn't it? Well, you're right. Right on the money."

He bowed his head, like he was praying. I saw the others do it, so I did it too.

The man in the white shirt, he kept watching us.

♣

After the leader left, the man in the white shirt took out a clipboard. He wrote something on it, then he kind of pointed at the guy who was with him the first time I saw him. The guy with the shoulder holster.

That guy explained what we were going to do. Some of the guys asked questions—you could see it was okay to do that with the leader out of the room. The way they talked about it, it was like this army thing.

But what they were going to do, it sounded like the same way they send a message in the city.

♣

We went in three cars. I was in the back of a station wagon, Murray was next to me. He kept squeezing a set of those handgrips, the ones with springs, to make you stronger. Over and over, switching them from one hand to the other. The handles were red, wood.

They had asked me what kind of gun I wanted—they had a whole bunch of them spread out on a table. I took one that looked like the one the Indian gave me.

The roadhouse was like a long, dark diner. Neon sign

outside: Rebel Inn. The parking lot had mostly pickup trucks in it. You had to walk this dirt path around the back to get to the trailers.

There were three of them, like the leader said, one standing off by itself to the left.

"Twenty-two hundred hours, right on target," one of the men said. The guy in the white shirt had said we should be there by ten o'clock, but I didn't say anything.

The three guys with the rifles went in first. We had to wait for them to finish so they could stand guard. It didn't take long. We all got a turn. I knocked on the door to the trailer. A skinny old woman with a big blonde wig let me in. It cost thirty bucks. The room was like a closet. The girl in there was tired and she smelled bad. You could hear the people grunting in the next room over—the walls were made of some cardboard stuff. I finished quick.

When we got together outside in the parking lot, the one they called Billy checked us over. He pointed to the house on the left, told me and Murray to take that one. The other ones fanned out.

"You see one, shoot him," Murray said. "They all carry razors and they'll cut you in a minute."

"Okay," I said.

Murray knocked on the door. A woman in a red dress opened it—she was fatter than the door opening. We climbed up the steps and went inside. We took out our guns.

"Get your hands up," Murray told the fat woman.

She did it. She looked bored.

"How many girls you got back there?" he asked her.

"Three."

"They all busy?"

"Two are. Mary's alone in her room."

"Where's the phone?"

"There's no phone here. We use the one in the tavern." The fat woman sat down, lit a cigarette. Murray looked mad, but he didn't say anything.

The fat woman dragged on her cigarette. I could hear a radio playing. Country music, it sounded like.

"Call her out . . . this Mary. Get her out here."

The fat woman started to get up, then she sort of shrugged, yelled "Maaary!"

Another fat girl came out, this one was younger. She was wearing a shortie nightgown and high heels. When she saw the guns, she went and sat down next to the other one, like she was half asleep.

"You try to run, I'll blow you away," Murray said to the women. They didn't look like they could.

The hall was too narrow for two of us. Murray went first. He stood outside a door to the left, pointed to my door on the right. He stepped back and kicked the door. It made a loud noise but it held. He kicked it again. I heard a scream. I turned the handle of my door and it opened. Inside there was a man just getting off a woman. They were both naked, except he had socks on. I pointed the gun at them.

"Get out," I said.

The man kind of jumped into his pants, grabbed up his clothes and ran out. The woman just laid there.

"There's gonna be a fire," I told her. I walked out of the room and I heard a shot. I looked through the open door. Murray was aiming at a man—I couldn't tell if he hit him or not.

"Come on," I yelled at him. "It's going up."

He followed me out. The two fat women were still sitting in the front room.

Another shot, from one of the other trailers. A man in a red jacket came in the front door. He had a stocking mask over his face and a metal gasoline can in one hand. He started splashing the gasoline all over—the smell was choking me.

The two fat women ran out. When the fire man got to the back of the trailer, the other two women came out too.

We went back to the parking lot. There was a big *whooosh!* from between the three trailers. A fireball went up, then it shot out in three arms. You could see it rip toward the trailers. They all went up. It sounded like a war . . . explosions from inside, popping, then a big bang. People were running out of the tavern. There was a lot of shooting, but it was all up in the air. Two men ran to a corner of the parking lot. They stuck a cross in the ground. The guy in the red jacket lit that too.

That was all. We got in the cars and took off. Nobody tried to stop us. I couldn't hear sirens.

♣

The car I was in had a police radio in the front seat. I couldn't understand it with all the crackling, but the guy next to the driver said the State Police were rolling toward the tavern. By then we were miles away.

When we got back, they dropped us off near the dorms. The guy in the shoulder holster was waiting. He told me and Murray to come with him.

We walked to another building, where the guy in the white shirt was waiting.

Murray went in first. The guy with the shoulder holster told me to wait.

When it was my turn, the guy in the white shirt asked me what happened. I told him.

"Good work," he said.

♣

I was walking back when I saw Murray ahead of me. He must have been waiting—I was in with the man in the white shirt for a while.

"What'd you tell him?" Murray asked me.

"What happened."

"About the niggers?"

"What niggers?"

"At the place . . . the niggers. I told him I . . . shot one. A nigger. In the room with a white girl."

I didn't say anything. All the men in the house had been white.

Murray put his hand on my arm. I let him do that—he was scared of something.

"John, did he ask you . . . if there was any niggers there?"

"No."

"You won't tell . . ."

"Tell what?"

"You're my true brother, John," Murray said, squeezing my arm hard.

♣

On the TV the next day, they said it was the KKK who set fire to the trailers. Some of the guys watching cheered.

The fire man rubbed his hands, watching the tape of the burning.

♣

It was another ten days or so when Murray came by. All excited again. Worked up.

"We going to an Action Team, John. I just heard. They tell you yet?"

"No."

"Hey, it's true. I got it straight from HQ. You'll see, both of us got tapped."

He was pacing around in a little circle, really happy.

The only thing I knew about the Action Team was what the leader said in one of his talks. He talked about Partition again. He said the niggers wanted their own land too, but, like all niggers, they wanted the government to just give it to them. Like Welfare. Our land, he said, our land would come from our own labor. We would pay for it. The Action Teams, they were the way they got the money.

♣

The guy in the white shirt, he was the one who told us about the Action Team they picked me and Murray for. Hijacking was what it was. An armored car, carrying a factory payroll from a bank. He knew everything about it. Everything. You can't shoot out the tires on one of those armored cars—the guards would just stand inside and call the police on their telephone. Roadblocks are no good either. What you have to do, he said, is hit them while they make a transfer. While the door is open.

He said they were experts. They did dozens of these, all around the country. It was the only way to get the money they needed.

♣

Me and Murray were watching TV. They just arrested this guy in Milwaukee. They found all kinds of bodies in his house. The announcer was saying the guy was maybe the worst serial killer ever. The fire man came in. He listened for a minute, getting excited.

"How many women did he kill?" he asked Murray.

"He only killed boys," Murray said.

"He's a sick bastard," the fire man said, getting up and walking away.

♣

One day, Murray asked me if I wanted to go work out with him. There's a weight room in one of the buildings. I told him no.

"John, come on, man. You're too skinny. I mean, I'm not coming down on you or anything, but I can see you got good musculature . . . a good skeleton, see? If you was to work out with me, I guarantee you, maybe six months, you wouldn't recognize yourself."

"Thanks anyway," I said to him.

He sat down next to me. "John, if I made you feel bad, I'm an asshole. That wasn't what I meant. This whole thing . . ." He waved his arms around. "This whole thing, it's not just for race pride, you know what I mean? Like . . . why did you join up? How come?"

"I hate niggers," I told him.

"Yeah, I know. Me too. As much as anybody. But . . . part of it, I guess . . . I wanted to have friends, too. Real friends. You understand me?"

"Sure."

"So forget about the iron work, okay? I just wanted to say, you got anything I could help you with, you just gotta ask me, okay?"

"Okay, Murray."

He punched me hard on the arm, but I could tell he wasn't trying to hurt me.

♣

The guy in the shoulder holster came by one afternoon. He said the leader wanted to see me.

I followed him over. The leader was in his big room, in his chair. The guy in the shoulder holster left us alone. I measured the distance. I saw the dots start to pop out on him. The door opened behind me—the guy in the white shirt came in.

"You are the young man who knew how to tell a transvestite from a real woman, aren't you?"

"Yes," I said.

"You know why that's so important?"

"No. I don't, I guess."

"The homo-sex-ual doesn't think with his mind, son. He thinks with his sex . . . whatever that is. They're bad apples. One of our great leaders once said, a man who won't fuck won't fight. That's why they don't let them in the army. Just one of them . . . a single one, he can destroy a whole movement. You know, the white power movement didn't start last week. It has a long, honorable history, ever since Reconstruction. . . . You know what that is?"

"No sir."

"After the Civil War, the niggers, the same ones who used to be slaves, they took over the South. Took it over. They were in charge. They owned the land, they owned the women. Naturally, white men could not tolerate this. That was the start of the Klan. And we've been moving forward ever since. Yes, there have been setbacks. But our real enemies have never been the niggers. Our real enemies have always been traitors. Traitors from within. We've got our list, and there's more whites on it than blacks, I can tell you. Judges, senators, FBI agents. All traitors to the race.

"That's why those homo-sex-uals are so dangerous, son. Did you know that one of the real heroes of our movement was actually assassinated by one of his own men? Now that would be hard to explain except for one thing . . . it was a damn lovers' quarrel! You understand? One fag jilted another fag, and we had a shooting. Now, the public doesn't know this, but it's a fact. The worst thing about a fag is how he thinks. So a queer can never be truly white, because he could fall in love with a nigger just like that!"

His fingers made a bone-crack sound when he snapped them. I looked close at him, like he wanted me to.

"You know why I'm telling you all this?"

"No. But it's good to know."

He looked over at the guy in the white shirt. Then he turned back to me.

"You pretty good friends with Murray?"

"I guess."

"He ever . . . act funny around you?"

"No. I never saw him do that."

"You know what I'm getting at?"

"Sure. I seen them before."

"In prison?"

"Yes."

"In prison, you ever see a man with big, huge muscles, tattoos . . . and he's still a queer?"

"Sure," I told him. It was the truth.

"Keep your eyes open," the leader said.

♣

After that, we had meetings every day. Like classes, with teachers. They had this big table, so big we could all fit around it. On the table they had little model cars, roads, and everything. Even a little armored car. They had maps. Not like maps you get in a gas station, black and white maps so big you could see the streets on them.

Some days, the man in the white shirt told us how to do it. Other days, the leader told us why.

♣

They went over it again and again. Every time, they would ask a different guy the same questions. The man in the white shirt pointed at Murray. "What's the procedure if you're captured?"

"I just say I want a lawyer. I don't answer any questions. I just say I want a lawyer."

"Good! One of our lawyers will get to you eventually. Just remember, you may get some Jew Public Defender or something until we can get to you. Don't speak to him either, understand? Wait for the word to get to you."

He looked around the room some more. "Billy, you've got the cash in the getaway car, okay? But when you approach the drop-off point, you see it's covered. What do you do?"

"I find someplace to hole up. I get off the road as soon as I can. Then I call the number and do whatever they tell me to do."

"Right! Now, what if you got a clear shot to make it back here with the money . . . ?"

"We never come back here. Never."

"Why?" the man said, turning his face so he was asking me.

"So the cops don't have an excuse to come in here," I said. I knew all the answers by then, from listening.

"Yes! This is sacred ground. We are all safe here. This is *private property* . . . remember how we talked about that? No cop, no FBI agent, no Treasury man, nobody from ATF . . . *nobody* comes in here without our permission. It's like John here said . . . we can't give them an excuse."

After the meeting, Murray slapped my hand, like he was proud of me for getting it right.

♣

I was watching a nature show on TV. It was quiet in the dorm. They showed different insects that looked like they were dangerous, but they weren't. It was so other animals would leave them alone.

Murray came in. He took off the little weights he wears around his ankles. He wears them around his wrists too. He came over to where I was. The show was just going off.

"How old are you, John?"

"Thirty-four," I told him. Sticking as close as I could

to the truth, like they had told me. The truth is I don't know.

"I'm twenty-nine."

I didn't say anything.

"You were in prison, right?"

"Yeah, I was."

"More than once?"

"Yes."

"I was never in prison. Never in the army either. Or an ex-cop, like some of the guys."

I lit a cigarette. A show about some kind of dancing was coming on.

"You think it matters?" he said.

"What?"

"What I was *saying*, John? Not being in the joint, or the service . . . you know . . ."

"No."

"You know, John, I don't mean to hurt your feelings or nothing, but some of the guys, they think you're not too bright. But me, I know better. You're just quiet is all. I know you got a brain, that's why I ask you stuff."

On the TV, people in white costumes were jumping around. Sometimes the men would catch the women in the air.

"I never forget what you did, John. What you didn't say, I mean. About the stuff in the trailer. We're partners, you and me. Anybody fucks with you, they fuck with me."

He stuck out his hand. I shook it.

♣

There was a lot of training in the place. Everybody was always being trained for something. The men, anyway.

There were women around, but I never saw them being trained.

They practiced so much with the guns. Sometimes the noise was like a wave, it just kept coming.

The Action Team was different. It was quiet. "They look at us different," Murray said to me one time. "Because they know we're on the team." He meant some of the other guys. They looked at us all right—I saw that myself. But I didn't think Murray got it.

In the dorm, it was pretty much okay. There's a bigger place over a few houses down. Like a tavern, I guess. They serve liquor, any kind you want. No charge. And they have a big-screen TV, pool tables, even waitresses. With their clothes on. It's open all the time, I think, but people mostly go there only late in the day.

Murray was always after me to go there. Most of the time I said no. One time I went with him. Some of the guys from another part of the camp were watching us. I always know when someone's watching.

Murray was wearing a black T-shirt, real tight, with the sleeves cut up high. It was a mistake, but I didn't know how to tell him.

I thought they'd start with him, but it was me. One of them banged a shoulder into me as I was carrying a couple of beers over to our table. The beer slopped over and some of it got on him. The guy who pushed me had long hair. A tall man, with fat, loose arms. He told me to watch where the fuck I was going, jabbed me hard in the chest with three fingers held together. I backed up. He came after me, shoving those three fingers at me, calling me names. Murray walked over, moving fast, tapped the guy on the shoulder. The man stepped away from me, three of his friends got up.

"You want to play?" Murray asked the man.

"I don't play with faggots," the man with the fat arms said. His friends laughed. Murray hooked him deep in the stomach. He didn't know how to put his weight behind it —the whole punch was with his arm, but it was enough. The man went down to one knee, trying to breathe.

Two of the man's friends started toward Murray. I cocked the pistol in my hand. It made a loud noise, because everyone was listening. They all stopped.

"Just them," I said.

"Come on, tough guy," Murray said to the man on his knees.

The man didn't get up.

♣

"He's a homo-sex-ual," the leader said.

"A fucking queer," the guy with the shoulder holster said.

"He's on an Action Team. He knows the plans," the guy in the white shirt said.

"It's up to you, son," the leader told me. Then he walked out of the room.

♣

"He has to go," the white shirt said.

"You down to do it?" the shoulder holster asked me.

I looked at him like I was stupid. But it only made things slower, it didn't stop them.

"It's for the cause, John. For the Nation. This Murray, he's dangerous. Probably a government agent."

"A government agent wouldn't kill a nigger," I told him. The acid test, like the crazy man said.

The white shirt looked at the shoulder holster. He put his hand on my shoulder. "Maybe you're right, John. But it doesn't matter. Queers are unreliable. Like the leader taught us. They can't be trusted. Murray . . . that's a Jewish name too, I think. He's gotta go, it's already decided. I know the leader would personally appreciate it if you took care of it."

"All right," I said.

"It's part of the price we pay, John. To be warriors of the white race. It's not his fault he's a queer, but that doesn't matter . . . he's a danger to us all."

They gave me the same gun I had taken with me to the trailers. It was just killing. I felt like I didn't want to do it. I never felt like that before. I thought of Shella. How long I'd been there already. The leader.

If I told them I didn't want to kill Murray, I'd never get close to him alone.

♣

I walked in the dorm. Murray was lying on the bed. He had his shirt off. His hands were locked behind his head. When he does that, the muscles bulge in his arms and his chest. I walked over to him. He smiled. I raised the gun and pulled the trigger. I shot him in the chest three times. Then I shot him twice in the face.

I heard people running out of the dorm.

I sat down in the chair next to my bunk.

# SHELLA

♣

The guy in the shoulder holster came in, two other men with him. He took the pistol out of my hand. Gave me a cigarette.

He was talking to me. I wasn't sure what he was saying. I heard one of the other guys whisper, "Just walked in and fucking blasted him right there. . . ."

They rolled Murray's body up in the blankets he was lying on and they carried him out. They took his bunk out too. One of them dumped Clorox on the floor and mopped it around. It made my eyes sting.

The shoulder holster walked over to me. "You did great," he said. "The leader said you were the right man, and he's never wrong about people."

♣

I went for a walk. Nobody said anything to me. In the woods, I saw a butterfly. A big one, black with little spots of yellow and blue. When I was a kid, in one of those places they kept me, I saw a butterfly come out, get born from a shell. I remembered it then, when I was walking. What I saw. It was brand new, wet. It flapped its wings to dry them off. I was watching it happen. One of the bigger boys came up. He was mean and nasty, asked me why I was crying. I didn't know I was, until he said it. He grabbed the butterfly before it could fly away and he crushed it in his fist. He thought it was funny.

They taught me not to cry in there.

♣

The next day, they took me to see the leader. This time, they searched me. Real close. Not as much as they did the first time, but they still touched me everywhere.

"You're gonna be alone with him," the shoulder holster said.

They opened the door and we walked in. The leader got up from behind his desk. He came over to me, stuck out his hand for me to shake. He looked over at the shoulder holster. They kind of nodded to each other and the shoulder holster walked out. He closed the door behind him.

I was alone with the leader.

He sat down behind his desk, pointed me to a chair.

"You are a true warrior of the right, John," he told me. "Sometimes it's hard to do what is necessary . . . a man shows his true color under fire. You showed white. You showed right. On behalf of our people, I appreciate what you did."

"Thanks."

"You're going to be spending some time with me every day from now on, learning some things. How's that sound to you?"

"Good." Black dots jumped out on his face. Faint dots. I watched his mouth move while he talked, waiting for the dots to get darker. The door opened. The man with the shoulder holster came in.

"There's a call," he said to the leader.

The leader stood up. He made a sort of salute at me. I walked out. They both stayed in the room.

♣

I went over there every day. They always searched me. Nobody was allowed to be near the leader with a weapon, they said.

One day, the leader got up, made a motion like I was to come along. We walked all around the compound. He was talking to me. About the race. Loyalty. A true white man. The shoulder holster was always close.

Near the back of the compound, there was a whole lot of men standing around.

"Here's a treat," the leader said. "Come on, John."

Men were standing around a ring. I thought it was going to be fighters until we got close. They stood aside so the leader could step up. I was right next to him.

The ring was maybe fifteen feet across. A wood wall went all around it. It came to just past my knee. The floor was canvas. There was lines drawn on it.

"You ever see one of these before?" the leader asked me. I saw the dogs then. "No," I told him.

He looked at his watch. "Roscoe's the next match?" he asked the shoulder holster.

The other guy nodded.

It was quiet for a minute. Then men climbed into the ring, carrying dogs in their arms. The one closest to us was a big black dog with a white patch on his chest. The guy holding him said something to the leader—I couldn't catch what it was.

"That's him!" the leader said.

The other dog was white, with a black patch over one eye. One ear was black too. He was smaller than the black one. The guys with the dogs were rubbing them. One put his dog in a tub and gave him a bath. Money was flying all around, people betting.

A man climbed in the ring, stood in the middle. He pointed at each of the men with dogs. They both nodded. Picked up their dogs and carried them forward. There was a line in the center. The referee stood on it. Each man came up to another line. They put their dogs down, held them between their legs, facing each other. The dogs were crazy to charge.

"Go!" the referee said, and both dogs ran together.

They fought hard, ripping. They locked together a couple of times, and the referee used a stick to break them apart.

People were screaming. "He can't be beat!" the leader yelled, right in my ear.

Sometimes they would take the dogs into their corners. The men holding them would face them away from the center, looking at the wall, so they wouldn't get crazy. They then would pick them up and bring them back to the center. When the referee said "Go!" they let the dogs free.

They fought a long time. The white dog's muzzle was all ripped, one of the black dog's eyes was gone, somewhere on the floor. When they brought them back, the white dog couldn't stand up.

"Go!"

The white dog crawled toward the black dog, ready to die. The black dog leaped on him. The white dog rolled on his back and nailed the black dog in the neck. Blood was all around his muzzle, but he couldn't keep the hold.

I figured it out. Every time they broke the dogs, it was a different dog's turn to move forward first. If they didn't go forward, they lost. If they did, one had to die.

The black dog won every time they hit, but the white dog never quit.

They faced them again, and the white dog crawled forward. He kept crawling. The black dog stood there, watching him. The white dog stopped. People screamed at him. A long time passed. The referee waved his arms.

"He quit!" one guy yelled near the wall. He looked mad.

"He's dead," another one said.

The man was holding his white dog in his arms. I could see he was crying.

The man with the black dog came over to the leader. He held up his bloody dog like a prize.

"Never defeated!" the leader said.

We stayed there. After a while, the other guy came over to the leader, carrying his white dog.

"You should be proud of him," the leader said. "He was dead game."

The guy kissed his dead dog. "You hear that, Razor? You hear that? Dead game, boy! That's you! Dead game!"

He was crying when he walked away.

♣

I was mostly in the dorm by myself, nights. Sometimes I went for a walk, looked at the dark woods. I could never see anything.

I was alone a lot with the leader, days. But I could never get the rhythm, never could tell when someone was coming in.

"You learn anything from the fight?" the leader asked me.

"I don't know."

"Dead game, what that means for pit bulls, it means they never quit. That's the quality you want, gameness. You know why we fight the dogs?"

"To watch them?"

"No, son. I know it must look like that, people screaming, betting, and all that. But the reason is to improve the breed. If you want a dog to be game, you have to test him. Only the true champions get to breed. . . . That way you get rid of the curs, the ones that will quit. You breed only game dogs, you get only game puppies, see?"

"The white dog, it was game?"

"All the way. Not a drop of quit in that beast."

"But it won't breed."

"Well, no. It won't. Only the best, John. Only the very, very best. What you want is pure."

♣

He talked a lot to me about Valhalla. Where warriors go when they die. If they die the right way. It's a perfect place for a man, he said.

He told me about dying. How it can be perfect. A perfect sacrifice for the race.

He said the white pit bull died for love. Love of its master. That's why they fight to the death, he said. For love.

He was talking about race when there was a knock from behind him. I didn't know there was a door there. He didn't act like he heard it. The knocking came again.

Finally, he got up and opened the door that was behind a curtain. A young woman came in. Pregnant, real heavy in front.

"John, this is my daughter, Melissa."

She kind of giggled at me. He talked to her, quiet-voice. She was touching his arm, patting at it. There was a button on his desk. He reached over and pushed it. The door opened behind me and shoulder holster came in. He looked at the leader, said "Come on" to me, put his hand on my arm to take me out of there.

As I was going, the girl looked at me. I saw her eyes and I saw what Shella must've seen.

♣

The more I practiced with the guns, the more they watched me do it. Every time I held a gun in my hand, I would feel it. What it could do.

I could do it too—I just had to be close.

I kept the gun with me all the time. So they'd expect it. Once, I was looking for a place to put it while I took a shower. They give us plenty of room for things here—not like in prison. Some of the guys had foot lockers, some of them had trunks. Most of the guys, they didn't stay in the compound anyway, they just came and went. I was the longest man in the dorm.

I couldn't think of a place to put the gun. I didn't want to leave it on my bunk. There was a row of metal lockers against the far wall. I looked there, but they all had locks on them. Then I saw it—Murray's trunk. I remembered it because it was this dark-red color, with black bands around it. It was all covered with dust, just sitting there in the corner.

Nobody was around. I didn't break the lock, I unscrewed the plate. Shella told me how to do that, once when we were trying to get into someplace.

Inside the trunk Murray had his clothes. And his little weight things for his wrists and his ankles. There was a bunch of letters. He had them tied with a ribbon. They looked old.

He had a jacket in there. It was black, with big white sleeves. It felt like silk. On the front, over the heart, it said *Ace* in little white letters, like writing. On the back it said the name of some gym.

I put my gun in his trunk while I took my shower. I fixed the lock plate so I could just pull it off with my fingers when I came out.

♣

"Who brought him in?" the leader asked the guy in the white shirt. Like I wasn't there. It didn't make me mad—people always do that.

The white shirt always has the long flat aluminum box with him. When he opens it up, there's pads and stuff inside. He looked there for a minute. "Mack," he told the leader.

The leader looked at me. "Mack say anything to you about the Lightning Squadron?"

"Yes."

"What?"

"He said he was a scout."

"Anything else?"

"No."

The leader gave white shirt one of those looks I never understand—it could mean anything.

♣

Every day was the same after that. Every day I would get up and walk around. Sometimes I would look at the posters. THE JEWS ARE THROUGH IN '92, was one I saw a lot. Then I would take my gun and go over and practice. After that, I'd walk back to the dorm. More people would be out by then. There would be kids too, dressed up like the older people in soldier suits with little guns. Some of them wore armbands . . . red with white circles and the black crooked cross inside . . . and they said nigger and kike and spic and that kind of thing like they were learning their ABCs or something.

They were always beating the kids. With sticks and belts. And slapping them. I saw a man whipping a little boy. The boy was screaming. The man's wife said it was good discipline and everyone standing around nodded. I walked away. When I looked back, the others were watching the little boy get whipped.

I would look at TV until one of them came for me. They would walk over with me. Then they would take my gun and search me so I could go inside with the leader. Sometimes there were other people there, sometimes we were alone. Sometimes his daughter came in. He never talked on the phone they had in his office. When it would ring, somebody else would take it.

I never knew if I would be alone with him. I never knew how long it would last.

Every day, the same talk from him. Master race, masters and slaves, serving the master. The Lightning Squad, it would strike like lightning at the enemies of the race. Some of the members, they wouldn't get out. But they would go to Valhalla for sure. Guaranteed.

Nobody ever talked so much to me. Nobody ever explained things like he did, except maybe Shella.

On one wall of his office, he had pictures. Pictures of men. Each one was in a metal frame. He said those men gave their lives for the Nation. They were heroes. Heroes of the race. The children who went to their schools would memorize their names.

He said the niggers weren't human, so you couldn't really blame them for the animal way they acted. The Jews, you could blame them. They knew what they were doing. They were a different race, even though they looked like us. You could tell the difference, but only if you knew them real good.

The leader told me that we were going to win, because we were superior. And because the niggers were starting to really hate the Jews and the Jews were going to have to do something about it.

He gave me books to read. One was a little red book, some kind of story. One of them said PROTOCOLS on it. I tried to read it. I'm not stupid. But I couldn't understand it. When he asked me, I told him the truth.

He said that was okay—the important thing was, would I do the right thing when the time came?

I always said I would.

Once in a while, they would ask me if I wanted a woman. I always said I did.

When I was fucking one of the women, I wondered if they had ever asked Murray if he wanted one.

♣

Every day, it got dark quicker at the end. It started to get colder. I didn't have a jacket with me, just what was in my duffel bag. When they searched me one day, before I went inside to be alone with the leader, they said why wasn't I wearing a jacket. I told them it wasn't that cold yet.

They must have a way the men outside could talk to the leader, because he asked me if I had a jacket. He said, if I didn't, I could grab a ride into town with Rex and pick one up. I didn't know who Rex was, but I figured out he meant the guy with the shoulder holster.

I never found out the name of the guy with the white shirt and the clipboard.

I told the leader I already had a jacket. He said I should start wearing it, otherwise I could catch a cold.

♣

The next morning, I remembered what the leader said before they came over to get me. I went into Murray's locker and got his black-and-white jacket. It was way too big for me when I put it on.

The men who searched me hadn't seen the jacket before. They made me take it off. They went through it real careful, but there was nothing in it.

They kept my gun. I carried the jacket inside with me to be with the leader.

It was never going to get any better. I knew that. It wasn't that I couldn't wait—I can always wait. But it would never change, I could see that.

He was talking and talking. I moved around a little bit,

listening to him, always watching his face. He kicked back in his chair, put his feet on the desk. I never saw him do that before. I guessed there was a button he could push, bring the other men inside. There's always a button like that in back rooms. He put his hands behind his head, the way Murray used to do. But there was no muscles bulging.

The way his hands and his feet were, he couldn't push a button real fast.

I got up, started to walk around a bit. I did that before. It didn't make him nervous anymore.

When his head tilted back, I saw the black dots pop out on his Adam's apple. The place where you can tell the real men.

I walked just past his feet, so close I could smell him. My back was to him for a second. I planted my foot and spun around. His mouth came open. I hit him so hard in the throat he couldn't make a sound even if he was alive. I pushed his face against the desk and held him there while I broke his neck from behind.

I didn't have a plan to get out. I started choking him. He let go while I was still squeezing—I could smell it.

His daughter walked in. Just walked in, didn't make a sound. She had a denim shift on, barefoot, a red scarf around her neck. Her belly was really big. She looked at me. I saw the blue marks high on her arms, where someone had grabbed her hard. I moved to her before she could get out the way she came in, but she just stood there.

She didn't say anything. Then she moved her hand, just a little bit. I stepped next to her, put my hand on the back of her neck. I gave it a little squeeze. Not to hurt her, just to tell her.

When I took my hand away, she didn't move.

I picked up Murray's jacket and put it on, watching her.

Something told me, told me so I knew. If she screamed, it wouldn't matter. Even if she screamed, the guards wouldn't come in.

She turned around, away from me. Started moving out the way she came in. I was right behind her. It was a whole apartment in one big room. A kitchen against one wall. The ceiling was very high. There was a platform on the wall, with chains holding it, like a bed in an old jail. A ladder so you could climb up there, maybe to sleep. I could tell it was just for her—the leader didn't live there.

I pushed her to a chair. She sat down without me having to do anything to her.

I looked out the window. It wasn't far to the woods. I stayed close to her. The red scarf around her neck, I took it off her, tied it around my head.

I couldn't take her out the window—she'd never make it up and through. I looked for something to tie her up with. She stood up quick, opened a door. There was a platform there, a little platform with steps to the ground. I saw a man with a baseball cap turn around when he heard the door open. I never saw him before. He had a machine gun on a sling over his shoulder.

"Come on," the girl said, and started down the stairs.

I came right behind her. I had to get close to the man with the gun. He started coming toward us, but his hands were away from the gun. I had my hand just behind her, on her waist. Soon as he came near enough . . .

The woods were close. Real close.

The man stopped. Too far away. "What's going on?" he said.

"He's just taking me into town. In the truck. To buy some things," she said.

"The leader didn't say anything to me about that."

"So what? You think I need his permission just to go into town?"

"Yeah, you do," a man's voice said. A voice from behind us.

I knew it then—I'd never see Shella.

♣

"Get your hands up, boy! Fast!"

I raised my hands.

"Step away from her . . . move!"

I did that too. The man who'd been behind us stood to one side. He had a pistol, a big chrome one. Aimed right at me. The guy in the baseball cap, he had both hands on his gun too.

"He told me to watch out for you," the guy with the pistol said. I could tell, the way he said it, he meant the girl.

"Let's take them both back," the man with the machine gun said. "Let the leader decide. You . . . let's go," pointing at me with his chin.

It didn't matter, but the woods were so close I had to try. I stumbled a little so I could get next to him, but the guy stepped back and then I heard something like a real quiet motorcycle trying to start and both of them went down, blood and bone flying from their heads.

I ran for the woods.

♣

I got over the fence in a flash. When I dropped down on the other side, there was nobody there. I ran away from the fence, hard as I could.

The Indian was there. Just standing there. I couldn't see where he came from. He had a rifle in his hand, a long rifle with a tube over the barrel. He moved his hand, like in a wave, and I followed him.

There was a Jeep at the end of the trail we went down. A black Jeep. I got in the back with the Indian—there was two men in the front seat already. We took off.

The Indian picked up a phone, touched one button.

"We're off," he said. "It's still quiet here. Check with the post, get back to me."

The driver was going through the woods like it was a street.

The phone made a noise. The Indian picked it up. "Go," he said. Then he listened.

"They found the bodies," he said to the men in the front seat. "They can't get a ring up in time. Sam's team will give 'em something else to think about in a minute, but we gotta go through the roadblock on our own."

The man in the passenger seat reached up over the windshield. He pulled something down, like a window shade. Only you could see it was metal. There was a thin slit in it. The driver leaned forward, looking through it. There was shades like that for the windows too, even the back window. I pulled mine down.

The Indian opened this case he had on the floor. I saw grenades, one of those little machine guns, some other stuff. It made metal clicking sounds when the Indian snapped it all together.

"Get on the floor," he told me. I did that and then there was this explosion. Like a bomb. From somewhere behind us.

"One more corner," the man in the passenger seat said.

The Indian slid up his metal window shade and poked a gun out the open window.

I felt the Jeep slide around a long corner and then it was nothing but blasting. Bullets smacked into the Jeep but all I could hear was the guns. The Jeep kept moving. I felt it hit something, then we were through.

The Jeep came to a stop.

"Come on!" the Indian told me.

We got out. The Jeep was smoking, one tire was off. There were two cars at the roadblock and a lot of dead people.

♣

We got into the woods again. The man who'd been in the passenger seat went first. Then the driver, then me, then the Indian.

We stopped after a bit. The driver was bleeding down one side of his face. He didn't seem like he knew it. The Indian took a little box out of his pocket. He pushed a button on it and there was a booming sound. We started off again. Then there was a loud sound like a firebomb.

"Gas tank," the Indian said to me. He took the phone out of the holster, pushed a button. "Six," is all he said. Then he listened.

The others looked at him.

"They're there," the Indian said. Then he took the lead and we followed him.

♣

Near the edge of the woods there was a big gray Ford. Me and the Indian got in the back seat. I saw the other two guys get in another car, a brown Chevy. There was another Jeep there too, a white one.

When we came onto the paved road, the white Jeep was in front and we followed.

The Indian lit a cigarette, offered me one.

"Nice jacket," he said.

I touched Murray's jacket with my fingers.

"They'll remember it," the Indian said. "We should of left it there."

I didn't say anything.

He waited, smoking his cigarette.

I leaned forward in the seat, took off Murray's jacket, and handed it to him.

"We'll hold it for you," he said.

♣

They didn't say much, but you could feel how tight they were. When the Indian moved in the seat next to me, I could see the little sparks all around him. I thought we'd go to their camp, but we drove all the way back to Chicago, straight on through. The car stopped in front of the apartment house where I stayed before.

When we got upstairs, it looked the same.

"I'll be back tonight," the Indian told me. "I'll tell you everything then."

♣

I took a shower, changed my clothes. There was food in the refrigerator. I listened to the radio, but there was nothing about what happened in Indiana. Maybe they bury their own dead.

I knew the Indian would come back. Otherwise, they would have just left me after I did the job. Left me right in that compound.

I wondered why they didn't. Maybe Indians don't do that.

After a while, I found a nature show on TV.

♣

I heard the Indian let himself in but I didn't move. The only light was the TV screen, but he came through the apartment like he could see.

He sat down across from me. "You did it perfect," he said. "Glided in right under their radar."

"Where is she?" I asked him.

He took some paper out of his pocket. Handed it to me. It was pages from a magazine, black and white. One page was folded back at the corner. A woman was standing there. In the light from the TV, I could see she had high black boots, something in her hand. There was another woman next to her, kneeling on a couch or something.

I turned on the light. The woman standing was blonde. Her hair was long. Her arms and shoulders were heavy. Big. Almost like Murray's. The woman kneeling next to her had a dog collar around her neck. She was stripped naked. The big woman was holding a leash in one hand.

A little whip with a lot of strings on it in the other.
It wasn't a real good picture, but I could see enough.
"That's her?" the Indian asked.
I told him it was.

♣

Later he showed me a lot of other stuff. Mostly pictures.
Shella with a girl over her knee, like she was spanking
her. Shella whipping a man, his hands tied way above his
head. Shella with her hands on her hips, like she was giving
orders. He showed me some ads too. Mistress Katrina.
Discipline lessons, private. In one picture, Shella had a
girl all tied up, clothespins clamped on the tips of her
breasts, a gag in her mouth. It was all Shella, even if she
looked different every picture.

"We don't have any close-ups," the Indian said. "The
crazy man said all this stuff was old, at least a couple a
years, okay? But if that's her, we know where she is now."

"Where?"

"We'll take you to her," he said.

♣

The next morning, he was back. "It'll take a couple a days
to set it up, all right? We got a long way to travel, we have
to make all the arrangements."

He had more papers with him. A police sheet with arrests
on it, all different names. Girls' names. He said that was
Shella too.

"I wasn't there every day," he said after a while.

"Where?"

"In the woods. We figured it out, finally. Where you were going every day. It had to be his house. But he didn't live there. He went in the same door you did. The front door. Every day. There's no angle on it, even from the woods, it's shielded by the other buildings, like in a tunnel. No way to get a shot off. The back, that was easy, but he never went there. The woman, the pregnant one? She would go outside sometimes, but she never got far."

"Did she . . . ?"

"We didn't shoot her. She didn't scream either."

I didn't say anything. After a while, he started talking again.

"When we saw you come out with the bandanna on your head, we knew it was done. If you'd gone out the front, you wouldn't have made it. No way we could cover you. And we couldn't get a message in. All we could do is wait."

"It's okay."

"He's dead. I guess you know that. There wasn't nothing in the papers, but the crazy man, he found out. He said he's satisfied. That's when he turned over the information . . . about your woman."

"We're going soon?"

"Day after tomorrow."

♣

The next day, he gave me an envelope full of money. "We sold your Chevy," he said. "Everything else too. It's all gone. You're starting over. This is all new ID, like he promised. You can buy whatever you need when you decide."

"Decide what?"

He just shrugged, like I knew what he was talking about.

♣

Three of them came up the morning we left. The Indian stepped to one side. "This is Joseph. This is Amos," he said. They held out their hands and we shook. I knew them—they were in the front seat of the Jeep when we came through the roadblock. Amos was the driver.

"They're volunteers," the Indian said.

Downstairs, we got in another Jeep. A red one. They really liked Jeeps, the Indians. They had all kinds of stuff piled in, even stuff on the roof.

"Hunting trip," the Indian said to me.

We took off.

"Better to stay off planes," the Indian said. "I don't think they know anything, but they might have a picture or something. They won't look for long—they're not professionals. For now, this is better."

We just kept driving, like Amos never got tired. The Indian talked. Sometimes Amos talked. Joseph, he just watched.

By the time they decided to stop, we were someplace in Nebraska.

♣

Amos and Joseph took one room in the motel. I guess they always stayed together. The Indian and me had a room too.

"We got about another day's drive," he told me. "Five, six hundred miles. We'll leave first light, time it so we get there next morning coming."

"Okay."

It was quiet in the room. The Indian told me about his tribe. I listened with my eyes closed. When he stopped speaking, I opened my eyes.

"The crazy man kept his word?" I asked him.

"Sure. We're just taking you to her ourselves to finish —not because we don't believe him."

"But you want to see for yourselves?"

He looked across at me, nodded his head.

"What about the rest?"

"The rest?"

"Hiram. Ruth's brother. Did they transfer him?"

The Indian didn't say anything. He looked at me for a long time. Then he dropped his eyes, played with a cigarette until he got it going.

"You remembered his name . . . ?"

I was surprised too. I didn't know I even knew his name until I said it out loud like that.

The Indian got up, walked around a little bit. I closed my eyes again. I felt him come close to me, sit down on the bed near my chair.

"Hiram was transferred the next day. They must have been typing the papers the minute the body hit the ground. They moved him into a Level Three joint. Cake. We can go in and get him anytime we want. It'll take a while, set it up properly. But our brother has spent his last winter behind the walls."

"Then . . ."

"He wouldn't cheat us, John. It wouldn't be worth it to him. But he might not know how things are. . . . You're with us, understand?"

"With you?"

"Until it's done. You did your piece. You did it perfect.

We think she's there. But we're not walking in the front door waving a sign. She's there, it's done. Like we agreed. She's not there . . ."

"What?"

"We'll find her. All of us."

♣

Amos kept the Jeep near other cars all the time, always rolling in the middle. He'd move from pack to pack, so smooth you could hardly feel it. He held the wheel loose in his hands, just flicked it a little bit when he wanted to move. Every couple of hours, he would move the seat. Forward, back. Up, down. Every time he did that, he would move the mirrors too.

I saw the overhead signs—we were in Arizona. Joseph turned around in the seat.

"No more problems, brother. Plenty of places to disappear to now."

The Indian looked at him. "They'd rat us out just as fast on the damn reservations. We only have ourselves."

Joseph nodded, turned around to look out his window.

We found a motel. Amos dropped us off, went away to get some stuff for the car.

"She's close," the Indian told me. "We go in tomorrow, soon as it opens up."

"What?"

"A hospital," he said, looking at me. "A hospital in the desert."

♣

The Indian was on his bed, smoking with the lights out. It was late, past midnight. I could see the red tip of his cigarette.

"Wolf?"

"What?"

"You think she's there?"

He smoked the whole cigarette through, ground it out in the ashtray. After a long time, he said "Yes."

# SHELLA

♠

In the morning, I felt like I should do something different, but I couldn't think of what it should be. It was still dark. The Indian wasn't in his bed.

He walked in about an hour later.

"You want some breakfast before we go? Some coffee?"

"I'm okay."

"What're you doing?" he asked me, looking at the bed where I had my stuff laid out.

"Packing."

He nodded his head, walked out again.

By the time he came back, I was ready to go. But when I put the duffel bag over my shoulder, the Indian shook his head.

"What?" He was looking at the room key in my hand.

"We're not going by the front desk. It's paid for a few days, but if things don't work out, we're gonna keep rolling. . . . You don't check out, they'll think you're coming back."

"Who would?"

He just shrugged his shoulders . . . not like he didn't know, like it didn't matter.

♠

Amos pulled the Jeep over to the side of the road on a long curve. I could see a bunch of white buildings on the right.

"Stay with Amos for a little bit," the Indian said. "We'll be back soon."

I saw the flash of a shoulder holster on Joseph as he climbed out the front seat. I guessed the Indian had one with him too. They started walking away.

Amos drove off, with me in the back seat. "It's all right," he told me. "We checked it last night, top to bottom. Just wanted to be sure, one more time."

He circled around, a long loop. No matter where he drove, I could always see the white buildings.

It took about half an hour. Then Amos pulled to a bus stop. The Indian and Joseph were sitting on a bench, like they'd been there for days. They climbed back in the Jeep.

In the parking lot, the Indian took a bunch of papers out of his coat. He smoothed them on his lap, pointed out a name to me. Olivia Oltraggio.

"That's the name she's using," he said.

I looked at it deep. Said it to myself over and over, so I'd know it. I couldn't say the last name. The Indian said it for me. Slow. In four parts. It sounded Italian. She had been there almost three months . . . I could see that from the papers. It said Ward Four. The Indian turned over the papers, tapped his finger again. She was in Room 303, starting a few days ago.

"It's a private room," the Indian said. "They had her moved once it was done."

I reached for my duffel. Felt the Indian's hand on my arm. "Leave it here," he said. "Outside her room, right

next to it, there's a staircase. You have to get out of there
fast, go down the staircase. *All* the way down, to the basement. Turn to your left, go past the laundry room, there's
a fire door there, a red door. You know the kind . . . you
push the handle and the alarm goes off . . . emergency
exit? You push it, nothing's gonna happen, no noise, but
the door'll open, okay? We'll be outside, keep you
covered."

"I'll be—"

"Right to the end," the Indian said. "You come out the
front door, there's no problem, just get into the Jeep, drive
it away yourself. Here's the keys. Your stuff'll be in the
back. Go back to the motel, go someplace else, it's up to
you."

I heard a door open. Joseph was already out, moving to
the front of the building.

"When you get inside, just get on the elevator, the one
right past the front desk. Go on up to the room, understand?"

"Yes."

The Indian nodded at me, and I got out too. When I
walked in the front door, I couldn't see Joseph.

♠

I went over to the elevator. Thinking it's good that people
never pay attention to me. There were people in white
coats on the elevator, talking. I stood to the side. Got off
on the third floor.

There was a sign there with an arrow. I walked down
the corridor. People were going in and out of the rooms.
It smelled like a prison with flowers.

The stairway was at the end. Room 303 right next to it.

There was one of those thin holders on the door, where they slide a piece of plastic in it with a person's name. To tell you who's inside. The name she was using was there. White letters on the blue plastic. It looked strange.

The door was closed. I pushed it open—it made a little hiss. The back wall was all glass. A bed was there, parallel to it. The sun slanted in—it was hard to see. The door closed by itself behind me. I stepped over to the bed and a face turned to me. It was all eyes, shrunken.

"I knew you'd come," Shella said.

♠

My legs locked. I moved toward her. . . . I felt like the white pit bull, crawling to the line. There was a brick in my chest. Right in the center of my chest, not over my heart.

I got there. Her hair was long, more white than blonde now, like dead straw, thin. Everything about her was thin, her arms were sticks. As she turned, the nightgown fell away. . . . her breasts were almost gone. Her cheeks were sucked in, big splotches on her face, dark ones. . . . I couldn't see the beauty mark I made for her.

I saw her teeth. I couldn't tell if she was smiling or snarling. She held out her hand.

I moved closer. I could hear a crackling in my chest, like when you crush the stuff they put around cigarette packs in your hand. I got close enough to touch her. She looked up at me.

"Hello, John," she said, real quiet. "If you came to kill me, you're too late."

♠

I just stood and looked at her. Shella. It was Shella.

"Same old motormouth, aren't you?" she said. She shifted her hips under the sheet, patted the bed for me to sit down.

I did that. She put her hand on my thigh, the way she used to, like it was hers. The sun came in on her hand. I could see every bone in it.

I closed my eyes. Breathed as slow as I could. I could feel her doing it too.

When I opened my eyes, hers were still closed, but she wasn't asleep.

"What happened?" I asked her.

♠

She didn't say anything for a long time. I didn't move. "You don't look any different," she said. "I knew you wouldn't. You're not gonna die slow."

"What happened, Shella? Why did you go?"

"Ah, who knows?" she said. "I got a whore's heart. Maybe I just got bored. What does it matter anyway?"

"I've been looking for you . . . for a long time."

"Why?"

"For you to tell me the truth."

She opened her eyes. "The truth-truth? The real thing?"

"Yes."

"I was afraid of you."

"Of me? Of me, Shella? I never did . . ."

"I know. When I took off, in the car, with everything

. . . I didn't go far. I drove for about an hour, and I got a room. The next day, I got out of the motel and I rented a furnished apartment. A nice studio. There was nothing in the papers until the next day. I could see it was gonna be a while before you went to trial. I figured I'd get work, wiggle my big butt enough to make some money, get you a good lawyer. I knew you wouldn't want me to come and visit in the jail. . . . They might be waiting on me . . . know you had a partner."

"A partner . . . sure, that's right."

"Yeah. Anyway, I started working. The next thing I knew, you were gone. I found out you pleaded guilty. After they took you down . . . oh Jesus, John . . . you expected me to be there, didn't you? Waiting for you when you stepped out of the gate."

"I thought you would stay," I told her.

"I *couldn't* stay, you fucking moron! What was I gonna do? Buy a house, get a job at McDonald's . . . what?"

"I don't . . ."

"People like us, we can't stay in one place. It's bad rhythm, dumb. You know *that* much, right?"

"I guess. . . ."

"I was never that far away. Not in my mind. I called the PD, told him I was your sister. He ran it down for me. I knew how much time you had to serve. . . . I went out on the track, got lost in the scene for a while."

I must of looked stupid at her when she said that—she kind of shifted gears with her voice. "You remember Bonnie? That skinny bitch I owned back when we had that beach cottage?"

I nodded.

"Like that," she said. "Most of them, just like that. I did some men too, but not many."

I looked around the room. It was a nice room. Big and clean. There was a TV set on the end of a metal arm, a stand-up shower over to the side. Behind the bed I could see a pair of tanks, like for propane gas. I took out a cigarette.

"Go ahead," Shella said. "It doesn't make any difference."

I lit the smoke. "Give me some," she said, the way she used to, moving against me. I handed her the smoke. She took a deep drag, handed it back. She was watching me close. She kept watching until I took a drag myself, then she lay back and closed her eyes again.

I thought maybe she was tired, but she started to talk again.

"By the time I came up for air, they had cut you loose. I took a plane, I was in such a hurry. I didn't think it would be so bad, so hard finding you. Some man would know where you were, on parole. I could always make men tell me things. I got a room in a real nice hotel. I had a whole bunch of money too, John. Your share. I kept your share for you, all the time. I was all excited. Like maybe the other stuff was over, I don't know."

"I—"

"Shut up. Talking makes me tired. Let me finish this piece. I called the parole office. When I asked for your PO, they made me wait a long time. That's the way they do, anyway. . . . It didn't spook me. But when the man came on the line, he wouldn't give me your address. Not over the phone, he said. I'd have to come in. I knew it then. I put down the phone. It only took me a couple of nights to find the right guy. A guy on parole. I promised him some pussy and he came back to the same joint in a couple of days, after he reported in himself. He told me you hung

up the parole . . . that you were a fugitive. There was a
warrant out for you. . . . When they got you, you'd have
to serve the rest of your time. A crazy move, not like you.
So I figured you were coming after me. I ran. I kept running. . . ."

"Shella . . ."

"I'm tired now, John. Real tired. I just drift off when I
get like this. They're gonna come in with my shots soon
anyway. Just let me go, now. Come back in a couple of
hours, okay?"

"Sure. I didn't . . ."

"I'm not going anywhere," she said, closing her eyes.

♠

I don't remember walking out of the hospital. I think I took
the elevator, but I don't remember. The next thing I knew
I was on the bench. The bench where you wait for the bus,
where the Indian and Joseph were before. A bus came, but
I didn't move. Other people got on, but I didn't. I knew
people were looking at me after a while. I knew it was
stupid to stay there. I knew I was stupid.

I got up and walked. Around and around. I knew that
was stupid too. People would notice me. I couldn't find a
dark crowd.

I saw a sign. TOPLESS. Inside, the cold came right at me.
It must have been hot outside. It was the same as all the
other places. The daytime girls are never the best. They're
tired, like they have jobs at night too.

I bought drinks and didn't drink them, like always. They
didn't really have acts in that place. The girls came on and
danced to records. Men watched. Nobody was laughing. It
was quiet watchers, mostly.

All the girls looked alike, but I knew that couldn't be. I guess I wasn't paying attention.

I sat at the bar until time passed around me. There was no clock there, and I didn't have a watch.

After a while, I got up and went back outside.

♠

I went in the hospital like I was going in the first time again. The elevator was there. Everything was the same.

Her door was closed. I pushed it open. She was sitting up in the bed, watching. There was a chair next to her bed. She saw me and moved her hand, like I should sit down. I went over and did it.

"You know what I have?" she asked me.

"I . . . guess."

"Yeah. I'm gone, John. My T-cell count's down below two hundred."

"You have money?"

"Money? It doesn't make any difference now. That's why they moved me to this private room. That's the way they do things here. It bothers the other patients to see someone go out—makes it harder to swallow all the bullshit about a positive mental attitude."

"How . . . ?"

"How *what?* What difference could it make now?"

I didn't say anything for a while. "I did a lot of things," I told her. "I did a lot of things, trying to find you."

"You always did a lot of things, John."

We stayed quiet after that. I smoked a couple of cigarettes, shared them with her. Nobody came in. The sun shifted lower in the sky but it was still coming in her window.

Maybe I fell asleep. I heard her voice like it was in the middle, like she'd been talking for a while.

"I went too far, honey," she said. "I went too far. I hated them so much. I still hate them."

"Who?"

"My father."

"Did you . . . ?"

"No. I never saw him. But I kept seeing him. You understand what I'm saying? I just kept seeing him. I was working as a domina. I never had sex. I never had sex since you went down, John. You believe that?"

"Yes. I was just . . ."

"What?"

"I was . . . confused."

"That's you. Confused. You're always confused, aren't you? I'm surprised you made it this far. People always use you. . . . I thought you'd be used up. All used up. It's funny, huh? I know how things work, you don't. And I'm the one—"

"Shella—"

"I never had sex with any of them. Not real sex. I never made a whore's mistake, either. Whores're stupid. They think because a man will pay them to piss on his face they can laugh at him. I knew a whore got herself killed doing that. You can't laugh unless you've got control. . . . It doesn't matter who's paying."

"It doesn't—"

"Everything matters. Everything gets paid for. My tricks, they could get off being whipped, when I hurt them. Sometimes they'd finish themselves. But I never let anyone inside me. I could have stayed on the phones. There's real money in that. Talking to freaks. Plug in a credit card and close your eyes and you get what you want. But some of them, they wanted the real thing. And they paid more for it. A lot more. It used to help me too. It was enough, for a while. I'd put on my outfit and make them lick my boots, tie them up, blindfold them. It felt . . . powerful. But as soon as it was over, they'd get dressed and they wouldn't look at you. They'd go back to being in charge. They got what they paid for. No matter what you did to them, they were calling the shots. Using you, the way they always do."

I touched her arm. The bones in her arm. "You don't have to do that anymore. . . ."

"I never *had* to do it, John. Remember what the little gangster in New York used to call you? Ghost? That's what I was, a ghost. It wasn't real. Spanking. That's what some of them call it. Spanking. Like the way you'd do a kid. Some of them did it. To kids, I mean. Some of them go both ways. Like AC-DC, but with the whip. Switch, they call it. If you're a switch, you'll give it and you'll take it. I never took it."

"I know."

She acted like she didn't hear me. "I worked the dungeons first, but then went out on my own. They have such a cute name for it. Domestic Discipline. One day, I had one of them tied up. Before we started, he showed me pictures of his little girls. Two little girls. Told me how he spanked them when they were bad. He had pictures of them. With their pants down. He told me maybe he'd bring them over to me. For discipline, he said. He wanted to watch. I was working on him. Saying the words. Like dancing. I saw his face. It was him. My father. Tied up and he couldn't move. I could see his hard-on bulging and I wanted to cut it off."

"It's all right," I told her.

"Shut up! I need to finish this. You came all this way to hear the truth. . . . Sit there and take it. Take it!"

I moved my fingers along her arm, trying to find a vein. Her skin was so pale I could see through it.

"I beat him to death. Halfway through, he got it. Knew I wasn't going to stop. There was a gag in his mouth. A good gag, big rubber ball. I don't know if he choked to death on the vomit or his heart just stopped or what. But I could smell when he died. I ran out of there then. I was scared. Scared of myself. But I went back. Right back to it. I did a lot of them, John. A lot of them. All over the country."

"It's okay."

"Okay? Yeah, it was okay. I could have kept going forever. Worked my way through every freak in the world. I never would have gotten sick. I was taking a lot of pills. For the pain. I had to keep moving, once I got started. I wasn't running from you anymore, just running. I had to do a lot of them before I'd find the right one. See his face. But once I got one done, I had to go. Right then, go." She took a deep breath. Something rattled inside her when she did it. "They knew about it. They had to know. They knew. One of them even asked me, are you her? They knew someone in the underground was killing them. But I never had any trouble getting clients. Never. I got bigger, stronger."

"I saw a picture," I told her.

"Yes?" she said. Then she closed her eyes. I thought she was going to sleep again. I sat there, watched her. Then she started talking again, but it was a whisper. Not like she was weak, just telling secrets.

"I got to need it. More and more. I saw his face all the time. Once I must have passed out when I did it. When I came to, he was there, all tied up and bloody. I left him there, went into the bathroom to take a shower. Then I saw it. Blood. On my mouth. All over my mouth. Then next time I did it, I stopped pretending. Stopped playing. I drank their blood. It was the best, sweetest, purest thing I ever did. That's how it must have happened."

It was getting dark in the room. When she went to sleep, I stayed right there.

♠

She didn't sleep so long. I had time, though. Time to think. When she opened her eyes, I told her.

"I can get you out of here," I said.

"What?"

"You can come with me. You don't have to . . . die here, Shella. We can go someplace. You can talk to me. Like it was. I can find him, too. Take him out before you go."

Her eyes were real soft, like they used to be, sometimes. I felt her hand on me. "Who, honey?"

"Your father. Like I promised."

"He's dead, baby. Long time dead. I found out. Once I started my march, I knew I could do him. Do him myself, the way it should be. He never left where he was—it was easy to find out. He just died. In his sleep. He was an old man. Just died. There's nothing left to do."

"We could still . . ."

"I don't want to be here. I don't want to go anyplace either. I want to be done. Out of this."

She looked at me. A hard straight look. Shella's look.

"One more deal, my partner. One more deal. You came a long way to hear. If I tell you what you want to know, will you do it?"

I lit a cigarette to get some time. She tapped my hand for a drag. I held it to her lips. She couldn't sit up anymore.

"Will you?"

I just nodded—I couldn't talk.

"I love you," Shella said.

Her neck snapped like a dry twig.

♠

I walked out the front door of the hospital. It was getting dark. The Jeep was sitting there. Like Duke's radio, with new batteries in it.

I got behind the wheel, started the engine. I sat there for a minute.

Then I put on the headlights and pulled out of the parking lot, driving slow.

When I got to the highway, I headed east.

Going to pick up my jacket.

# A NOTE ON THE TYPE

This book was set in a digitized version of Caledonia, a typeface designed by W. A. Dwiggins (1880–1956) for the Mergenthaler Linotype Company in 1939. Dwiggins chose to call his new typeface Caledonia, the Roman name for Scotland, because it was inspired by the Scottish types cast about 1833 by Alexander Wilson & Son, Glasgow typefounders. However, there is a calligraphic quality about Caledonia that is totally lacking in the Wilson types.

Dwiggins referred to an even earlier typeface for this "liveliness of action"—one cut around 1790 by William Martin for the printer William Bulmer. Caledonia has more weight than the Martin letters, and the bottom finishing strokes (serifs) of the letters are cut straight across, without brackets, to make sharp angles with the upright stems, thus giving a modern-face appearance.

W. A. Dwiggins began an association with the Mergenthaler Linotype Company in 1929 and over the next twenty-seven years designed a number of book types, the most interesting of which are Metro, Electra, Caledonia, Eldorado, and Falcon.

Composed by PennSet, Bloomsburg, Pennsylvania
Printed and bound by R.R. Donnelley & Sons,
Harrisonburg, Virginia
Designed by Virginia Tan

# TIME TRAPS

## PROVEN STRATEGIES FOR SWAMPED PROFESSIONALS

## Todd M. Duncan

NELSON BUSINESS
A Division of Thomas Nelson Publishers
*Since 1798*

www.thomasnelson.com

Published in Nashville, Tennessee, by Thomas Nelson, Inc.

Nelson Books may be purchased in bulk for educational, business, fund-raising, or sales promotional use. For information, please e-mail SpecialMarkets@ThomasNelson.com.

Unless otherwise noted, Scripture quotations are taken from the HOLY BIBLE, NEW INTERNATIONAL VERSION®. Copyright© 1973, 1978, 1984 by International Bible Society. Used by permission of Zondervan Bible Publishing House. All rights reserved.

The "NIV" and "New International Version" trademarks are registered in the United States Patent and Trademark Office by International Bible Society. Use of either trademark requires the permission of International Bible Society.

Jacket design: The Design Works Group, Inc.

Front cover image: Steve Gardner, Pixelworks Studio

Interior design: Walter Petrie

Previously published as *Time Traps: Proven Strategies for Swamped Salespeople*

**Library of Congress Cataloging-in-Publication Data**

Duncan, Todd, 1957–
    Time traps : proven strategies for swamped professionals / Todd M. Duncan.
      p. cm.
    Includes bibliographical references.
    ISBN 0-7852-6323-3 (hardcover)
    ISBN-10: 0-7852-8833-3 (trade paper)
    ISBN-13: 978-0-7852-8833-6 (trade paper)
    1. Sales management. 2. Time management. I. Title.
HF5438.4.D857 2004
658.8'1—dc22                                  2004023129

*Printed in the United States of America*
06 07 08 09 RRD 4 3 2 1

# Contents

# CONTENTS

THE ONLY TIME THAT COUNTS IS THE TIME
THAT YOU MAKE COUNT. TIME MATTERS, TODAY
MATTERS—MAKE IT YOUR MASTERPIECE!

# Note from the Author
# on the Second Edition

In November of last year, I asked seven people to meet for half a day to talk about the first edition of this book. In the room sat the vice president of a large logistics company, a life coach, a publisher (not my own), a salesperson, a former marketing consultant for Home Depot, my writer, and the CEO of my company. Each had read the book and were there to offer feedback.

It was my original intent to write *Time Traps* for all the salespeople I teach and interview throughout the world. This is why the first edition contains the subtitle: *Proven Solutions for Swamped Salespeople*. However, the purpose of the meeting I mention was to discuss a new edition.

After *Time Traps* became a *New York Times* best seller, the comment I kept hearing from radio interviewers, letters, and personal encounters was: "You don't really have to be in sales to make use of this book . . . My friend (or spouse or colleague, etc.) is a such-and-such and she applied the principles to her life with great success."

I heard the comment enough times that I began to wonder if I shouldn't expand the scope of the book in a new edition—this time with some thoughts and insights for a more general audience: all professionals, not just sales professionals.

I mulled this over for a while and then I spoke with my publisher, and they posed the same idea. It was confirmation, and so I set out to complete a second edition of *Time Traps* with a new subtitle, *Proven Solutions for Swamped Professionals*, and new content.

It would have been easy enough to simply change the subtitle of the book and modify all the references of "salespeople" to "professionals," but I wanted to do more. So I asked those in the November meeting to offer candid feedback. What about the book needed to be changed so that *all* professionals would find it very helpful? What parts of the first edition didn't apply to someone, say a corporate attorney, who wasn't part of a sales force but nonetheless struggled with a hectic schedule? What needed to be added so that professionals from surgeons to teachers to athletes to accountants could learn to get themselves out of the swamp they are in and onto high ground where they have plenty of time to live out the lives they desire?

I looked to the seven for answers because they are part of this broader audience, and I felt they could tell me what they and the professionals they knew needed.

Their candid input, along with some revisions and updates, make this second edition all-the-more useful. I believe *Time Traps* now contains the principles and practical applications required for *any* professional to step out of the swamp and gain more freedom to do what they really want to do with each day.

My experience and my heart tell me this is still achievable for anyone—for you—no matter how busy or behind you are now. My main hope as you begin this book is that you will find more time and greater freedom in your life after reading and applying what you learn. Trust me, there's still hope and there's still time. Enjoy this ride, and then experience your freedom.

*Chapter One*

# Time Matters All the Time

## When Does It Matter to You?

*"The problem with life is that it's daily."*

— JEFF DUNN, PUBLISHER

You could hear the wind screaming past the open door. My executive team and I were two-and-a-half miles above the earth and it was time to jump. The man standing by the large opening in the plane's side shouted over the noise. On zero you could *not* hesitate. We had practiced on the ground all day; we had studied how to jump and what to expect; our packs were secure and tightly fastened, and we had donned our helmets. Now it was go time. We were as ready as we were going to be. The four of us smacked our hands together and hollered in out-of-character fashion the way guys do when they're acting courageous. Then came the moment of truth.

"Three—two—one—Go! . . . Go! . . . Go! . . . Go!"

One by one, we dropped from the plane like bombs from a B-52 and sped toward the ground at 120 miles an hour. Whether we liked it or not, our lives were now in our own hands. The time we spent rehearsing was past. All that mattered now were the next sixty seconds, three seconds at a time. We had to pay attention; it was life or death important. To pull the rip chord too early would endanger a fellow skydiver and send you well off course. To pull the chord too late was, well, far worse. Time matters in such moments, and my watch remained well within sight.

On another occasion, my wife and I rented a dive boat with a group of friends to view the best underwater spots around the Fijian islands. One morning we were on a deep-water dive to observe several species of sharks. We dove down and down and down, and the light at the surface became dimmer and dimmer. When we reached the bottom of an undersea canyon I glanced at my computer and it read 130 feet. I remember peering up toward the surface and the heavy feeling that I was thirteen stories below. When you're that far down and you know that you only have a certain amount of air and that once you start to ascend you can only rise a few feet every few seconds, time does not pass indiscriminately. You are very aware that if you ascend too late you will run out of oxygen. Too fast and you'll get the bends, which can kill you just as quickly. Time matters a lot in such moments, and my flippers didn't sweep the water once without serious consideration.

It may sound odd, but I think our time *off* work teaches us a great lesson about our capacity to make the most of our time *at* work. The two previous examples are from my vacation experiences, but here's an example we can probably all relate to.

Think about *your* last vacation. Chances are good that as the date for your departure neared, you became more purposeful about your time. You probably said no to invitations you'd normally say yes to, and you likely became very efficient about finishing tasks, because you knew that if you did, you could fully relax when you stretched out on your chaise lounge.

Time matters before vacations because the return is immediate: if we are very productive before we leave, our freedom won't be hindered while we're away.

In this light we seem to have a double standard with our use of time. We squander it in one instance—maybe in most instances while on the job—and we squeeze productivity out of every last second in another, especially right before we're taking time off. Vacations expose this double standard that, oddly enough, offers us some hope.

## BEHIND THE TIMES

It would seem by the way most of us act that time only matters in critical moments or cost-effective moments. In other words, for most of us time only seems to matter:

1. *When it has to*—like when you're two miles above the earth or 130 feet below the sea . . . or working with your boss looking over your shoulder, or
2. *When it offers immediate rewards*—like when you're about to go on vacation or when you're vying for a big promotion.

We seem very adept at making our time count in those moments. Yet in all the other moments of our lives—which are predominantly spent on the job—many of us seem to have great difficulty stringing together ten productive minutes. Why is this so?

I don't think being swamped would be so frustrating if deep down we didn't sense we could do better—if deep down we didn't know that we *had* done better with our time when it really mattered. We probably wouldn't say things like, "That meeting was a waste of time" if we didn't know that the week before we had been able to say, "I had the time of my life!"

The fact that we have valued every second of our time at some point in our lives—even if it was just before vacation or just after we jumped out of a plane—proves that we at least have the *capacity* to make time matter. This knowledge ought to give us some hope. In fact, I believe it is this hope (which is usually subconscious) whispering to us that somewhere, somehow, there is a way to enjoy success at work and freedom in life without getting swamped.

What dulls this hope are the many obstacles that keep us from making time matter on a regular basis. I call the obstacles Time Traps, and most of our lives are full of them.

## DON'T SURRENDER

Many of us have given up trying to control our schedules and have accepted an existence in which chaos and catch-up are the status quo. One clever woman summed up her surrender this way:

> The clock is my dictator, I shall not rest.
> It makes me lie down only when exhausted.
> It leads me to deep depression, it hounds my soul.
> It leads me in circles of frenzy for activity's sake.
> Even though I run frantically from task to task,
> I will never get it all done, for my "ideal" is with me.
> Deadlines and my need for approval, they drive me.
> They demand performance from me, beyond the limits of my
>    schedule.
> They anoint my head with migraines, my in-basket over-flows.
> Surely fatigue and time pressure shall follow me all the days of
>    my life,
> And I will dwell in the bonds of frustration forever.
>
> MARCIA K. HORNOK, PSALM 23, ANTITHESIS

We laugh because we can relate all too well. But who wants to live in the "bonds of frustration forever"?

Think about the last time you enjoyed a wonderful evening with one of your favorite people doing one of your favorite things. Even if it was only a dinner at a great restaurant with a close friend, wasn't it refreshing and uplifting? Didn't you feel more alive afterward? We all want more times like that.

Maximizing time feels good, no matter how it is enjoyed. Wasting time feels bad, no matter how it is wasted. Unfortunately, the reality for most of us is that we're prone to feel bad more often than we feel good. We're busy and we're going someplace and it may be a good place to go. The only question is: are we leaving anything (or anyone) behind? Will we get to that place we are going to and then wish we had taken a different path or different companions, or used a different map?

*Wasting time feels bad, no matter how it is wasted.*

The obvious (and seemingly impossible) resolution is to work in a way that allows us great success on the job *and* major freedom and pleasure off the job. I'll admit that sounds like a hugely overambitious task, but I know it can be done, in a much less complicated fashion than you might realize. I see it happen in the lives of hundreds of professionals every year.

Depending on your particular circumstances, there are specific and immediate actions you can take to move your business and life to a place where you are no longer swamped and where you can enjoy more freedom with your time, every day.

In each chapter I will present these proven solutions to you as a resolution to the time trap being discussed. You may not find yourself in every chapter. With such chapters, education is your best strategy. Therefore, in chapters that speak directly to your struggles, dig in and apply the solution as soon as possible. In chapters that don't quite apply to what you're going through, safeguard your future days by learning how to avoid the traps being described because they are very common and you are prone to fall into them at some point in your career. In fact, nearly every professional I know has struggled with the eight traps we will discuss.

## THE TOUGHEST CHALLENGE WE FACE

Freeing up your time can be a frustrating thing, especially in the working world where much of our time is shared with others who may not value what we do. But we can and should fight for our time—and, though it often feels like an uphill battle, it's not a lost cause. Consider the victory won by a client of mine named Tim.

He wasn't being productive with his work time, and he knew it. He was going in early and coming home late and he was tired of missing out, so he came up with a plan. He determined that for three weeks he would tally the amount of time he spent at the fax machine and then multiply his weekly average by the number of weeks he worked in a typical year to come up with an annual total of hours spent faxing. He figured that once he saw how much time he was spending carrying out menial tasks, he would be extra motivated to improve. He wasn't sure how he would improve, but he knew he would figure out a way if he were provoked.

When the annual tally came in, the result nearly made his eyes pop out of his head. The total was much larger than he had anticipated. He punched the numbers into the calculator one more time. Same result. By his modest estimation, he spent approximately *336 hours per year* inserting paper, fishing out jams, gazing at flashing fax numbers, and refaxing misfaxes. Divided into eight-hour increments, this meant he piddled away forty-two work days a year by standing over a fax machine.

The discovery would have been more amusing if it weren't so telling. The bitter truth was that Tim literally faxed away one-fifth of his work year, and now he understood why he hadn't been able to take a real vacation in two years.

Many of us may find ourselves in a similar place, wondering how much better things could and should be, how much less stressful, how much more enjoyable, if our days weren't so stinking busy. And not just with simple tasks like faxing. With other, more important, more critical tasks that cannot just be pushed to the side.

Nearly every professional has a challenge with time. It is the most repetitive and pervasive problem I've come across in fifteen years of speaking and training, and it doesn't just go away. The details of our stories may be different—some of us struggle hourly or daily, and others only now and then—but the results are predictably similar. What didn't get done today overflows into tomorrow. What was meant for tomorrow gets reshuffled to the next day or the next week or month. To-Do Lists never get done on the day for which they were intended. Post-It Notes lose their stickiness, and the dream of productivity fades into a state of harried and hurried multitasking.

Most of us who are swamped have at some point found ourselves wishing there was a way to drive success on the job while simultaneously enjoying a lot of free time off the job—and most of us have concluded there isn't. Work success comes at the expense of free time.

I thought this.

But then, like Tim, I began tallying how I spent my time at work, and I realized that most of what I did had little to do with increasing my job success and even less to do with increasing the quality of my life. I realized I was climbing a ladder and climbing as best I knew how, but the view at the top of that ladder wasn't going to be any better—and maybe it would be worse. This frustrated me at first, and then frustration turned into motivation.

I vowed to make some changes to the way I worked and the way I used my time. I wanted to invest my time, not merely spend it. And I wanted those investments to give me more free time off the job to do whatever I wanted to do, even if it was only an hour more a day.

Initially, some changes worked, some didn't. But I continued making changes until eventually I figured out a way to be productive with about three-fourths of my work hours. Consequently, I got more done in less time, and this allowed me to spend fewer hours at the office. That was benefit number one. Benefit number two was that I became more successful. I was a mortgage specialist, and because I was more productive I was able to give more clients better service and close more loans in less time. But benefit number three was the most important: I had a lot more free time off the job—some weeks I had four times more than before. What would you do with twenty more hours of free time each week?

With my free time I learned to scuba dive with my wife, and now we take dive trips each year. I started going to afternoon baseball games with my boys. I began playing more golf and learning to play the piano. I began writing books and seeing friends more often and volunteering at my boys' school and dining slower and observing longer. And sometimes I reinvested my free time back into my career. The point is that I finally had the choice to do whatever I wanted with my time.

Eventually I got to the place where I could say that the two main tracks of my life—working and living—became one. Today when I work, I am fulfilled because I love what I do. When I'm not working, I am guilt free and unhurried. I am living, and I am enjoying life.

To tell you that getting to this place was an easy undertaking would be patronizing. But to tell you it is not also possible in your life would be a lie. I believe your results could be very similar to Tim's.

As a result of applying the principles and practices you will read about in the coming chapters, Tim now sells $80 million in home loans every year by working about eighty days. Once a workaholic logging seventy-plus hour weeks, he's now an enigma in an industry where late nights and long hours are fashionable and seem necessary. Yet Tim holds no secrets or special powers. He's no different than you or me. He's an ordinary professional who was once seriously swamped. Then something happened. He came to understand a little something about time, and he let it transform his life.

What he learned and what he is now reaping are what this book is all about: gaining freedom with your time and beginning to live the life you desire, on and off the job.

## EXECUTIVE SUMMARY

If you look at the way most of us carry ourselves throughout life, it would seem that time only matters in critical moments or cost-effective moments. In other words, for most of us time only seems to matter:

1) *When it has to*—like when you're dropping from a plane two miles above the earth or working with your boss looking over your shoulder, or

2) *When it offers immediate rewards*—like when you're about to go on vacation or when you're vying for a big promotion.

We seem very adept at making our time count in those types of moments. Yet in all the other moments of our lives—moments which are predominantly spent on the job—many of us seem to have great difficulty stringing together ten productive minutes. Why is this so?

The fact that we have valued every second of our time at some point in our lives proves that we at least have the *capacity* to make time matter. This knowledge ought to give us some hope. In fact, it is this hope that whispers to us that somewhere, somehow, there is a way to pursue success at work and freedom in life without getting swamped.

What dulls the hope for many of us are the numerous obstacles that keep us from making time matter on a regular basis. These obstacles are called time traps, and our lives are typically full of them. The key to having more freedom with our time is learning how to sidestep these traps.

*Chapter Two*

# Fighting Back

Will You Fight?

*"What will you do without freedom? Will you fight?"*

— WILLIAM WALLACE IN *BRAVEHEART*

I t's the most critical and oft-repeated scene of the film. The small Scottish army is haggard and hopeless. They stand in a muddled mass and gaze across the green Falkirk battlefield at the swelling English army as they take position in perfect lines. The foot soldiers, the archers, the cavalry. They wear chain mail and finely woven uniforms and sit atop armored horses brandishing giant swords and long spears. The Scots wear only garments of wool, leather, and fur and wield weapons of wood and metal fashioned by hand. It appears that a slaughter is imminent. "The English are too many!" says one young Scot, and he's right. They are outnumbered and outmatched. No army in two centuries has overcome the odds they face. They are better off tucking tail and heading home, and so they do. They begin to leave the battlefield, and then something happens. William Wallace rides up with his face painted ready for battle.

In the film's most memorable monologue, Wallace steers his horse before the sullen, outnumbered band of Scots and asks them a question:

". . . What will you do without freedom? Will you fight?"

"Two thousand against ten?" a Scottish veteran shouts. "No! We will run and live!"

"Yes!" Wallace shouts back. "Fight and you may die. Run and you will live, at least awhile. And dying in your bed many years from now, would you be willing to trade all the days from this day to that for one chance, *just one chance*, to come back here as young men and tell our enemies that they may take our lives, but they will never take our *freedom?!*"

With this moving speech, Wallace reminds the Scots that one day, one hour, one year of freedom is still better than a long life in captivity, alive but not really living. His words stir in their hearts and move them to finally face their enemy head on, despite the seemingly impossible odds. At his command, the weary Scots lift up their handmade weapons and slaughter the bigger, more powerful English army and thus pave the way for their eventual freedom.

## PAVING THE WAY

Fueled by frustration and taught by trial and error, Tim and I discovered that there is a way out of the captivity-of-busyness that so many of us find ourselves caught in. I want to share this way out with you now. But I first have to explain something very important: your freedom will not come by practicing better time management. In fact, time management is a waste of your time. It's like chasing the wind.

*Time management is a waste of your time. It's like chasing the wind.*

The notion that we can manage something fixed is completely fanciful. You can't manage or tame or control time any more than you can lasso the wind and tie it to a fence post. Yet for years that's the gist of nearly every solution we've been given to help us deal with the incessant demands of our more-than-full-time jobs. *Just manage your time better; that'll do the trick.* What does that mean?

Despite our best efforts to manage our time we still show up late for meetings, we forget appointments, skip lunch, miss dinner, work weekends, and in general we get ourselves seriously swamped. If I gave you five minutes right now, I bet you could think of five things you should get done today but won't.

Being swamped can be extremely frustrating. And here's why.

Most days, time takes more life from us than we take from it. That's because time is more consistent than we are. Time is predetermined, set in perpetual motion by God "in the beginning," and there is no slowing its pace or altering its consistency. That's why managing time is unrealistic.

> *We cannot manage time, but we can manage the thoughts and actions that fill our time.*

Time management is not just a play on words either. It represents a flawed understanding of time that affects how we react to our swamped schedules. We may attempt to reclaim our time and tame our time and take back our time, even make up for time. But the truth is, we can't. These busy days require a different solution—one that takes into account the fact that we *cannot* manage time, but we *can* manage the thoughts and actions that fill our time.

In one way or another we all are trapped by the relentless, ever-diminishing nature of time, and we often feel doomed to work more than we should to accomplish less than we could. In sum, many of us are frustrated that there never seems to be enough hours to do all that we intend to do. Many professionals accept this as the norm, but you will soon see that it is not the way it has to be. I can recall many stories that prove it.

## CHANGING TIMES

In my career as a speaker, it was a first. A middle-aged man approached me as I prepared to speak to six hundred sales professionals for the third day of a three-and-a-half-day event. He reached out his hand and gave me a folded five-page note, then looked at me with glassy eyes and said thank you.

Sensing the significance of the moment I immediately opened the note. My eyes went to the top right corner of the page where he recorded the hour when he'd begun to write: it read "4:00 AM."

I began reading and noticed dried splotches of blue ink dotting the first page. This was no ordinary letter. Then I came to one paragraph that seemed to say it all:

> The tears are from the joy of knowing that over the last year I have received more business than I ever dreamed possible—but more importantly, I have a life. My wife and kids cannot believe the change. I am more balanced than ever and cannot describe adequately for you how this new view on time has changed my life forever.

The remainder of this proud man's letter described all the positive transformations that had taken place and how much freedom and joy his life now had. Greater productivity with fewer hours on the job, always work-free weekends and stress-free vacations, a stronger family, and an appreciative, appreciated spouse. It is wonderful story. Also, it is a story that is not uncommon.

For fifteen years, this is all I have attempted to do. I have strived to help professionals realize that there is a better way to work and live—and it has everything to do with how you use your time. As I pore over the letters I have saved over the years, I am struck by how critically important it is that I convey to you in these opening pages that you *can* be highly successful on the job without working yourself to death and without giving up the things that are important to you.

The people whose testimonies I am reading are no different from you or me; they are women and men, professionals from their early-twenties to their late-fifties, first-year employees and tenured CEOs. Each of them with different career paths but all with similar circumstances: work took up most, if not all, of their time, and they were fed up with life passing them by. With some encouragement, a few unique skills, and a new perspective on time, all of them turned their lives around and now enjoy more success and freedom. I believe the same results are available to you no matter how backed up things are now. So far, no one was too far into the swamp that they couldn't be pulled out.

From here on out, as you turn each page in this book and we begin discussing how to get out of the most common time traps, let the echo of the following people's words give you hope that things can and soon will improve in your life.

"It's 6:18 AM. For months I have pounded excuses into my head as to why I have been unable to accomplish what you teach. But what I once thought was impossible is now a reality."

---

"Drinking after a few years started to consume my life. I didn't know my wife or my children and I was in trouble. Then I read your book—what a life changing event . . . I was so excited that after three chapters,

I quit reading it. That was all it took . . . I quit drinking and started planning the rest of my life. My wife and kids gave me another chance. I never dreamed that marriage and being a dad could be this good. And business has never been better."

---

"In light of his death, I find great satisfaction in knowing he spent his four years as a husband and one month as a father putting his family ahead of his work. As busy as he was, he would leave the office every day at 5:30, knowing he was leaving for something more important. For this I thank you."

---

"I must tell you that I was in no way prepared for how deeply you and your teachings would touch my soul. The insight you have given me— about me—is incredible. Thank you so much for taking the time to identify and clarify . . . real success."

---

"I can't believe I let myself slide to such a low level . . . My days had become so dysfunctional and nonproductive that I was going home every night with a bad attitude that I always justified as a product of my daily stresses. I spent my days reacting to problems and not doing the important stuff. At the end of the day I always seemed to have two choices: neglect my work and go home or neglect my family and do the work I should have done all day. I would generally go home but angrily because I had no sense of peace about the loose ends I was leaving at work . . . Two years have now passed since your seminar and my business is totally under control. Most recently I asked my wife to answer a question: How do you feel about me? I've sent you a copy of her answer." *(His wife wrote an eight page letter that gushed with love, admiration, praise, and appreciation for her husband).*

---

As we embark on this journey together I want you to know that my motivation for writing springs from my commitment and resolve to make a difference in your life—not just your career. I want to help set you free from the traps that sap your best energy and steal your most precious commodity. I want to help you free up your time so that you can live the life that until now you may have written off. Because that life is still possible. Think of it now.

## Your Time Is an Open Book

Imagine you are a writer and an anonymous source has hired you to write a masterpiece. The topic and title are unknown; you've only been told that you should expect to receive more information in the mail—research information, you're guessing, that will explain the details.

The mail arrives one day and with it a manila package. You open it and discover an attractive book bound in soft, chocolate leather and with it a note. You open the note at once. It's only one sentence that reads:

*This is your story to write however you desire.*

You finger through the pages and find that every one of them is blank except for a small inscription centered in the middle of the first page. It is your full name and directly beneath it is the current year with a long dash next to it—the final year yet to be determined.

What story would you tell? Would it be a romance or an adventure? Maybe a bit of both. Who would be the other characters in your story? How would your story end?

Whatever you might decide, that book is real, and the one asking you to write it is me. We all have a story we'd like to tell, and I will do my best to put a pen back in your hand. You may feel that your story is not worth writing yet—but I believe it will take a dramatic turn in the coming chapters. Keep reading, and I'll show you how.

# Executive Summary

Nearly every professional has a challenge with time. It is the most repetitive and pervasive problem I have come across in fifteen years of speaking and training, and it doesn't just go away. The details of our stories may be very different, but our results are predictably similar. In one way or another most of us feel trapped by the relentless, ever-diminishing nature of time, and we often feel doomed to work more than we should to accomplish less than we could. Worse still, most of us accept this as a necessary evil, but it's not how it has to be.

There are specific and immediate actions you can take to free up your time on the job in order to free up your options off the job. In each chapter I will present these actions to you as the solutions to what I call Time Traps: those habits of time use and abuse that keep us swamped at work and dissatisfied at home.

While our careers tend to be full of time traps, there is plenty of hope. In fact, our own experiences prove this to be true. Consider the weeks preceding your last vacation. You probably said no to things you'd normally say yes to; you probably completed tasks efficiently and didn't waste time piddling. Why? Because you knew if you didn't, your vacation wouldn't be a vacation.

We can make better use of our time because we have made better use of it at some point. The trick is to do this naturally and regularly. I believe you can, and in the following pages you will be shown how.

Chapter Three

# The Organization Trap

Wasting Time Juggling Unnecessary Tasks

*"Society often demands more of a man's nature than he can give."*

— THORNE LEE

*"What if we put in shorter hours and got the work done anyway?
Don't laugh. Some people are doing it."*

— AMY SALTZMAN

It varied the older we got—but when we were young there was always a prerequisite to having free time. Completing our chores, finishing our homework, cleaning our room. Something like that, right? Whatever it was, the gist of the message was that we couldn't do what we really wanted to do with our time until our work was done and things were in their place. It was a rule meant to teach us a sense of order. Work came first, and only after work was done came play or whatever else we might want to do.

I've noticed that many people still hold themselves to the same rule.

The problem is that in the grown-up world, work is *never* done. At the end of the day there is always one more call to make, one more e-mail to send, one more contract to draw up, or one more report to finish. The working world does not shut down when the clock hits

5:00 PM. Many days it seems we are flooded with more To-Dos every hour, and trying to get organized feels like trying to stack rocks in the middle of a raging river.

## THE RIVER OF RESPONSIBILITIES

The Klamath begins as a river should with a tall waterfall cascading from the south edge of a lake set amidst the pristine pine mountains of southern Oregon. From beneath the falls the river begins its southwestward decent toward the California border. It flows through the Topsy Reservoir and into northern California and Copco Lake and eventually through the Iron Gate Reservoir on its way toward the Pacific. It is to this seventeen-mile stretch south of the Iron Gate Reservoir known as the Upper Klamath that whitewater rafting enthusiasts flock in late spring when the snowmelt and April showers swell the river beyond its borders and the heavy water tumbles at eighty-five feet per mile.

During mid-May the Upper Klamath is typically at it highest and most treacherous level. Its water rushes deep and wide over the volcanic canyon floor forming some thirty mammoth rapids. Rocks that normally arch above the surface untouched are instead veiled beneath and behind dashing white shrouds of current. Certain shaped boulders force portions of the surface inside itself creating sink holes spread randomly along the river like mines in a field. If your raft crosses one just right, the downward suction can yank the entire boat under and keep it there for days. The river guides will tell you of tragedies so you don't forget the gravity of the ride. The Upper Klamath is not a place for beginners. On the contrary, it is a stretch of river that commands respect, and one that has taken the life of many careless enthusiasts.

But for those who know how to guide their raft atop its May current, the Upper Klamath is as exhilarating a ride as you'll ever experience.

It's much the same in the working world.

Some days your river of responsibilities flows steadily and predictably. You can easily pace yourself and complete your tasks without difficulty. You can foresee the obstacles in your path threatening to slow your productivity and easily maneuver around them. If mistakes are made you can correct them with minimal loss of time. It is very feasible to get to work at a regular morning hour and still be home for dinner. But let's face it—such days are a rare exception.

On most days your river of responsibilities rages like a mid-May, flood-high current that threatens to drown you. The more tasks bubble up, the more disorganized and out of control you become. Even if you see obstacles, you rarely have the time or the energy to avoid them. Furthermore, getting organized at this rapid pace is at best a daunting task, at worst a lost cause.

That's more like it, right?

It seems the bane of our existence: a fast-running, oft-raging current of responsibilities that rises high like a river in spring. I understand this state of affairs because I've been there. I've put in the long hours and still felt as though it wasn't enough. I have felt overwhelmed by the amount of tasks I had to accomplish in a day. In fact, this is a circumstance I still must work to avoid, as do most professionals. And maybe that's because we typically aren't the most structured people.

## You Have an Excuse . . . Sort of

When I ask professionals to tell me the one thing they struggle with the most, the vast majority of them tell me they are swamped and lack the time to catch up. As a result, they scramble to get work done every day but often at the expense of great inefficiencies and gross errors. It's a trap of sorts. To get organized takes time. It takes thought-out decisions and purposeful actions, but what hard-working professional has time for that? Once you're in the middle of the river and the current is sweeping you along, stopping to get organized can compound the problem. The river will pile up behind you, and eventually its weight will take you under.

To make matters worse, many professionals are disorganized by nature.

It may relieve you to know that there are actually psychological reasons for your hectic work ethic. An excuse? Not really. But it's at least a possible explanation for how easily you seemed to get where you are.

Most ambitious professionals—especially sales professionals—test out in the highly driven or highly relational personality categories according to the DISC model.[1] Not surprisingly, people in these two

| | Driven Worker | Interpersonal Worker |
|---|---|---|
| Basic Descriptors | Daring<br>Direct<br>Dominant<br>Decisive | Inviting<br>Inspiring<br>Infectious<br>Indomitable |
| Emotional Default | Anger | Optimism |
| Characteristics | Risk Takers<br>Need to Lead<br>Desire to Win | High Emotions<br>Need to Interact<br>Desire to Be Liked |
| Quick Indicators<br>1. Extrovert/Introvert<br>2. Task/People Oriented<br>3. Direct/Indirect | Extroverted<br>Task Oriented<br>Direct Communicators | Extroverted<br>People Oriented<br>Indirect Communicators |
| Value to the Team | Challenge Oriented<br>Self-Motivators<br>Forward Thinking | Highly Optimistic<br>Team Players<br>Motivational |
| Possible Limitations | Overstep Authority<br>Impatient<br>Argumentative | Oversell<br>Impulsive<br>Lack of Detail |

categories have the most difficulty when it comes to achieving organization. Take a look at a snapshot of these two personality types to see if you fit into one or both categories.[2] According to leading international coaching firm Building Champions, indicators are very high that you do.

The highly driven worker is a task-oriented, outgoing individual who thrives on getting things done. The problem is that this person tends to be impatient and move on to the next thing if a task is dragging or not reaping an immediate and tangible reward. As a result he is always changing priorities and thus overloading his plate. Once swamped, the driven worker succumbs to a multitasking strategy that he sees as a challenge. Unfortunately, this pattern leads to a decrease in work quality and an increase in work time. Deep down this angers the driven worker, but he keeps telling himself, "Hard work pays off in the end."

The highly relational worker is also outgoing, but instead of being task oriented she is people oriented and thrives on influencing people by building relationships. The problem is that the highly relational worker tends to be impulsive and overcommit. Furthermore, while this person excels through communication skills, she tends to overlook the details required for good follow-through. As a result she is constantly shuffling priorities to satisfy people, which ultimately monopolizes her time. Thus she never gains a real sense of control to her days. However, she continually tries to look on the bright side. It is the interpersonal worker who claims, "Being busy is a good problem."

Do you see yourself in one of these people? Maybe both? While this information might explain some of your tendencies and blunt some of the frustration you've been experiencing, it doesn't solve the real problem. I wanted you to see this data because I believe it affirms our need to take strong measures to get our days under control. Our tendency is to remain out of control and resign to working harder in order to counterbalance the disorder, but there are far more productive measures we can take.

## LESSONS FROM A RIVER GUIDE

Brent, my writer, spent two summers guiding the Upper Klamath River, and a couple of the lessons he learned provide us with some great insight for beginning to overcome our incessant flood of responsibilities.

I don't want you to worry about what actions to take yet. For now, just consider the truth of these two lessons and allow them to construct a mental foundation for cleaning up your days. Then you will be primed to take the necessary steps to achieve a place of sanity and simplicity in your schedule.

Here are the lessons my writer learned as a river guide:

**Lesson #1:** *Acknowledge the power of the river.* One of the requirements of Brent's training was jumping into a Class III rapid with waves that crested at about six to eight feet. In case you don't know, the rapids in western states are generally classified from I–V, Class V being the most dangerous. A Class III is a rapid whose danger often lies in the sheer power and volume of the water. Often there are not large rocks that pose a serious threat, but the mere pace and power of the Class III current can take your breath away if you're not careful—it can effortlessly flip a ten-person raft.

It was into this type of current that Brent was required to hurl his body, inhaling big on the peaks and holding his breath when the rapids forced him under. He says it was a struggle just to keep his head above water. He also says that after the experience he plainly understood how easily a big current can take a person's life.

Early on in a career it might seem like a winnable challenge to take on everything that comes your way. But the longer you work, the sooner you realize that the pace of a professional career doesn't slow down involuntarily. The more responsibility you assume, the faster the river travels; eventually it can drown you if you underestimate the force of its current. Usually it leaves you struggling just to keep your head above water. You must first acknowledge the life-sapping power of your river of responsibilities if you are to ever muster the courage to overcome its unforgiving current.

**Lesson #2:** *When the river is high and fast you must scout what's ahead.* This often requires that you pull out of the current and determine the right path to take.

On a steep section of the Upper Klamath looms one of its most daunting rapids. Large boulders on each bank force the path of the swift current through an opening barely big enough for one raft. Normally this funnel effect would make for a fun ride and require simple technique, but there is one very big problem: a canine-shaped boulder reverently named "Dragon's Tooth."

Only ten feet beyond the small funnel-like opening, a giant granite tooth shoots out of the whitewater forcing the guide to pick a side or be eaten alive. The tooth isn't cordial; it stands dead center of the rushing current's path daring the guide to avoid it. It couldn't be more in the way. As a result, the powerful current rushes smack into the tooth's rough face. For a raft to follow suit is perilous. The water is too powerful and the rock is immovable. For this reason, the most seasoned guides paddle ashore upriver to walk the banks beside the tooth and scout the best route to take. This isn't a cowardly move; quite the contrary, it's what every wise guide knows to do in order to protect and preserve their life and the lives of those in their raft.

If you're swamped, you've probably come to a place where your "Dragon's Tooth" is in view. You know you have to do something, anything, or your condition is about to get worse—completely out of control. Maybe as a result of working so much, your family is beginning to fall apart. Or maybe your long hours have caused you to put on weight and put major stress on your body. Maybe you're just sick of working so much and you are about to crack if something doesn't change. You probably want to get back to spending time on other things you love; or to at least have some choices with your time.

Now is an ideal time to pull off this raging river of a job, if only for a few moments, and survey the scene in order to determine how to make it through this in one piece. From the bank, things become a little clearer.

## DAMMING YOUR WORKLOAD

When you get out of the chaotic current of your job long enough to give it an honest look, you find there are only three ways to manage your raging river of responsibilities:

1. You can turn in your raft and paddle and call it quits,
2. You can learn to guide yourself through the rapids and attempt to avoid the obstacles as best as you can, or . . .
3. You can build a dam.

Some take the first option and find another job. Being an ambitious lot, most professionals typically go for the second option. The floodgates are opened when we take our first job, and for the rest of our careers we do our best to avoid drowning. It's not necessarily something we face every day, but it probably describes a lot of our days.

It's not entirely your fault if you chose to take on the mighty river. Many of our first managers teach us that "it doesn't matter how it gets done, just get it done," and so it's likely that when you started working you were thrown into the river and forced to learn on the go. It's the proverbial sink-or-swim management technique. As a result, you probably developed techniques that weren't the most efficient but that got you by—techniques that allowed you to just barely keep your head above water. Now, whether you've been at it six months or twenty years, you might still utilize some of those diligent-but-not-so-efficient strategies.

The foundational problem with option two is that you can't very well manage the flow of the river when you're in the middle of it yourself. The sink-or-swim technique may teach you how to keep your head above water, but it doesn't teach you how to manage the flow of the water. This is why so many people still struggle to maintain organization in their days. When the current is sweeping you along, the best you can do is keep your head up and avoid the rocks and trees. But you can't change the current while you're part of it.

The only way to truly slow the pace of your river is to take option three and build a dam. Only then can you temper its relentless flow.

## The Blueprint of Your Dam

Dams are constructed to regulate the flow of a body of water. Essentially, they act as boundaries that safeguard against an excessive flow at any given moment and maintain a predictable, manageable current. If your desire is to regulate the floodwaters of your frenzied work schedule, you must construct a similar boundary.

I've said this for years: if you don't put boundaries on your business, you won't have balance in your life. In other words, without boundaries on your work responsibilities you won't have free time for your life responsibilities and opportunities. On the other hand, *with* boundaries regulating your flow of tasks, your time for life has far greater potential. Let's talk about how to begin constructing this dam to temper the crazy pace of work that you're currently caught in.

First, you have to understand that since you cannot manage your time, the only way to organize your day is by managing your daily tasks. Task management—not time management—is the foundation of organization. If you can learn to harness the tasks that crowd your days, you will realize more freedom with your time. Put another way: to free yourself from the traps that are monopolizing your time you must manage the things that occupy your time: *tasks*.

With that said, let's begin with the basics of putting boundaries on your tasks. I will usually refer to this process as "building your dam."

*If you don't put boundaries on your business, you won't have balance in your life.*

## COMMENCING CONSTRUCTION

The construction of your dam happens in four phases. Each phase represents new task boundaries—or additional levels of the dam— that you must construct in order to slow the rapid pace of your river of responsibilities. If you complete these phases in succession, in the end you will have raised up a sturdy dam that will allow you to regulate even the greatest flood of tasks. The four phases are as follows:

1. Accumulation
2. Admission
3. Action
4. Assessment

Let me briefly explain each phase so that you can understand the whole scope of what we will accomplish in this book. Then we'll back up and begin constructing the first phase of your dam.

## PHASE 1: ACCUMULATION

This is the foundational phase of your dam. In this phase you will learn to block all *unnecessary* tasks before they require your attention and sap your time. In other words, the primary goal of the Accumulation phase is to set up boundaries that will prohibit interruptions or distractions from entering your river. The construction of these boundaries is the key to overcoming the Organization Trap. We'll get back to this in a minute.

## PHASE 2: ADMISSION

Once you've stopped *unnecessary* tasks from sapping your time, you must set up boundaries that will help you prioritize and schedule the tasks that still require your attention. That's why this phrase is called Admission—here you will determine how to *admit* acceptable tasks into your schedule in the most efficient manner possible. It is also in this phase that you will learn to decipher the difference between *necessary* tasks and *productive* tasks and then set up boundaries that will allow you to maximize your time each day for what is most productive. (This phase covers the Yes Trap.)

## PHASE 3: ACTION

In this phase you begin to carry out the tasks that are either *necessary* or *productive* based on the boundaries you've set up in the Admission phase. In the Action phase of construction you will learn to increase your overall productivity. Upon completion of this phase, you will have completed construction of your dam. (This phase covers the Control Trap.)

## PHASE 4: ASSESSMENT

Once we get to this phase, you will already have a solid system of boundaries, a dam in place that will provide you at least four more productive hours a day. However, because you can still fall into habits that hinder the productive time you've created the Assessment phase helps you avoid those obstacles and teaches you how to remain focused on the tasks that are not only the most productive to your career but also the most beneficial to your life. (This phase covers the Identity Trap, the Technology Trap, the Quota Trap, the Failure Trap, and the Party Trap.)

There's not much to the system. In fact, as we continue you may find that you have constructed part of your dam already. If that's the case, I encourage you to treat those sections in the book as review and a chance to evaluate the effectiveness of your boundaries. As for the remainder of the book—keep with it. This system is simple to implement, and it will not only change the pace of your days, it will change the look of your life. In the end, the value of creating more time is gaining more life—so that's what we're ultimately after.

Now, if you're ready to pick up some tools and build this dam of yours, let's get going. We have no time to waste, literally.

## DAMMING TASKS BEFORE THEY DAMAGE YOU

The first two phases of construction— Accumulation and Admission— are the foundation of your dam and represent steps you will take to either eliminate or regulate tasks from entering your river. Placing boundaries that prohibit wasteful actions from requiring your attention is the primary key to organization, no matter how out of control you are now.

For now let's focus on damming unnecessary tasks before they can get to you and demand your attention. This will immediately help you gain a sense of order to your days.

## Phase 1: Accumulation

So often people pile stress and extra work on themselves by taking a reactive approach to tasks—in essence, doing whatever falls on their plate. This is highly unorganized and allows unproductive interruptions to constantly litter your river and monopolize your time.

To begin to clean up your chaotic work schedule and get yourself better organized, there are five guidelines you should follow for constructing boundaries that regulate or eliminate the most common unnecessary tasks that fill your river. Applying these guidelines will lay the foundation of your dam.

1. *Don't give your personal digits to customers or coworkers.* I'm talking about your cell phone number, your home phone number, and your personal e-mail address. This is a common mistake, and you know why? Because people use them. If someone gives me their personal digits and I can't reach them at work, I try to contact them with the other means they've provided. Why wouldn't I? They've given them to me. Don't you do the same thing? Yes, we don't want to miss out on important calls—but if you don't begin to put boundaries on customers' and coworkers' ability to get in touch with you, you're never going to be able to leave your work at the office. A nice salesperson gave me a business card the other day that listed seven ways to get in touch with her. Why give people so many options? Make it simple for them and sane for you. Here's what I tell

*Don't give your personal digits to customers.*

people at my events: give customers and coworkers only one e-mail address and one phone number. I know it's tempting and easy to justify giving out more contact information, but don't. Ask yourself this: would I rather be known as easily accessible or worth waiting for?

2. *Don't give your work digits to friends.* If they already have them, ask your friends to use your personal lines instead. If the problem persists, ask your boss if you can change your digits (e-mail and/or phone number) and explain that you are working toward increasing your productivity. I know you may be thinking that this is a bit extreme, but how many ways do our friends need to get a hold of us? If you have a personal cell phone and a personal e-mail address and a home number (which most of us do), your friends already have three ways to get in touch with you and leave messages. That's more than enough. The thing you have to realize is that if there is an emergency (the excuse that many people use for giving out their work digits to friends), people can get in touch with you no matter where you are. The idea is to avoid taking all the nonemergency calls and e-mails from friends during work that encompass about 99.9 percent of the total. If you're a relational person this will be like pulling teeth at first, but ask your friends for help. Develop a system of communicating only on breaks and during lunch, or train them to wait until after work for your response.

3. *Turn off the instant message and e-mail alert functions on your work computer.* I shouldn't need to tell you to do this, but I've found that many people keep one or both functions on while at work. If you are checking and retrieving your messages at specific times (we'll discuss this in the next chapter), you don't need to know if you have messages until those times. The last thing you need is one-liners and alerts popping up on your screen all day. They are too tempting, and they will whittle away your time quicker than you realize.

**4. *Don't answer the phone unless it is someone you are expecting*.** Be honest. How many of your unexpected calls end up being critically important? Very few, if you're like most. You don't need to be answering the phone every time it rings. In fact, unless you are in an industry whose business is run via phone or you are expecting a call, you shouldn't have the ringer on. You may even want to cover the red message waiting light with black tape and turn the message waiting beep or vibrate off on your cell. I know that may seem antisocial of you—especially if you're in a big office with lots of coworkers—but the fact is that if it isn't an expected call, you don't need to answer. People will find a way to get in touch with you if it's really important.

**5. *Don't check your personal e-mail during work hours*.** This is probably discussed in your five-hundred-page company policy manual, but let's stops pretending. Very few abide by that rule, and it adds to your work hours—sometimes several hours a week. Not only that, it adds tasks to your river of responsibilities, like e-mailing so-and-so with a phone number or calling so-and-so with directions or checking out a new Web site or answering a question that can be answered after work. Again, your friends will generally support you when they understand that you are taking steps to be more organized so that you will have more free time in return. If you don't have a laptop or a home computer this can be a difficult step to implement, but there are two ways to remedy this: (1) talk to your manager and request a laptop to replace your desktop. Most companies lease their computers so this may be more feasible than you think. Or (2) invest in a home computer. Nowadays, there are several complete desktop systems that are extremely inexpensive or that you can pay off with monthly payments. (For tax purposes this can also be considered a nonreimbursed business expense.) If you can't afford this route, you can also lease a laptop for less than the cost of your cable bill and use it at home to catch up with friends when you're off work. Whichever way you decide to go, your increased productivity at work will generally offset the expense in no time.

## WORK WITHOUT INTERRUPTIONS

Permit me to skip over all the obvious escapism tasks that we get into like surfing the Web and playing computer games and shooting pool with coworkers in the lounge. I don't need to tell you these tasks are a waste of time and should be eliminated if you desire to spend less time at work. Those mentioned in the previous section represent the most pervasive, but often overlooked, time sappers. There are others of course: needless meetings, straightening up your work area incessantly, reading the paper in the bathroom (let's be honest, guys), constantly "freshening up" in the ladies room (you're not off the hook either, ladies), snacking every hour, fixing the broken copier, checking stocks, sports scores, or shopping malls online . . . Have I made my point? There are seemingly endless unnecessary tasks that can saturate our days. As trite as they may seem, you'll be surprised at how much time is freed up by simply constructing boundaries that keep such tasks from ever entering your river of responsibilities.

If in modest estimation you currently spend the following amounts of time each day on the five most pervasive tasks, take a look at how much time you will free up over the course of a year if you are able to dam them:[3]

| Task | Time Wasted | Time Freed |
|---|---|---|
| Personal e-mails to work address | 30 mins/day | 115 hours/year |
| Personal calls to work phone(s) | 30 mins/day | 115 hours/year |
| Answering every call | 60 mins/day | 230 hours/year |
| Customer calls to personal digits | 60 mins/day | 230 hours/year |
| Instant messages & e-mail alerts | 15 mins/day | 57.5 hours/year |
| **Total time freed up** | **3 hours/day** | **747.5 hours/year** |

If you're thinking these are high estimates, I challenge you to tally your time for three weeks. I think you'll find the figures are not far off.

Can you imagine how much more you could accomplish with 747.5 more hours a year? That's almost nineteen more weeks!

Imagine the possibilities.

But of course freeing up your time is more than keeping unnecessary tasks from interrupting you. As you know, certain tasks cannot simply be eliminated. Organization, then, is also regulating the scheduling of tasks that you must carry out, but may or may not be highly productive. This is the next phase of construction and the subject of our next chapter.

## Executive Summary

Most days, getting organized feels like trying to keep your head above water in a fast and high river. Often, your river of responsibilities rages like a mid-May, flood-high current that threatens to drown you. The more tasks rain down, the more disorganized and out of control you become. Even if you see obstacles, you rarely have the time or the energy to avoid them. Furthermore, staying in control at this rapid pace is at best a daunting task, at worst a lost cause. And to make matters worse, hard-charging, relational professionals are characteristically unorganized.

The majority of disorganization, however, is not the result of character flaws, too much work, or too little time. It is primarily the result of investing time in meaningless tasks. Therefore, the first step to cleaning up your days is creating boundaries that keep unnecessary tasks from sapping your time. There are five boundaries you should construct:

1. Never give your personal digits to customers or coworkers.

2. Don't give your work digits to friends.

3. Turn off the instant message and e-mail alert functions on your computer.

4. Don't answer the phone unless you are expecting a call.

5. Avoid checking your personal e-mail during work hours.

Metaphorically speaking, these five boundaries represent the initial construction of a dam that will eventually slow the current of your river of responsibilities. This initial phase is referred to as damming your Accumulation of tasks.

*Chapter Four*

# The Yes Trap
Wasting Time Saying Yes

*"I'm just a girl who can't say no."*

— RODGERS AND HAMMERSTEIN,
SONG FROM *OKLAHOMA*

*"The ideal worker is someone who enters the full-time, now
overtime, workforce in early adulthood, and, if he or she can,
lifts their head forty years later . . . Ideal workers are hostages
to their jobs . . ."*

— JOE ROBINSON

It has been estimated that a typical worker has 170 interactions every day.[4] If you break this estimation down based on a fifty-hour workweek the numbers are telling: 170 interactions per day multiplied by five workdays per week equals 850 interactions. Divide these 850 weekly interactions by fifty work hours a week and you find that you have about seventeen interactions every hour. Or, in other words, you have about three minutes to focus on any one thing without interruption. Even if you work eighty hours a week to catch up, you will still only have about five minutes to focus on one task without interruption.

Not only is this rarely enough time to get anything done *right*, it's rarely enough time to get anything done *period*.

The problem is simple: most people take on too many responsibilities, and this not only increases time on the job it increases propensity for stress and oversights. One busy woman I read about purchased tickets to the World Series for some high-profile clients. She told the broker from whom she purchased the tickets that she wanted to attend a game on either Tuesday or Wednesday night, but preferably Wednesday. Imagine her embarrassment when she met up with her clients at the gate on Wednesday night and was turned away because she held tickets for the night before. In a flurry, she had forgotten to verify the date.[5]

The busyness dilemma shows up in many ways: tardiness, forgetfulness, inconsistency, inefficiency, frustration, stress . . . there are many more, but busyness is rooted in only one thing: we say yes too often. As a result, we end up starting more tasks than we finish, and the tasks we do complete are often riddled with errors or inconsistencies. This is only the beginning of the woes, as you may know, for when tasks are done wrong, more time must be used to revise or redo them. Furthermore, if tasks are begun and not completed one day, they spill into the next day, compounding the workload and flooding your river of responsibilities high and fast until you are forced to either put in marathon days to catch up or concede to a whirling, flailing pace of work every day. And we all know that catching up is somewhat mythical, somewhat unattainable. It is being done by the super heroes of the working world who, legend has it, move so fast their actions are invisible to the naked eye. But is anyone *normal* catching up? Studies suggest that we aren't.

> *Busyness is rooted in only one thing: we say yes too often.*

### A typical day in the life of Superworker

| Monday 9:01 AM | Monday 9:02 AM | Monday 9:03 AM |

## THE NEW "YES" ECONOMY

According to a 2001 phone survey of working American families conducted by the Families and Work Institute, the following conclusions were made:

◆ 55 percent are overwhelmed by how much work they have to accomplish.

◆ 45 percent feel they have to carry out too many jobs at once and multitask too often in order to keep up.

◆ 59 percent admit they are unable to reflect on and perfect the work they are doing.

◆ 90 percent strongly agree that they work "too fast" and "too hard" and they "never have enough time to get a job done properly."

We have become a laboring nation of yes-men and yes-women for whom no task is too much to ask and every task is commenced "right away, sir" with a "consider it done, ma'am" attitude.

It's easy to fall into the Yes Trap. Climbing the ladder means granting requests and taking on tasks to gain rapport and never turning down an opportunity to impress. It necessitates a can-do attitude. And it takes a big investment of time. It requires you to become what Joan Williams, a law professor at American University, calls the "ideal worker." In *Work to Live*, Joe Robinson summarizes what this person looks like:

> The ideal worker is someone who enters the full-time, now overtime, workforce in early adulthood, and, if he or she can, lifts their head forty years later.

However, there are problems to this label; Robinson explains one of them:

> Ideal workers are hostages to their jobs, which makes them non-parents . . . The ideal worker role is a time bomb that blows up marriages, and kids are the collateral damage. The divorce rate is higher in overwork industries . . . In the end, the kids and all of us pay, says Williams, because 40 percent of divorced women wind up in poverty, and the children along with them, since most will live with the mother.[6]

Robinson calls this current working condition a "world where parents can't make a living and be a parent at the same time . . ." It's tragic. But even if you're not a parent, the effects are extensive.

According to the National Sleep Foundation, 63 percent of American adults don't get the recommended eight and a half hours of sleep necessary for good health, safety, and optimum performance; nearly one-third report sleeping less than seven hours each weeknight. The study discovered a direct correlation between loss of sleep and the number of hours worked, indicating the need for Americans to find a way to scale back our hours on the job or suffer the consequences.

Most of us can admit to not getting as much sleep as we should. Unfortunately, we usually fail to make any headway on scaling back our workload and therefore continue laboring in a constant state of stress and fatigue. It's not for lack of wanting, however.

Another NSF poll found that most workers indicate they are concerned about the impact of sleepiness and fatigue on a person's job performance. The poll found widespread support for limiting work hours for many professions that affect personal safety. Specifically, the poll found that:

◆ 70 percent believe the maximum number of hours worked each day by a doctor should be ten or less.

◆ 86 percent agreed that a pilot should be allowed to take a nap to overcome drowsiness while flying if another qualified pilot can take over; 63 percent said a pilot's maximum workday should be eight hours or less.

◆ Almost 50 percent supported limiting workdays of police officers, truck drivers, and nurses to a maximum of eight hours.

These results indicate our acknowledgment of the need for change when one is spending too much time on the job. They also indicate our general agreement that long hours and sleep-deprived nights don't enhance job proficiency. At least that's what we think when it comes to doctors, nurses, truck drivers, police officers, and pilots. It's a different story when it comes to ourselves, isn't it? We feel trapped.

With an ever-rising flood of responsibilities, it seems impossible to scale back hours without shrinking our potential. But that's just how it *seems*. The truth is that if there are not limits to what you undertake, there are always regrettable consequences, and they're often worse than losing a few winks of sleep.

At one of our recent events Tim Sanders, the chief solutions officer of Yahoo!, revealed that about eight million working Americans suffer from what he calls NEDS. It stands for New Economy Depression Syndrome, and it's one adverse effect of the Yes Trap.

## Scaling Back without Sacrificing Potential

There are only two ways to scale back your busy workload and free up more time: (1) sacrifice success, or (2) say no more often. If you choose the first option, you are simply deciding that decreased career accomplishment is a fair trade-off for gaining more simplicity and sanity *on* the job and more freedom *off* the job. This is an admirable route, and if you choose it, I say more power to you. But it's not the most effective route—nor is it necessary.

My company's research has given us one piece of data that remains fairly consistent from year to year. It is that most professionals we work with are productive for only one-fourth of their workday. According to other studies, my statistics may be slightly modest.

In a recent book Brian Tracy writes that in 1928, *Sales and Marketing Management* conducted a survey that revealed that the average American worker in a sales industry was productive only ninety minutes a day or about 20 percent of their time at work. In 1988, thinking the increase in training would surely have increased American workers' productivity, the same magazine conducted a repeat survey. The results, however, were the same: the average worker still managed to grunt out only ninety productive minutes a day. Nothing had changed in sixty years.[7]

Many of the people I speak to each year are salespeople, and I've found that they may be among the most swamped of all professionals. In the very least, they provide us with a good benchmark for measuring what happens when one gets seriously swamped. Recently, I came across a study conducted by Proudfoot Consulting™ that confirmed this notion.

Each year Proudfoot studies the work behaviors and performance of professionals around the globe. For the first time since initiating the annual study, in 2003 Proudfoot looked specifically at salesforce effectiveness.[8] They found that in every country surveyed (Australia, France, Germany, South Africa, Spain, the UK, and the US) professionals holding sales-related positions are extremely bogged down and on average only spend 20 percent of their time on activities that affect the bottom line. Take a look at the study's breakdown of time use by general category:

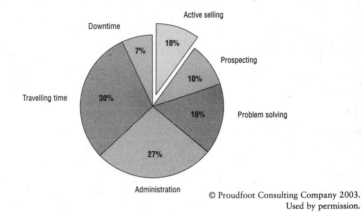

© Proudfoot Consulting Company 2003.
Used by permission.

Now take a look at the breakdown of time use in the world's most prominent sales industries. Note the far left column that indicates the average percentage of actual productive time in each industry.

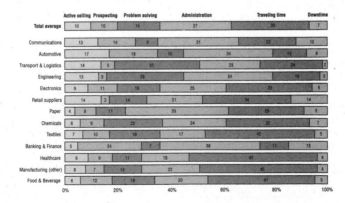

| | Active selling | Prospecting | Problem solving | Administration | Traveling time | Downtime |
|---|---|---|---|---|---|---|
| Total average | 10 | 10 | 16 | 27 | 30 | 7 |
| Communications | 13 | 14 | 8 | 31 | 22 | 12 |
| Automotive | 17 | 3 | 18 | 10 | 34 | 18 |
| Transport & Logistics | 14 | 5 | 32 | 23 | 24 | 2 |
| Engineering | 13 | 3 | 29 | 34 | 18 | 3 |
| Electronics | 9 | 11 | 16 | 25 | 33 | 6 |
| Retail suppliers | 14 | 3 | 14 | 21 | 34 | 14 |
| Paper | 4 | 8 | 11 | 39 | 29 | 9 |
| Chemicals | 6 | 9 | 22 | 24 | 32 | 7 |
| Textiles | 7 | 10 | 19 | 17 | 42 | 5 |
| Banking & Finance | 5 | 24 | 7 | 38 | 11 | 15 |
| Healthcare | 9 | 9 | 11 | 18 | 49 | 4 |
| Manufacturing (other) | 8 | 7 | 14 | 22 | 45 | 4 |
| Food & Beverage | 6 | 12 | 16 | 20 | 41 | 5 |

© Proudfoot Consulting Company 2003.
Used by permission.

Whether or not you hold a sales-related position, you can learn from these statistics because the same holds true for nearly every professional my company has studied and trained. The vast majority of swamped workers, when they come to us, are spending between 70–80 percent of their workdays carrying out tasks that are either unnecessary or not highly productive. Conversely, they are investing only 20–30 percent of their workdays on tasks they would consider highly productive to their job potential and career success. In other words, if you are swamped, your daily activities may look different from the chart above, but it's very likely that your river is equally full of tasks that are not highly productive.

## THE VALUE OF SAYING NO

In the last chapter we discussed how we aimlessly take on tasks that monopolize our time. It's a trap we called the Organization Trap. To avoid it we must construct boundaries that regulate the Accumulation of unnecessary tasks. This is essential to shelter your time and keep inconsequential, disruptive tasks from flooding your river.

In this chapter we're talking about something different. We're talking about our inability to spend the majority of our time carrying out the most productive, bottom-line tasks. Clearly it's a problem and has been for some time. I call it the Yes Trap, and it is rooted in a worker's inability to say no.

If we take a detailed look at the general tasks that we are saying yes to, we'll not only pinpoint the source of the problem, we'll discover a fresh solution you can use right away.

In the grouping of tasks that we carry out over any given day, there are generally three categories:

    1. Unnecessary tasks

2. Necessary tasks

3. Productive tasks

To make this easy to remember, think of the three categories as the three descending colors on a stoplight. Here are brief explanations; we'll break each one down more thoroughly in a minute.

◆ *Unnecessary tasks* are *red* because they represent activities that prohibit your career from moving forward and therefore are a waste of time. Such tasks include e-mailing friends, answering unexpected phone calls, chatting with coworkers, instant messaging, making personal phone calls, Web surfing, and playing computer games. These are the tasks you need to stop.

◆ *Necessary tasks* are *yellow* because they represent the activities that have the potential to move your career in a positive direction but at a less productive pace than other activities. These activities are a good use of your time but not the best use. Such tasks include goal setting and planning, observation and evaluation, some company meetings, and necessary paperwork and communication. This is your caution zone. You need to regulate your time investment in these tasks.

◆ *Productive tasks* are *green* because they represent the activities that most effectively move your career in a positive direction and are the best use of your time. They are often the action(s) that reflect the discoveries you have made completing necessary tasks. Generally, you will only have one or two activities in this grouping, and if you could spend the majority of your time on them you would reach your potential much quicker. They are your "go" tasks.

UNNECESSARY TASKS

NECESSARY TASKS

PRODUCTIVE TASKS

Let's discuss the details of each task category and determine how to construct boundaries that enable you to effectively utilize them.

## UNNECESSARY TASKS

We dealt exclusively with the most pervasive unnecessary tasks in the last chapter so I won't say much more here except to remind you that your boundaries in the Accumulation phase are the foundation of your dam. You must maintain regulation of these time wasters through disciplined boundaries, or you will never temper the current of your river of responsibilities. Initially, this should require no more than 5 percent of your work hours. Once you have cemented your boundaries and are comfortable with their effectiveness (this should take three weeks or less) you will no longer have to spend time on regulation in this category. Your dam will do the regulating for you.

That said, let's examine the other two categories and how you can set up boundaries that will help you spend the majority of your work time on tasks that reap the greatest return in productivity and free time. Now we are on to the next phase of construction.

## Phase 2: Admission

### NECESSARY TASKS

The category of greatest struggle for most people is necessary tasks. This category includes tasks that offer some value to your career and *can* free up your time if carried out properly; but if too much time is given to these tasks you will not have much time to spend on your most important tasks. Proceed with caution on necessary tasks; this is where many good workers hit a ceiling on their productivity. A client named Linda found herself in this place when she sought out coaching help. As it turned out, she'd been spending an average of 185 minutes a day on necessary-but-not-productive tasks. Finding a solution for decreasing the amount of time she was spending on these tasks became the focus of her coaching and the main reason she eventually improved her career and increased her free time. That may be where you need to start as well.

The goal with necessary tasks is to spend high-quality time on them but not a high quantity of time. Let's highlight the main tasks in this category and briefly discuss the boundaries we must construct for them.

### NECESSARY TASK #1: PAPERWORK

[TOTAL TIME INVESTMENT:
*30 minutes every other hour, or 2 hours total per day*]

This is a major time killer if boundaries are not in place because it encompasses so many different tasks: filling out paperwork, faxing paperwork, copying paperwork, filing paperwork, etc. This is the most common bog-down area for workers.

The fact is that most of us have paper trails that are necessary to do our jobs. While this is never the best use of our time, there are some ways to spend less time on paperwork. Remember, the point of the Admission phase is regulating necessary tasks so you can complete them in a highly efficient manner.

By far the best way to accomplish this is to delegate your necessary paperwork to an assistant or team member. I will discuss this solution in the next chapter as it requires more explanation than we will take time for here. For now, let's assume that an assistant or team is not yet an option for you. The next most effective way to regulate time spent on paperwork is to block specific periods each day to deal only with these tasks—this way you are never interrupting your momentum on more productive tasks.

| Time | Monday | Tuesday | Wednesday | Thursday | Friday |
|------|--------|---------|-----------|----------|--------|
| 9:00 | Tasks | Tasks | Tasks | Tasks | Tasks |
| 9:30 | Paperwork | Paperwork | Paperwork | Paperwork | Paperwork |
| 10:00 | Tasks | Tasks | Tasks | Tasks | Tasks |
| 10:30 | Tasks | Tasks | Tasks | Tasks | Tasks |
| 11:00 | Tasks | Tasks | Tasks | Tasks | Tasks |
| 11:30 | Paperwork | Paperwork | Paperwork | Paperwork | Paperwork |
| 12:00 | Tasks | Tasks | Tasks | Tasks | Tasks |
| 12:30 | Tasks | Tasks | Tasks | Tasks | Tasks |
| 1:00 | Tasks | Tasks | Tasks | Tasks | Tasks |
| 1:30 | Paperwork | Paperwork | Paperwork | Paperwork | Paperwork |
| 2:00 | Tasks | Tasks | Tasks | Tasks | Tasks |
| 2:30 | Tasks | Tasks | Tasks | Tasks | Tasks |
| 3:00 | Tasks | Tasks | Tasks | Tasks | Tasks |
| 3:30 | Paperwork | Paperwork | Paperwork | Paperwork | Paperwork |
| 4:00 | Tasks | Tasks | Tasks | Tasks | Tasks |
| 4:30 | Tasks | Tasks | Tasks | Tasks | Tasks |
| 5:00 | | | | | |

## Damming Your Paperwork

A good place to start is to block out thirty minutes every other hour for paperwork tasks. During this time—and only during this time—

complete all necessary paperwork (which includes filling out and filing forms online) that has accumulated over the previous hour and a half. With your time blocked accordingly, your weekly calendar would look like the previous chart (for now we will just say the remainder of your work time is filled with "tasks").

Obviously, the less time you spend on paperwork, the more time you will free up to invest in productive tasks. Therefore, if you find that you don't need two hours each day, scale it back accordingly. I know people who block the thirty minutes before their lunch break and the thirty minutes before they go home to do paperwork tasks. These seem to be productive periods, as eating and leaving are great incentives to get the work done efficiently. Whatever you decide, make sure that you block your paperwork time strategically so that you won't have too much to complete in that designated period. One way to ensure this doesn't happen is to set up a simple filing system that helps you separate what needs to be done immediately from what can wait. I use a system I call the Nifty Fifty that can be set up like this:[9]

1. Pick up 50 hanging file folders.
2. Divide them as follows (the particular colors in each grouping are not significant and are merely those I chose when I started—you can substitute your own colors):
3. Get 4 purple folders and label them Family, Fitness, Finances, and Fun. (We won't discuss these here, but this is where all your ideas for these categories go. They are reviewed annually and go into the system described below.)
4. Label and number 31 green folders 1–31 for the days of the month.
5. Label 12 yellow folders January through December.

6. Label 2 blue folders with the current year and the following year followed by the word *Planning*.

7. Label 1 red folder with the words *Improvements and Surveys*.

Here's how it works: When you have an upcoming paperwork task, you drop the necessary papers into the appropriate yellow monthly folder according to when you need to complete it. On the last workday of the month, take out the next month's yellow folder and sort its paperwork into your thirty-one green daily folders. At the beginning of your blocked paperwork time each day, you will simply take out your appropriate green daily folder and complete the paperwork filed there. You will be clearing a green folder every day.

Once this system is underway, it flows smoothly and makes it easy to stay on top of all your paperwork with minimal effort. If you have an assistant, have that person use the same filing system. You can then delegate to his or her folders and free up even more time. If you travel, take the green daily folders for the days you will be gone, as well as the next month's yellow folder. If you have a vacation scheduled, don't file anything in the folders of the days you will be gone.

## NECESSARY TASK #2:
## PLANNING AND GOAL SETTING

[TOTAL TIME INVESTMENT:
*8–24 hours per year; 15 minutes per week*]

Spend one to two days planning once a year. Do this during a period when you will not be distracted by social plans or professional obligations. I usually do it between Christmas and New Year's—but if December is a long way off as you're reading this, then schedule it sooner.

During this time you will not only review your progress (or lack thereof) from the year that is about to end, you will also set goals for the upcoming year for your career and life, and then determine specifically how you will accomplish these by recording specific daily, weekly, or monthly steps on paper. File these papers in one folder labeled with the current year and the word *Planning* and review them every Monday morning before you begin working. If there are planning ideas for next year, keep them in next year's blue folder.

Your Monday morning reviews should take no more than fifteen minutes as your plans should be concise enough to be typed on one to two pages. Mondays are not time for evaluation; they are simply to position your goals and values at the front of your mind as you begin your week. Here are a few examples of questions you might want to be answering as you begin your week: What new things do you need to learn? What people do you need to foster relationships with? What are your most important tasks?

If you isolate yourself during your annual planning sessions and are careful to set realistic, value-centered goals, you will not have to spend time amending your plan throughout the year. Instead, you will focus on constantly keeping your goals in mind so that your actions support attaining them.

## NECESSARY TASK #3: SURVEYING CUSTOMERS AND COWORKERS

### [TOTAL TIME INVESTMENT:
*5 minutes per sales transaction or 30 minutes per month (if not in sales)*]

If you do not work with customers, meet with a close coworker once a month for thirty minutes to ask specific questions about yourself and how you might improve. To make this time effective and efficient, design a standard survey that asks the questions you need to be asking this person who should at least be familiar with your work habits, your weekly schedule, and your job requirements. Allow your coworker the freedom to give honest feedback on the survey and then use the monthly meeting to discuss the feedback and advice openly. Here is a simple survey you might ask your coworker to complete:

---

### SAMPLE PROGRESS SURVEY

1. On the following scale, circle your honest opinion of my work habits over the last month:

   1 — Poor
   2 — Been better
   3 — Average
   4 — Better than usual
   5 — Excellent

2. On the following scale, circle your honest opinion of my attitude over the last month:

   1 — Sour
   2 — Been better
   3 — Typical
   4 — Good
   5 — Inspirational

13. On the following scale, circle your honest opinion of my time use over the last month:

   1 — Wasteful
   2 — Inconsistent
   3 — Busy
   4 — Consistent
   5 — Purposeful

---

If you are in sales, my advice is to not let this task build up. Design or have designed a strategic survey that elicits the information you desire from your customers and then ask for their feedback *before* you close the sale so that errors are quickly pinpointed and addressed. One of our favorite restaurants does this between the time you finish your entrée and before dessert and coffee are served.

---

### AN EXAMPLE OF A SURVEY

Honest, critical feedback from you is the best way for us to stay in tune with your needs. Learning how we did after your order is fulfilled is valuable, but as a team we feel it is more important to understand how we are doing currently. If we are off, we want to correct our efforts now so that you have a good experience from now on. If we are on target, then we want to stay the course.

Please take just a few moments to answer 7 very brief questions using a scale of 1 (Poor)–5 (Best):

Have we done a good job of determining the right product solutions for your specific needs?

    1    2    3    4    5

Have we returned your calls promptly?

    1    2    3    4    5

Have we answered your questions to your satisfaction?

    1    2    3    4    5

Have we kept you informed of the status of your order?

    1    2    3    4    5

Have you found everyone on our team to be courteous and professional?

    1    2    3    4    5

Are you pleased with the service our other departments are providing?

    1    2    3    4    5

Can you make any suggestions on how we might serve you better?

_____

_____

Thank you for taking the time to help us. We appreciate you!

---

The last thing you want is a customer who pays but feels bad about the service he received. That's why surveying is a necessary task. It's productive but not the most productive use of your time, so come up with a survey that is quick and to the point.

Once completed, keep your surveys in your red folder labeled with the current year and the words *Improvements and Surveys.* You want these saved and easily accessible because they provide great material for evaluating your progress during your observation and evaluation time. This is the next necessary task.

## NECESSARY TASK #4:
## OBSERVING AND EVALUATING

### [TOTAL TIME INVESTMENT:
*5 minutes every 60 minutes of your workdays for the first month; then, when you're highly productive, spend 1 hour every month*]

Early in my career a man who worked for a national insurance firm told me that he takes five minutes out of every sixty to evaluate his productivity. If you work eight hour days, spending forty minutes throughout the day making sure seven hours and twenty minutes goes well is a good idea. I recommend that you follow this model for the first month or until you feel that you are sustaining momentum. Then spend one hour on the last workday of every month observing and evaluating your progress against the goals you've recorded in your planning session. You can also use your customer or coworker surveys as aids here—they will often help you decipher some good and bad trends and show you how to improve. Record your observations and necessary improvements on a sheet of paper (you can type and print these as well) and file them each month in your red folder labeled with the current year and the words *Improvements and Surveys.* If certain improvements come to mind that change your goals for the year, you can also move this paperwork to your blue Planning folder that you review every Monday morning.

## NECESSARY TASK #5: COMMUNICATION

### [TOTAL TIME INVESTMENT:
*30 minutes every other hour or 2 hours total per day*]

The final necessary task that steals so much of our productive time is communication. This primarily includes two tasks: e-mails and phone calls. When we discussed the Organization Trap in the previous chapter, I mentioned the need for you to set up boundaries to eliminate unnecessary communication: personal e-mails, personal phone calls, and giving coworkers and customers your personal information. Now we are talking specifically about communication that is required for you to carry out your job. Although these tasks are necessary, there are still boundaries that you should construct so they don't build up and breach your dam. These boundaries are also created by strategically blocking periods of time to dedicate to the tasks.

### *Damming Your Communication*

Most people check voice mail and e-mail every time they return to their work space. If there are no messages, this is a certain waste of time. If there are messages that require action, this often adds to the stress of the day, especially when you are tempted to return the message or carry out the requested task immediately. Caught in this cycle, the average worker wastes approximately two hours a day treating every message as an emergency that requires immediate attention. One salesperson I coached spent twenty-five hours a week listening to and returning messages before she built boundaries. After her boundaries were in place, her productivity increased by 200 percent because she had so much more time to invest in her main tasks.

The fact is that most voice mail and e-mail messages can wait—especially when you let others know of your explicit plans to return their communications. So instead of constantly checking for messages throughout the day and responding to them immediately and sporadically, determine two to four specific times each day that you will check and return messages. Also, indicate with a voice mail greeting and an auto-response e-mail that you will be doing so.[10] This will reassure your message leavers that you will call them back shortly, and it will help you not feel compelled to answer the phone.

Obviously the less time you spend on communication the better, but it's sometimes important that you don't appear rushed—especially if relationships are important to your success. Where e-mails are concerned, this is easier to avoid. When speaking in person, it's okay to be to the point, but don't be so time conscious that you are impersonal or rude. Make it your overarching goal in all work-related communication to be efficient, considerate, and professional. The best way to accomplish this without seeming rushed is to make a point at the beginning of the conversation to mention how much you value the other person's time.

Let people know you want to be sensitive to their schedule and they will generally let you proceed in a professional and efficient manner. However, don't overlook that any time spent on communication with a customer, colleague, or coworker is a chance to grow the relationship and must occasionally be regulated with a soft boundary. I'm not talking about allowing for meaningless chatter. I'm talking about instances in certain conversations when you will have an opportunity to further a relationship or close a deal that will aid your career. These moments arise at times, so be open to them.

My advice is to initially set modest boundaries with necessary communication tasks and adjust them as you get more comfortable with how much time you typically require. I usually advise people to initially spend the first thirty minutes of every other hour checking messages and returning calls, text messages, and e-mails. If we apply this to our schedule in-progress, your weekly calendar would look like this:

| Time | Monday | Tuesday | Wednesday | Thursday | Friday |
|------|--------|---------|-----------|----------|--------|
| 9:00 | Communication | Communication | Communication | Communication | Communication |
| 9:30 | Paperwork | Paperwork | Paperwork | Paperwork | Paperwork |
| 10:00 | Tasks | Tasks | Tasks | Tasks | Tasks |
| 10:30 | Tasks | Tasks | Tasks | Tasks | Tasks |
| 11:00 | Communication | Communication | Communication | Communication | Communication |
| 11:30 | Paperwork | Paperwork | Paperwork | Paperwork | Paperwork |
| 12:00 | Tasks | Tasks | Tasks | Tasks | Tasks |
| 12:30 | Tasks | Tasks | Tasks | Tasks | Tasks |
| 1:00 | Communication | Communication | Communication | Communication | Communication |
| 1:30 | Paperwork | Paperwork | Paperwork | Paperwork | Paperwork |
| 2:00 | Tasks | Tasks | Tasks | Tasks | Tasks |
| 2:30 | Tasks | Tasks | Tasks | Tasks | Tasks |
| 3:00 | Communication | Communication | Communication | Communication | Communication |
| 3:30 | Paperwork | Paperwork | Paperwork | Paperwork | Paperwork |
| 4:00 | Tasks | Tasks | Tasks | Tasks | Tasks |
| 4:30 | Tasks | Tasks | Tasks | Tasks | Tasks |
| 5:00 | | | | | |

(I know some people who retrieve voice mails one last time on their way home from the office, but I don't recommend this as it creates unnecessary anxiety and decreases the quality of your evening free time.)

You can obviously raise this boundary up or down based on how much your job depends on the phone and e-mail. But don't miss the point. By regulating your communication time, you increase the quantity of time that you can spend on your most productive tasks. That is the goal.

## PRODUCTIVE TASKS

We will discuss how to increase your efficiency in your most important tasks in the coming chapters. For now, you simply need to understand that productive tasks (green light tasks) don't need to be regulated. These are tasks in which you want to invest as much time as possible. In other words, it is to these tasks that you always want to say yes. But that can only happen when you say no to unnecessary tasks such as personal calls and e-mails, and place strategic boundaries on necessary tasks such as paperwork and communication.

If you kept to our working schedule above, your day would currently have four hours for your most productive, career-advancing tasks (assuming you are working eight hours a day). If you are around the national average for most workers—ninety productive minutes every eight hours—this means that by applying the boundaries we've just discussed you should already be able to increase your productive time by 167 percent. Not a bad start.

But I believe we can do even better.

## Executive Summary

Climbing the proverbial ladder in any profession generally means becoming a yes man or yes woman. To move up requires a can-do attitude and gung-ho work ethic and that takes a big investment of time. This often gets us swamped because it creates a constant, unprioritized influx of wants, needs, and obligations that cause our river of responsibilities to rise high and fast.

Some of these tasks are simply a waste of time—and in such cases need to be avoided—but other tasks are necessary in order to maintain a good rapport and carry out our job requirements with excellence. The best way to manage your fast current of necessary responsibilities is to place boundaries on the amount of time you spend on them or, metaphorically speaking, raise your dam higher. This includes regulating the time you invest in:

1. Paperwork
2. Planning and goal setting
3. Surveying customers and/or coworkers
4. Observing and evaluating your productivity
5. Communicating with coworkers, colleagues, and/or customers

This is the second phase of task management and the second level of your dam. It is referred to as damming your Admission of necessary tasks.

*Chapter Five*

# The Control Trap
## Wasting Time Hoarding Tasks

*"Master carries heavy burden . . . Smeagol knows. Smeagol carried burden many years."*

— GOLLUM FROM *THE LORD OF THE RINGS* TRILOGY

*"Whether a man is burdened by power or enjoys power;
whether he is trapped by responsibility or made free by it;
whether he is moved by other people and outer forces or moves
them—this is of the essence of leadership."*

— THEODORE WHITE

*"The man who is director of half a dozen railroads and three or
four manufacturing companies, or who tries at one and the
same time to work a farm, a factory, a line of street cars, a political
party and a store, rarely amounts to anything."*

— ANDREW CARNEGIE

S everal years ago, I was the president, sales rep, accountant, marketing rep, writer, and speaker of the Duncan Group. I had my hands on everything, and the company was growing at a rate of 2.5

percent a year. To be honest, the company's success was hardly worth mentioning—but I felt in control.

Then one day I met with my friend John, a very successful writer and speaker, with two *New York Times* best sellers under his belt and three highly successful companies. Four years earlier, he left a successful career to pursue speaking and writing full time. Since I had made the same leap, I wanted to get his take on things. How had he done so well? What were his secrets? How did he manage to take an enterprise he started in a friend's garage and develop it into two multimillion-dollar companies and one successful foundation? Furthermore, what was I doing wrong?

John wasted no time. He immediately told me I was shooting myself in the foot by trying to do it all myself. My success was being stifled, suffocated. There was only so much time in a day, he reminded me, and only so much I could do in that allotment of time. Therefore, the more tasks I controlled, the lower my ceiling of potential fell. He suggested that the only way to grow my business was to raise my ceiling, or in other words, to lift some responsibility off my shoulders.

I hated to admit it, but I was a bona fide control freak. It was the main reason my business wasn't growing the way I wanted it to, the way John's had. I was trying to expand a sales-based business with two hands and one mind—it wasn't enough. I was guilty of buying into some common misconceptions that essentially caged in my potential:

◆ If I want it done right, I have to do it myself.

◆ No one will work harder for me than I will.

◆ I cannot expect another person to take responsibility for my career.

◆ I am the only one I can truly trust with my livelihood.

My story is fairly common: what begins as an ambitious act of taking ownership often ends up as an unexpected (and often overlooked) burden that weighs us down, a lid that keeps us from rising higher in our endeavors and realizing our potential. It's a frequent mistake in self-starter professions and especially in new positions. Aren't we expected to pull up our bootstraps, take control of our futures, and make our job "our baby"? Yes, we are—but we *can* take it too far. When we do we end up trapped by the very things we are trying to control.

## HOLDING ON TOO TIGHTLY

In the jolly land of the Shire there was once a well-meaning hobbit named Sméagol. If you've only seen the first two installments of *The Lord of the Rings* trilogy, you're probably more familiar with his bug-eyed, skeletal alter ego, Gollum. But in Peter Jackson's adaptation of the final installment, *The Return of the King*, we are flashed back to the story's beginning, and it explains a lot of things, particularly Gollum's seemingly cursed existence.

The film begins with a young Sméagol and his cousin Déagol sitting in a small wooden boat on the river Anduin, surrounded by the lush green landscape of the Shire. Suddenly, Déagol's face lights up.

"Sméagol! I've got one! I've got a fish, Sméag!"

Both chuckle and Sméagol watches gleefully as his cousin struggles to pull in his catch. As Déagol continues to tussle with his bent pole, the fish at once gives a great tug, yanking him into the water. Sméagol is left gazing anxiously at his cousin's hat as it bobs on the surface. Underwater, a huge fish is pulling Déagol, eyes closed and cheeks puffed with air, along the riverbed. Finally, he lets go of the pole and opens his eyes just in time to catch a flicker of something on the river bottom. He reaches down and closes his hand over a patch of sand before kicking back to the surface.

As he re-emerges and begins to climb ashore, Déagol peers back into the shimmering water, and then, remembering something, opens his clenched, muddy hand and gazes at his discovery—a shiny gold ring.

In the background, nervous birds abandon their trees as Sméagol hurries to his cousin.

"Déagol! Déagol!" Sméagol approaches from behind and peers over his cousin's shoulder, eying the glistening ring.

"Give us that, Déagol my love."

Déagol closes his fist and turns to face Sméagol.

"Why?"

"Because it's my birthday, and I wants it."

Sméagol's smile fades slowly—then he snatches at the ring. Déagol dodges his attempt and the two laugh nervously and begin to circle each other. Sméagol lunges for the ring again, less playful this time. Soon the two are in an all-out skirmish. Sméagol bites at Déagol's arm and the ring falls to the ground. Both scramble madly along the ground but with a final lunge Déagol grabs hold of the ring then turns and closes five fingers around his cousin's throat. Sméagol lets out a scream and something snaps inside of him. His face turns pale and obstinate. Slowly, emotionlessly, he reaches down and closes ten fingers around Déagol's throat and presses from above him. There is only a brief struggle. Sméagol then climbs over Déagol's lifeless body and takes the ring from his loose fist. He fingers it close to his face and then slips it onto his finger and whispers in a guttural voice, "*My preciousss.*"[11]

## LETTING GO

Some things, if they're not let go, begin to control us, or worse, they begin to consume our time. The longer we hold on, the firmer they ensnare us—eventually they take us down. If the scene ended there, we might be left to assume that Sméagol was only a murderous thief and the ring merely a valuable treasure. But there is more to the ring and more in store for the one who holds it too tightly. If you've seen the trilogy you know that the ring Sméagol claimed as his own eventually begins to control him and ultimately destroy his life. It's the eventual fate of the control freak.

There are four basic reasons we maintain control even when it's detrimental to our success:

1. Ego—*No one can do it better than I can.*

2. Insecurity—*If someone does it better than I do, I will look bad.*

3. Naïveté—*I'm fine by myself; I don't need anyone else.*

4. Temperament—*Working with others is too complicated.*

It's true that our careers should be our babies. We all want to have a firm grasp on our direction and on the things that dictate our fate. But to realize our potential, we cannot hold on too tightly. There are limits to the value of control. Limits that if crossed can impart more damage than delight.

In the course of your career there are things you should control and there are things you should not. There are things you should make your baby—your *Preciousss*—and there are things you must let go if you are to ever break through the ceiling of average. That is the trap. You must take control of your career if you want it to take off, but if you wield *too much* control, you can stifle your potential and kill your momentum.

## TIME TO FOCUS

Success in any endeavor is a result of focused time. Rocky goes to the mountains of Siberia to train for his fight with Ivan Drago. Alejandro Murrieta takes to a cave with his mentor to learn the ways of Zorro. Rannulph Junuh learns to "see the field" and gets his swing back. And Billy Chapel "closes the mechanism" and pitches a perfect game. To become great at anything, you have to learn to focus your time on the main things—the more time you focus on one action, the more proficient and productive you will become at that action. Study any person throughout history who has achieved greatness and see if I am not right about this.

*Success in any endeavor is a result of focused time.*

This notion makes more sense when you understand that there is a compounding value to time. Multiple deposits of time on the same tasks can have a big effect. You experience this truth when you invest an hour at the gym each day for a few months. Over time, your sleep patterns improve, your body craves better foods, and you look better physically and feel better emotionally.

Conversely, there is very little value in haphazard deposits of time.

When you haven't worked out for several weeks, it will do you no good to spend three hours in the gym in one day. You cannot get in better shape by working out once every three months. Single deposits of time here and there have very little value. This is why multitasking is so unproductive. If all you have time for is arbitrarily doing tasks as they arise, you may get many things done but you will get nothing done with excellence. That is an inconsistent, reactive approach to task management and more is required if you want to climb out of the swamp and achieve a high level of success.

## THE RENAISSANCE IS HISTORY

Even Leonardo da Vinci's life is a testimony to this. I've read much about the original Renaissance man, and it's true that he was good at many things. He had many hobbies. His friends claimed he had the voice of an angel and was also a superb athlete, a brilliant mathematician, and an accomplished scientist. But despite his many talents, by what achievement is he known today? Only one. And as it so happens, it is in the pursuit of his art that he focused the overwhelming majority of his time. He too understood that greatness is a function of focused time.

To realize your potential you must get in the habit of focusing your time on only the few tasks that bring your career the greatest return, and then let go of the rest. That might require you to lose some control over other important (even productive) tasks. It won't necessarily be easy, but it's unavoidable if you are ever to reach new heights in your career.

## TAKING FOCUSED ACTION

In the last two chapters we discussed how to dam your Accumulation of unnecessary tasks so they will never enter your river of responsibilities. Essentially, this is the skill of interruption management—removing the possibility of needless disruption. We then discussed how to regulate the Admission of necessary-but-not-highly-productive tasks to your daily schedule. This is the skill of prioritization—minimizing your time on the lowest priorities so you can maximize your time on the highest priorities. These are the two primary skills you must learn in order to clear up your schedue for the most productive tasks. These two skills will dam your river of responsibilities and keep the current of tasks relatively manageable. But the river can still get out of control if you don't know how to focus the time you've freed up on what's most important.

## Phase 3: Action

Once you've set up boundaries that allow you to dam the Accumulation of unnecessary tasks and regulate the Admission of necessary tasks to your schedule, you must take Action on your most productive tasks. Therein lies a new problem for many people.

Even if you've built a sturdy dam that blocks unnecessary and less-productive tasks from your river, you can still get flooded with the amount of productive tasks you have left to carry out.

With the schedule we've been creating, you've dammed your river enough to give yourself four hours a day to focus on your main productive tasks. Let's take a look at it again (see page 71).

The problem lies in the fact that there's more to our main job responsibilities than meets the eye.

In the first edition of this book that I wrote to help professionals in the sales world, I diagramed the key steps to closing a sale. I want to share those with you here, whether or not you are in sales, because it serves as a good example of just how much can be involved in carrying out our "main responsibility." (See page 72.)

When I show this diagram to people I train, it's easy for them to see that even when a schedule has been cleared for productive tasks, it is still very easy to become swamped.

| Time | Monday | Tuesday | Wednesday | Thursday | Friday |
|------|--------|---------|-----------|----------|--------|
| 9:00 | Communication | Communication | Communication | Communication | Communication |
| 9:30 | Paperwork | Paperwork | Paperwork | Paperwork | Paperwork |
| 10:00 | Main Tasks | Main Tasks | Main Tasks | Main Tasks | Main Tasks |
| 10:30 | Main Tasks | Main Tasks | Main Tasks | Main Tasks | Main Tasks |
| 11:00 | Communication | Communication | Communication | Communication | Communication |
| 11:30 | Paperwork | Paperwork | Paperwork | Paperwork | Paperwork |
| 12:00 | Main Tasks | Main Tasks | Main Tasks | Main Tasks | Main Tasks |
| 12:30 | Main Tasks | Main Tasks | Main Tasks | Main Tasks | Main Tasks |
| 1:00 | Communication | Communication | Communication | Communication | Communication |
| 1:30 | Paperwork | Paperwork | Paperwork | Paperwork | Paperwork |
| 2:00 | Main Tasks | Main Tasks | Main Tasks | Main Tasks | Main Tasks |
| 2:30 | Main Tasks | Main Tasks | Main Tasks | Main Tasks | Main Tasks |
| 3:00 | Communication | Communication | Communication | Communication | Communication |
| 3:30 | Paperwork | Paperwork | Paperwork | Paperwork | Paperwork |
| 4:00 | Main Tasks | Main Tasks | Main Tasks | Main Tasks | Main Tasks |
| 4:30 | Main Tasks | Main Tasks | Main Tasks | Main Tasks | Main Tasks |
| 5:00 | | | | | |

Your dam may be regulating the tasks that shouldn't be filling your time, but if you can't properly utilize the time you've cleared up, you haven't made much progress. Water will back up and eventually rise over the dam making you just as flooded as you were before. To be successful with the time you've freed, you need to construct a top level on your dam. However, this level must have a spillway that allows *some* productive tasks to pass through—but not *all* of them.

## LETTING GO AND LIFTING UP YOUR BUSINESS

When you're a good worker, oftentimes you are given more responsibilities. But achieving productivity becomes difficult when you try to handle it all by yourself.

Sticking with the previous sample diagram, if we multiplied the seventeen steps by only three customers, one worker could

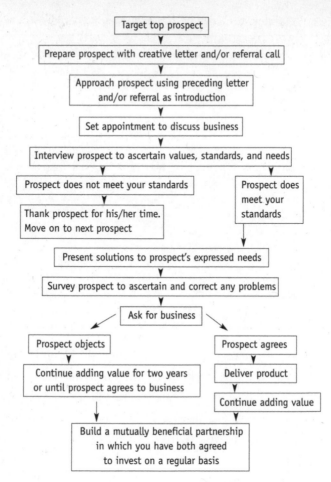

probably still manage every task; and that's how it is when we're first starting off in any job. We are in control and don't feel over-whelmed because we haven't yet been given much responsibility. But when we begin to climb the ladder higher (and I'm assuming that we want to) the rules quickly change; soon we are flooded with more tasks than we have time for in a day. It doesn't take much to get there either. For instance, in most sales-related industries if you multiply the seventeen steps in the sample diagram by ten customers, one can easily become a swamped workaholic if he or she is the only one carrying out the tasks.

The truth of the matter is that one is too small a number to achieve greatness in any endeavor.[12] You may be able to manage your river of responsibilities alone when you are starting off, but when your career begins to flourish there will come a point (and you may be there now) when you can't handle all of your responsibilities without sacrificing other important parts of your life. We need help to contend with the downstream current of success.

At the time of my conversation with John, I was employing anywhere from five to seven people. They each had job titles, but their job descriptions varied with the wind and hinged on what I didn't mind someone else controlling. I held on to the most important tasks. Most of my employees' duties were menial and involved making calls I didn't want to make or following paperwork trails that ended on my desk in the form of a report or confirmation. Phones were busy and paperwork was everywhere all the time—it was more like a newsroom than a corporate office—and I thought it was productive. But after John's candid advice I immediately began making changes that freed up my time to focus on my main task—speaking. Today the annual growth of the company is nearly twenty times greater than it was back then. In fact, we've grown so much that last year we purchased two of John's three companies so that he could focus his time even more on what mattered most to him.

The following four steps are based on the advice John gave me and are the keys to focusing your time and talents on the one or two tasks that bring you the greatest return in business. Not only will the steps multiply your potential for success, they will make it easier for you to achieve more by working less. To construct the third and final level of your dam, do the following:

**1.** *Answer the 100 percent question.* While thus far we've managed to free up four hours of your day to invest in highly productive tasks, your goal should be to eventually spend the entire day, every day you work, on your most productive tasks—this is the essence of the 100 percent question. Of course there will be other productive tasks that pass through your dam, and I will discuss how to manage those in a moment. For now, dream a little. Determine how you could best spend your time if given the opportunity. Ask yourself what your career would look like if you spent 100 percent of your work hours doing the one or two things that most advanced your career. Think about how much more you could make. How much less stress would you have? How much less would you have to work? How much better would your life be?

*Your goal should be to spend the entire day, every day you work, on your most productive tasks.*

Of course, you will not achieve this standard overnight, but by visualizing its results you will find it easier to make the necessary decisions to get there— and those are forthcoming in the remainder of this book. For now, so that you comprehend the value of this question, here's a snapshot of a client who sought out a 100 percent standard, gave up the necessary control, and over the course of four years gained the freedom it offers:

| Before | After |
|---|---|
| 70 hours a week | 40 hours a week |
| 15 sales a month | 40 sales a month |
| 2 weeks of vacation | 10 weeks of vacation |
| 1 location, solo effort | 3 locations, a team of 18 |

**2. *Assume a CEO mind-set.*** When I considered this step, the irony is that I was already the CEO in title. The problem was that I wasn't acting like it. A CEO mind-set is looking at your career as you would if you were the owner of a company and then determining what decisions need to be made in order to grow and ensure future stability. A CEO realizes that in order to take any endeavor to the next level and keep it growing, one must invest time wisely and form mutually beneficial relationships. When you see your job as a company you must run and grow, some important variables become clear—foremost, the necessity of good help that allows you to focus on what's important.

**3. *Delegate in increments.*** If we're honest, even with interruptions at bay and productivity climbing, four hours a day is barely enough time to complete every highly productive task. Eventually, we all come to a place where we accept that we must do one of two things to continue climbing:

1. Work more hours or

2. Lower our standard of success

Most of us don't consider the third option if it's not offered by our employer:

3. Seek help from other people

I'm not telling you to immediately go out and hire an assistant. You may not be able to afford it just yet. Since it is *your* business (CEO mind-set), the initial investments you make and the level of risk are up to you. However, I believe there are incremental steps that will help you work up to hiring an assistant and eventually a team to help you advance your career and gain more free time. These steps will eventually become necessary if you desire to maximize your time and potential on and off the job.

Take a look at these three delegation steps and determine at what point you should begin sharing some of your workload.

**Delegation Step 1:** *Hire yourself.* Essentially, you've already done this by blocking four hours a day to take care of necessary-but-not-highly-productive tasks. During these four hours, you act as your own assistant. For some, this alone might make a huge difference in your success. But this is only the start, as four hours a day is a lot of time to give to tasks that don't directly advance your success—especially when you consider that those hours could be used for the most productive tasks.

**Delegation Step 2:** *Utilize the help your company provides.* This is something often overlooked and underused. Many of us are employed by companies who already pay people to take care of some of the necessary tasks that we are carrying out. Before you consider what it would take to hire your own help, consider what help is available to you from your company, for free. You might be pleasantly surprised.

I also highly advise you to get your boss or board involved at this point. Request a short meeting to discuss your new productivity goals and what the company might have to offer in the way of help. Even if no in-house assistance is available, letting your boss or board know that you are actively taking steps to focus your time on greater productivity will be pleasing to hear. Furthermore, this conversation will lay the groundwork for your next step.

**Delegation Step 3:** *Hire a part-time assistant.* You have four hours of work each day that needs to get done, but that is not the most productive use of your time. If you delegated these tasks to an assistant, you'd only have to pay this person for twenty hours a week. At this point, the importance of the CEO mind-set really sets in. Some of you may be scoffing at the idea of hiring an assistant with your own money or even at the thought of having to train one; but if you're really interested in blowing the lid off your career potential, this is a necessary investment. And you need to see it that way—as an *investment*.

Remember Tim from the beginning of the book—the one who was faxing his life away? Hiring an assistant was his first step in letting go of some necessary tasks, and the way he did it is very effective.

Tim met with his manager and offered a deal: he would pay for his own part-time assistant for six months, and if after that period of time his productivity had increased enough to cover the cost of the assistant, the company would hire her. (Increased productivity was easy to measure since he is a salesperson. You will need to determine your own method of measurement.) Tim's manager agreed with his proposal. After only three months, Tim's extra time had already increases his revenue enough to defer the cost of his assistant. Convinced of her value to Tim's productivity, the company took over the cost three months ahead of schedule. When you consider the return on investment that a part-time assistant can bring, the decision is much easier to make. Even if you hold a set-salaried position, that doesn't nullify the point that hiring an assistant is a small price to pay for doubling the amount of time you can spend on productive tasks. Eventually, your monetary return will come in the form of a raise. But increased income is only part of the reward.

Think about what your life would be like if you finished all your responsibilities in five or six hours of work a day. Wouldn't it be nice to leave the office everyday at two o'clock? The monetary investment it takes to free up more of your day doesn't have to return money for it to be worthwhile. I know plenty of professionals who would not hesitate to net less money for more free time. Consider the following results from a fall 2003 poll commissioned by the Center for a New American Dream titled "Americans Will Take a Pay Cut for More Time, Less Stress":[13]

- More than half of Americans (52 percent) say they would be willing to trade a day off a week for a day's pay a week.

- Americans say they'd accept a pay cut to: have more free time to do whatever they wanted (27 percent); have more free time to spend with their family (21 percent); and to genuinely feel less pressure and stress in their life (20 percent).

If you really believe you cannot afford the cost of an assistant right now, consider sharing a part-time assistant with a coworker or colleague whose values you share. This will cut the cost in half and still free up ten more hours a week for you to use however you like. That's a start. And when you immediately begin to reap the benefits, you'll probably wonder why you didn't do it sooner.

Now, there's something else I want you to consider—in fact, you've already begun. It has everything to do with the fact that most of us would not hesitate to work less if we knew we could still advance our career and earn a better living than we are now.

**4:** *Begin building a team.* When I met Harry he was like Sméagol—he hoarded everything for himself. He employed a few people who simply took messages and scheduled tasks, but they didn't return calls or carry out any real work; that, according to Harry, was *his* baby. Then, at one of my events he was struck with what he calls a "blinding flash of the obvious."

*With a team, the sky is the limit.*

As I was sharing with the audience the bleak realities of being a control freak, Harry realized that he had been severely stifling his potential by keeping his hands on every important task. He was showing up to work early in the morning, at six or seven o'clock, and working until seven every night, with at least one weekend day to get caught up. A lot of hours, in other words. Needless to say, he was the wrong kind of busy—a bona fide control freak, like I was.

When Harry returned home from the event, he sat down and began to list what tasks should be delegated. He then had his employees shadow him for the next couple of weeks to learn every aspect of his job. Before long, each could handle every task that might arise, including the most productive tasks.

Today, Harry's team of four literally runs the show. He spends every minute of his work time on his most productive tasks. Everything else is taken care of and that has nearly cut his office time in half—from seventy-five hours a week to about forty-five—and it also affords him stress-free vacations whenever he wants them. He now typically takes six to ten weeks off a year. Additionally, his income has increased 400 percent since initially letting go. What Harry learned is that with a team, the sky is the limit.

When you're ready to initiate this final delegation step, here are the four things your team needs to succeed:

1. *A team needs a purpose to excite them.* If you've seen the film *The Rookie* you'll remember the key scene in the movie where Dennis Quaid, playing high school baseball coach and former minor league pitcher Jim Morris, is confronted by his team about his ability to pitch. They strike up a deal with their coach that if they win their league, he has to try out for the majors. It's the stimulation the team needs to succeed. When you begin building a team, make sure you give them something exciting to strive for that's as valuable to them as their help is to you.

2. *A team needs an opportunity to gel.* "Houston, we have a problem," says Tom Hanks in the film *Apollo 13*. He's playing the

astronaut Jim Lovell who has just discovered that fuel is leaking out of the spacecraft at a rapid rate. If Houston wondered how they would work together when it really mattered, their question was about to be answered. In the end, the team proves it has what it takes. The only way your team will gel is by having some big responsibilities. It's your job to give them the chance to come through.

3. *A team needs a coach to empower them.* Russell Crowe speaks power to his fellow gladiators by leading them "as one!" to their first victory in the Coliseum. Once you begin building a team, your role is to give your players the means to succeed. This requires you to define their roles, train them thoroughly, and encourage them often. If they fail and you haven't done your job, their failure is your fault.

4. *A team needs intimacy, honesty, and accountability to unite them.* You recall the scene if you've watched the film *Remember the Titans.* Denzel Washington, playing Coach Boone, is faced with the reality of leading an interracial football team in a segregated time. He takes the team on a mandatory morning run to the Gettysburg battlefield, where young men lost their lives fighting for the same thing—racial equality. The team is forced to come to terms with their issues and eventually unites as brothers. In the same way, set your team standards up front and hold each member accountable for their actions—good and bad. This is the best way to ensure unified success.

## Take the First Step

For some of you, building a team is several steps away. Spending half a day on productive tasks might be *huge*, a giant step forward. And if that's the case, you should go with that. Start where you need to and work your way up. But don't quit halfway because, trust me, it doesn't take long for the rewards of this stuff to kick in. I've always said that *if you have a dream and don't have a team, your dream will die. But with a team, your dream will fly.*

I know that some of the ideas in this chapter may seem revolutionary—even ridiculous—given your circumstances. For instance, if you work out of a cubicle, it would be a little awkward (and a little too cozy) to squeeze an assistant in there with you four hours a day. And then there may be company rules and liability issues. These are some of the things you

*If you have a dream and don't have a team, your dream will die. But with a team, your dream will fly.*

may have to take into account as you strive to maximize the value of your productive time. Like any endeavor toward success, there will be hurdles, and that's okay. My advice is to think outside the box and get your boss involved from the outset. When your boss understands what you are trying to do, he or she will more than likely be willing to help you take the necessary steps—even if it requires doing something out of the ordinary—because your success will make him or her look good, too. At the very least your boss won't be surprised by anything you try to do. Put together your best persuasive skills and make it your goal to get your boss on your side with this stuff. And if you want, like Tim, make an offer anyone would be a fool to refuse.

The encouraging news is that once you work you way to hiring an assistant—even if you're sharing one with a coworker—you will have already taken the first step toward building a team. And that is literally the beginning of the end for your days of being swamped.

But there's one more phase we need to work through in order to maximize your productive time. With the dam built, we now need to Assess your capacity to be productive. There are still some obstacles that can slow your raft and delay your progress downriver.

## Executive Summary

In the course of a growing career there are things you should control, and there are things you should not. There are things you should make your baby, and there are things you must let go if you are to ever break through the ceiling of average. You must take control of the most productive aspects of your job if you want to advance, but if you wield *too much* control you stifle your potential and kill your momentum. And that's because success in any endeavor is a result of focused time.

To realize your potential on the job you must get in the habit of focusing your time on only the few tasks that bring you the greatest return in work success and life freedom, and then let go of the rest. To do this you must:

1. Answer the 100 percent question.
2. Assume a CEO mind-set.
3. Delegate tasks in increments.
4. Begin building a team.

These steps conclude the construction of your dam and constitute the third phase of task management referred to as taking focused Action on the most productive tasks.

Chapter Six

# The Technology Trap

Wasting Time on Time-Saving Devices

*"My assistant says I'm hard to get a hold of, but I just counted: she has eight ways to get in touch with me. There's my cell phone that's always with me, but sometimes the battery goes dead. Then there's my work phone, but the voice mail box gets filled up pretty quickly. Then there are my two home numbers for which I have several cordless phones; the reception gets fuzzy only when I'm in the back half of the house. My wife's cell is usually on and if I'm with her she can reach me there—although her ringer is sometimes off. I have two e-mail addresses that I check when I'm in the office, which is about ten hours a week; but currently only one of them receives e-mail. The other one is for emergencies only. And then there's my PDA—it's wireless . . . I don't understand what the problem is."*

— TODD DUNCAN

During a period that we now call the Enlightenment, Sir Francis Bacon described a modern civilization that would emerge if we unleashed the power of science and technology. This unleashing, he was convinced, was the path to a society of unprecedented convenience, choice, well-being, and prosperity for all people. In 1624, he called this technological island paradise "The New Atlantis." Today we might call it America.

According to biographer William Hepworth Dixon, "Every man who rides in a train, who sends a telegram, who follows a steam plough, who sits in an easy chair, who crosses the channel or the Atlantic, who eats a good dinner, who enjoys a beautiful garden, or undergoes a painless surgical operation, owes [Bacon] something."[14] That was written in 1862. Nearly 150 years later, we might have Francis Bacon to thank for something else. I call it the Technology Trap, but it's been called by many other names. Maybe you've heard of them.

The computer. The lap top. The Internet. The PDA. The CrackBerry. The cell phone. E-mail. V-mail. The wireless router for your wireless laptop with a wireless card in it. The Wi-Fi for your PDA that allows you to check e-mail and v-mail from anywhere. The flash memory that makes your cell phone a stereo, video game, and camera in one. You get the picture.

Bacon led us to science, science led us to technology, and technology led us to the wonders of time-saving devices. But these days, the devices we laud as efficient may be stealing the very thing they were designed to save.

## THE TIME BANDITS OF TECHNOLOGY

I have nothing against technology. I'm not a Marxist, and I don't think machines are eventually going to replace humans in the labor force. Technological advances have done wonders for the world and will continue to do so. But in an ever-expanding era of gigabytes, Web sites, and satellites, many of us have become a little gadget happy. As a result we may be loosing more time with technology than the time we intend to gain.

In a *Seattle Times* article titled "Saving Time No Longer a Tech

Reality," columnist Paul Andrews asks the question, "Has technology become a time bandit?"

Part of the workday involves dealing with technology. That's where the concept of time thievery comes in. Bandits include computers, voice mail, e-mail, the Internet and automated processes where humans have been supplanted by technology.

I thought of time thievery the other day at the supermarket, where shoppers can now check out, pay for and bag their own groceries. You stand at a kiosk and pass your bar-coded groceries through scanners, which somehow also recognize fruit and other non-coded items. If I were in a hurry, self-checkout might be a way to avoid standing in line . . . [But] if supermarkets start requiring all shoppers to do self-checkout I won't be saving myself *any* time. There will be lines at the kiosks just as there are today at the checkout stands.

Plenty of other examples abound . . . I can remember when I began using PCs back in the early 1980s. They saved me enormous amounts of time. And e-mail was a wondrous advance over the drudgery of appropriately named snail mail. Fast forward to today's perception of PCs. Perhaps [today's] most notorious time bandits are the twin evils of spam and Windows viruses. If one isn't clogging our inbox, the other is crashing our PC.[15]

I can certainly relate.

When my writer and I were working on *Killing the Sale* his laptop got infected with a virus and he couldn't access any of his files. He spent over *twenty hours* on the phone with a tech expert over the course of two weeks, and no writing got done. When I asked him how it was finally solved, he said it wasn't. After reinstalling the hard drive three times, the tech expert gave up and ordered him a new motherboard—if you don't know, that's the equivalent of a new laptop without the plastic casing.

And thanks to those two weeks spent in a technology trap, the book was completed after the original deadline.

This year, it was something different, but the story is the same.

Brent purchased a new laptop altogether hoping to avoid any major setbacks, and he did—but of course, there is still *my* laptop.

About a month ago my e-mail crashed several days in a row leaving Brent without important feedback from me—one time, when I was on the road, he was without my correspondence for almost two weeks. This once again hurried our writing schedule.

Unfortunately, the Technology Trap is a regular and universal problem because even the most basic amenities can tie us down and steal our time.

Take e-mail, for starters.

While e-mail has offered us an efficiency of communication that we never knew before, when we consider the setbacks that can plague over the course of a day, it may prove to add more stress than time to our days—my recent experience illustrates this. I'm sure you could think of an experience of your own—maybe as recent as today.

The problematic potential of e-mail has become so great that a recent *USA Today* article began with these words: "For years, consumers and corporations raved about e-mail's potential. Now they're fretting about its future."

According to the article, our cyber-frustrations cost us over $15 billion in personal losses and workplace productivity last year alone. It cites the three most prevalent e-mail ailments and the huge costs associated with each. I think we can relate to every one of them. Take a look:

### Spam
#### (Unsolicited e-mails that plague your in-box)

*The stats:* According to national e-mail monitoring company Brightmail, in the month of May [2004] about 64 percent of all e-mail was spam—up from 58 percent in December of last year.

*The cost:* "It costs companies nearly $2,000 per employee a year in lost productivity, double from a year ago, says Nucleus Research." On average, spam alone results in a loss of about 3.1 percent of total productivity.

## Phishing

*(Spam that tricks consumers into surrendering their personal information)*

*The stats:* "Phishing attacks soared to a record 1,125 unique schemes in April [2004] . . . according to the Anti-Phishing Working Group."

*The cost:* Each attack can add anywhere from fifty thousand to ten million e-mail messages to or from your inbox.

## Viruses

*(Self-replicating programs that harm files and slow processor speed)*

*The stats:* There are currently 90,800 known viruses in cyber-space with the potential of infecting your computer each time you open an e-mail or surf the Internet.

*The cost:* If they're not crashing your computer or blocking access to important files, many viruses leave "security holes" in your computer allowing hackers to remotely send spam and phishing schemes to you and others from your computer. This includes your prospects, coworkers, and trusted customers.[16]

About five years ago, reality set it in. The tribulations of computer technology were costing us big time. Computer Economics in Carlsbad, California, reported that businesses worldwide lost a total of $7.6 billion in revenue and productivity in the first two quarters of 1999, at the hands of Melissa, the Explore.Zip worm, and other viruses.[17] This led to a global increase in computer security funding within corporations.

Today we're not only spending more time dealing with these dilemmas, we are spending more revenue.

According to *Entrepreneur* magazine, if our technology dilemmas continue at their current pace, the Radicati Group estimates that revenue and productivity losses from computer viruses "will reach $75 billion in 2007 worldwide—up from $28 billion [in 2003]." Radicati also estimates that by 2007, individuals and corporations will spend $6.1 billion for anti-virus solutions and $2.4 billion for anti-spam and content-filtering solutions—up from $1.8 billion and $653 million in 2003.[18]

Of course, we can talk in general, global terms about the time traps people get into with technology; but the reality is that if it doesn't affect us personally, we don't see the problem.

However, I'll be the first to admit that it does, in more ways than one. I have a feeling you're in the same boat.

During a recent workout, I noticed a Boeing commercial that began with the words: "Freedom rises on the wings of technology." I had been having trouble with my laptop, and I remember thinking, *The only thing rising on my wings of technology is frustration.*

And the challenges continue, not just for me but for everyone around me.

## TECHNICAL DIFFICULTIES . . . PLEASE STAND BY

In an airline's frequent flyer lounge, I recently asked why I had two membership cards. "One is for our new magnetic reader," the lady behind the counter explained. "But it isn't working due to technical difficulties. It will eventually replace your old card, but we can't use it yet."

Halfway through that same trip, I overheard another traveler telling the person on the other end of the phone that he had just spent thirty minutes trying to figure out how to adjust the volume on his cell phone. He ended the conversation by saying, "Let me call you back on a land line."

The other day I showed up at my friend's house and he was up in arms. When I asked him what was wrong, he said, "I've spent half the day trying to figure out how to use this new camera." It claims it's supposed to do everything—except, I suppose, teach you how to use it.

Another friend owns a sales business, and they are trying to convert everything to wireless technology. It's been fourteen days, and it's still not working.

A few months ago, I sat in a meeting with a few people from my publisher's office. They asked how this book on time was coming along. I told them fine as long as we didn't fall into any more traps. Everyone laughed, and then one of them admitted to having 619 unopened e-mails.

Technology traps are everywhere, and we fall into them everyday. They not only keep us constantly connected to our jobs making us slaves to others' schedules, they cut deeply into our time. Too often technology is a hindrance instead of a help. I don't think there's any question of that. But one question that needs asking is this: *can a solution for technology be found with more technology?*

By our actions we assume it can. Why are we almost *compelled* to purchase the latest, greatest edition of a techno tool we already own?

## Can Technology Solve Itself?

It's as though we think technology will at some point be flawless, without glitches and bugs. But our loftiest expectations are unfounded. Technology will never be perfect; it's created and maintained by people—flawed people, I might add. The fact is, until people are perfect, technology won't be. But that doesn't seem to stop us from anticipating technology to purge itself of its problems.

Even the government fell victim to this misconception. Early last year,

Congress sought out a technological solution to a technological problem when it proposed a national do-not-spam registry to follow in the wake of the do-not-call registry offered the previous year. According to *USA Today*, the Federal Trade Commission threw cold water on the idea stating that it would likely lead to more spam and greater vulnerability for users of e-mail. Furthermore, the FTC noted that managing a list with up to 450 million addresses would be a technological nightmare.[19]

You see, technology is not its own solution, and it never will be. And that's because technology is not the problem. We are.

In conclusion to his article *Seattle Times* columnist Paul Andrews reminds us: "To be sure, technology is not the culprit—technology is just a tool. But in many ways, it's become a tool the user can no longer control. Perhaps in addition to 'Take Back Your Time' [day], there should be a 'Take Back Your Tech' day to remind us of technology's original benefits and to strategize overcoming its abuses."

Spam, phishing, viruses, poor cell reception, and wireless hiccups will always exist. Technology is designed and advanced by men and women, and it will therefore remain fallible. A cell phone that gets perfect reception everywhere you go? Never. We'll always ask, "Can you hear me now?" E-mails will still slip through the cracks, computers will still get viruses and crash, PDAs will still fail to sync, and wireless technology will still only work so far from wires. The problem isn't technology; the problem is our unreasonable expectations of it and our dependence on it.

If we start there, a solution to the Technology Trap is within reach.

## REGAINING CONTROL OF TECHNOLOGY

I have to admit, I have been the first in line to buy the latest techno tool more than once. I want it to improve my productivity and help me be more effective at what I do. And honestly, it often does. But there are also moments—too often to count—when technology fails me and usurps my time. It's in those moments when I realize I need to be more strategic about how I use technology.

I'm not advocating that we toss our gadgets into a giant bonfire. I just want us to see that increased productivity requires that we put some parameters on how, when, and why we use technology.

## Phase 4: Assessment

I believe there are actions we can take in order to temper the Technology Traps that so often sap our productive time. Remember, we're on a river and the dam is now behind us. We've done a good job thus far in eliminating and/or regulating the many tasks that normally flood our schedules and keep us unproductive. We've freed up at least four more hours a day to be producitve—or possibly your entire day if you are able to delegate to an assistant or team. If you apply what we've discussed thus far, you can expect a much smoother ride downriver.

But as you know, when time is freed up, it can still be squandered. That's because when the current is calm there still arise obstacles that can slow your progress. Today, technology is likely the most common obstacle.

Consider an excerpt from a recent column by Michelle Conlin in *BusinessWeek* that describes a CEO named Marty Kotis whom the writer calls "one of them."

Marty . . . carries not one but two cell phones. That's so he can talk on one while simultaneously checking and sending e-mail on the other. His green BMW 740 is equipped with two LCD screens mounted above the front and back seats so he can hold mobile videoconferences. On the bimmer's back-seat bulges his 50-lb. go-back complete with a laptop, five external drives, an iSight camera, a digital camera, a digital video recorder, and a Bluetooth printer. At stoplights he downloads everything from aerial photographs of new site locations to songs like *Over and Over* by Tim McGraw and Nelly, which he plays wirelessly on his stereo through his iPod.

In Tokyo they call them the *oyayubi sadai*—the Thumb Generation. Here in the U.S., the multitasking mobs don't yet have a moniker. Instead they are known by their CrackBerry thumb splints and their Treo trances, their faces glued to screens as the sounds of *Ice, Ice Baby* ringtones fill the air . . . In Congress, BlackBerries have turned a slew of starched staffers into keyboard Cassanovas. CNBC anchor Alan Murray even confessed to viewers that he uses his handheld in church.

There's no doubt our multitude of tools can help us improve productivity. But they can also make us unproductive. "Can gadgets enable one employee to do the work of two?" asks Conlin. Her findings indicate otherwise.

The idea that gadgets make us more efficient "is a scam, an illusion," says David Greenfield, direction of the Hartford-based Center for Internet Studies. That's because at their heart, gadgets enable multitasking. And a growing body of evidence suggests that multitasking can easily turn into multislacking.

Conlin cites the following support:

According to University of Michigan psychology professor, David Meyer, gadget-induced multitasking can elongate the time is takes to accomplish the most basic tasks by up to 50 percent or more.

According to Harvard Medical School psychiatry instructor, Edward M. Hallowell, gadget-induced multitasking contributes to cognitive overload—a key factor in a new epidemic he calls ADT: attention deficit trait, which "dilutes performance and increases irritability" causing managers to become disorganized underachievers.

"As gadgets enable everyone to generate more and more work, raising the volume of material people have to process," explains Conlin, "the flywheel moves faster and faster."

"At some point," adds Hamilton College anthropologist Douglas Raybeck, "it becomes an insupportable loop."

Maybe signs of sanity are emerging, encourages Conlin in her concluding thoughts. "Teenagers are throwing cell-phone-free, no-text-messaging-allowed parties. As with all things technological, perhaps it's time for the executive class to take yet another cue from them."[20]

I tend to agree. Technology *can* be good thing—as long as we know how to keep it from usurping our time. Here are five ways to accomplish this:

1. *Shorten the leash*. At one of my events I appoint one attendee to be the cell phone "sheriff." I then tell everyone in attendance that if a cell rings while I'm on stage, the owner has to pay a fine to the sheriff on the spot: $20 for a first offense, $40 for second offense, and $100 for a third offense. Any money that is collected over the course of the three-day event is potted and then donated to a charity that the audience has voted on. The pot tends to get pretty big. At an event two years ago, the attendees set a new record giving out over $1200 in fines, which included $20 from my wallet. You'd think we would catch on—but we don't.

With most of us carrying at least two of the three: a cell phone, a laptop, and a PDA—we are attached to work twenty-four hours a day. As a doctor, police officer, or firefighter, this level of availability is often necessary. For you and I, it's not. In fact, it's usually detrimental. One of the biggest traps of technology is the ability it gives us to work anywhere, anytime. I'm not sure which is truer: technology keeps us on top of things or technology keeps things on top of us. When the latter is more accurate, we need to shorten the leash and give ourselves time free of the threat of work interruptions. Otherwise, two things will continue to happen: (1) we will never maximize productivity on the job, and (2) the life for which we are striving so hard may never exist.

2. *Substitute; don't stockpile.* According to *Newsweek*, "There are 1.5 billion mobile phones in the world today. Already you can use them to browse the Web, take pictures, send e-mail, and play games. Soon they could make your PC obsolete."[21] I hope so because the fewer tools we rely on to accomplish our work the better. But we would likely still have a problem.

When we add all the time we lose with technology problems, it makes sense to use the tools only as needed and not in unnecessary excess. You know what I mean. We buy techno tools all the time that we don't really need. Or we buy a new version of something we already have and continue to use the old one as well as the new—like the guy from the *BusinessWeek* story. My advise: if you have to buy a new gadget, get rid of the old one; don't try to use both. Substitute, don't stockpile. Donate your old cell phone to a women's shelter where the women can use them for Emergency-911 calls. Donate your old computer to a nonprofit company or a college student you know. Let a co-worker or customer have your old PDA. Use what saves you time and do away with the gadgets you've replaced. There comes a point when the more you have the less time you save, and it's not hard to get there.

3. *Ask directions.* Guys don't ask for directions, I know. And women usually do. So maybe this particular piece of advice is more for my male readers. Either way, if you want to waste a ton of time, try to figure out how to use your techno gadget on your own. I just spent seven hours trying to learn how to use a new MP3 player I bought. I picked it up because I can download lessons from the Web and listen to them on the road without having to keep track of several CDs. Not to men-

tion it's much easier to carry than a portable CD player. But because I didn't know how to use the thing I was seven hours in the red from the start. I should've taken advantage of the salesperson's knowledge and let him teach me. It probably would've taken fifteen minutes.

There's nothing genius about this piece of advice, but so few people use it. We buy gadgets and often take hours teaching ourselves to use them—this is a major time sapper. Then to compound the problem, we never figure out how to use all the functions with which we could ultimately save more time. How many functions on your CrackBerry or cell phone or laptop do you not know how to use? Too often, we make the false assumption that gadgets automatically equal time saved, when the truth is that they only saves us time if we know how to use them effectively. The quicker you get to that place, the sooner its value can kick in.

4. *Test your gadgets' efficiency.* Five years ago, I spent big bucks for a very nice laptop. The thing had everything I thought I might need to get my job done efficiently at home or on the road. It had floppy, zip, and CD drives, a big screen, and a top-of-the-line sound system with all the function buttons above the keyboard. It was heavy, but I figured that was a small price to pay for having an all-in-one laptop that would increase my productivity. About three months later, I wasn't using half of what the laptop offered because I either didn't know how or didn't need it. I was stuck needlessly lugging around this ten-pound wafer. In fact, I stopped traveling with it because I dreaded carrying the thing.

In the end, I gave the laptop to a friend who works from a home office and doesn't travel, and I bought a small laptop that offered only what I needed. I've been using it effectively ever since.

We all need to evaluate the effectiveness and efficiency of our technological tools. And we need to be honest about what we discover. Don't keep something because it looks good if it gives you all kinds of trouble or has many useless functions. It's wasting your time. Do some research and find a tool you feel will give you the biggest boost in time and then test it out. If it improves your productivity, stay with it. If it slows you down, dump it for something that makes more sense. And don't rule out the option of doing things the old fashioned way. Technology isn't always more efficient than you.

5. *Go backward to go forward.* I recently sat in a meeting that concluded with the scheduling of another meeting. As soon as a date was suggested, everyone checked their calendars. After thirty seconds, I looked up from my paper calendar that is filled out in pencil and replied that I was available. Then I watched as everyone else mashed buttons and poked wands for at least two more minutes. Eventually, they all chimed in that they were free.

*How* free is another question.

Sometimes technology isn't better. It's just prettier. I know that there's a subtle pressure to have the hippest, newest gadgets available. But if you can accomplish something more efficiently without a gadget, don't get one because everyone else has it. Besides, retro is in these days. It's the trend in clothing, cars, and houseware. Why shouldn't it be the trend in technology, too?

*Sometimes technology isn't better. It's just prettier.*

## LIGHTEN THE LOAD

When it comes to time and technology, we would all do ourselves good to remember the tortoise and the hare. So often we play the hare with our flashy, fast-paced gadgets designed to save us time and get us from point A to B much quicker, but only slowing us down in the end.

For now we need to heed the advice of the tortoise, who always tended toward a slower but more deliberate pace. It wasn't that the tortoise didn't want to go faster—he just understood the only way to do something right is to sacrifice some time on the front end to figure out the right path, and then move forward confidently and purposefully to the finish line. This is our lesson with technology, and it is our lesson from here on out: the essence of the Assessment phase is trading a small amount of time on the front end to reap a large amount of time on the back end.

The truth is that you can free up all the time in the world to advance your career; but if you don't know how to use that time effectively, you can still waste most of your days—and that may be worse after all.

It's bad enough to be swamped with tasks that needlessly fill your time and put a lid on your success—but you know how to overcome that now. It's worse to have enough time to succeed and squander it away in the name of productivity and efficiency. Misused technology is often the cause of this, but there are other reasons, too. Let's assess them one at a time, and in the end, with a dam behind us and a steady current before us, we'll be smooth sailing.

# Executive Summary

The Enlightenment led us to science, science led us to technology, and technology led us to the wonders of time-saving devices. But these days, the devices we laud as efficient may be stealing the very thing they were designed to save. Technology is not the problem, however—we are. In an ever-expanding era of gigabytes, Web sites, and satellites, many of us have become gadget happy. As a result, we are losing more time with technology than we intend to gain.

We've done a good job thus far in damming or regulating the many tasks that normally flood our time and keep us unproductive. We've freed up at least half a workday to focus on the most productive tasks (or an entire day if you are able to delegate to an assistant or team). You can expect a much smoother ride downriver. But when your time is freed up to prospect and sell, you can still squander it needlessly. Even when the current is calm there are still obstacles that can hinder your progress. Technology is one of the most common obstacles because most of us rely on it so heavily. Nevertheless, it *can* be a good thing— as long as we know how to keep it from impeding our progress. There are five ways to do this:

1. Shorten your technology leash.
2. Substitute new gadgets; don't stockpile them with existing ones.
3. Ask directions for maximizing the effectiveness of your gadgets.

4. Test your gadgets' efficiency.

5. Go backward to go forward; don't use new technology if an old, manual method is more efficient.

These steps represent the final phase of task management called the Assessment phase. In this phase you are assessing your use of the time you've freed up and removing any hindrances to your continued productivity.

*Chapter Seven*

# The Failure Trap

Wasting Time Worrying about Yesterday

*"When defeat comes, accept it as a signal that your plans are not sound, rebuild those plans, and set sail once more toward your coveted goal."*

— NAPOLEAN HILL

*"Failure should be our teacher, not our undertaker. Failure is a delay, but not defeat. It is a temporary detour, not a dead-end street."*

— WILLIAM WARD

At each of my events there are at least a half-dozen people who approach me to admit how regretful they are that they wasted so much time. Many quantify this by divulging the number of years they've wasted. I identify because I spent my first five years making poor choices professionally and personally. I worked twelve-plus hour days; I abused my body with drugs and alcohol; I compromised my integrity to make a buck; I turned my back on my faith; I spent money to make a statement . . . I thought I had it all, but I was wrong. I carelessly squandered more time than I can count.

When I look back on those years, I sometimes shudder at the man

I was. But that is yesterday, and there is nothing I can do to change it. Those years are
etched in my personal history and cannot be rewritten. The only story that
is still to be penned begins today and
ends when God says it does, hopefully many years from now.

*The only time
that matters today
is today.*

It's important that you understand
this, because the only time that matters
today *is* today. The rock band *Switchfoot* wrote
a song about this called "This Is Your Life," and it's a call to move
beyond the time you no longer possess and contemplate the time you do:

Yesterday is a wrinkle on your forehead
Yesterday is a promise that you've broken
Don't close your eyes, don't close your eyes
This is your life and today is all you've got now
Yeah, and today is all you'll ever have
Don't close your eyes
Don't close your eyes

This is your life, are you who you want to be?
This is your life, are you who you want to be?
This is your life, is it everything you dreamed that it would be
When the world was younger and you had everything to lose?[22]

If past failures slow you down, then failure is a trap that steals time
from today. But when you recognize that the only time you can do
anything about is the moment you are in now, failure takes on a different meaning.

Taking a cue from my friend John Maxwell, my failure probabilities have diminished greatly by creating my Daily Dozen. Each morning I review these things to help me gain perspective and increase the odds of success. Here they are:

My Faith gives me peace.
My Family gives me harmony and stability.
My Fitness gives me stamina and energy.
My Friends give me counsel and comfort.
My Finances give me options.
My Future gives me direction.
My Focus gives me growth.
My Feelings shape my attitude.
My Faithfulness gives me serenity.
My Freedom gives me choices.
My Fun gives me renewal.
My Fulfillment gives me joy.

## Good-bye to the Old You

At this point in the book you might be looking at your career—and even your life—and thinking, *I can't believe how much time I've wasted. I can't believe I let things get this way . . . I shoulda done this . . . I gotta stop doing that.* A young lady was at this same point after the first day at one of my three-day events. She stayed up all night to handwrite an eight-page document she titled "Good-bye to Me." Here are some excerpts from her letter:

*June 17, 2004*

*I am so at the bottom today that the only place I have is to go up. Last Monday my boss gave me a verbal warning to shape up or get canned. Do I have circumstances going on in my life? Yes . . . I have let go of* so many things: my business, my family, my Christ, my values. Where have I been? My husband left . . . I pushed his buttons . . . I told him I never loved him. I know I did. He was my first true love; we lived so much together. He stopped wanting to achieve . . . and began to not care . . . I guess I walked away, too. At first I was angry. Disillusioned. I even harbored resentment . . .

I haven't been happy in years—not sure how long, maybe three years . . . I have been writing my life plan for the last 2 years—I wonder if any other coach has been more frustrated as [mine] since he knows me and my potential. I have been promising, over-promising to my kids, my family, myself; and I come up short daily. [This] makes you realize, "Okay, I have short-changed myself daily for many years while having the tools to do all of this correctly. Forget the reasons; forget the excuses. I just wasn't ready to be successful."

Most people this evening worked on their mission statement . . . [Instead] I just wanted to say good-bye to a life lived by accident and reaction. It hasn't been much fun; it's been sad, frustrating, scary. I want to say good-bye to the woman who is ashamed to go to church on Sunday because she is going alone with two kids, the one who doesn't schedule her doctor appointments because she doesn't make her health a priority. I want to allow myself to cry in order to grow . . . I want to place value on my time . . .

The purpose of this letter is to say good-bye to all those things and actions that have not allowed me to reach my fullest potential in life . . . Good-bye, Old Me.


What my client came to understand that day is that, despite all her failures and setbacks, time was still moving on, and therefore so must she if she was to ever begin working and living as she desired. It's a lesson that many of us need to learn, as hard as it may be.

I imagine you have some misused time you'd like to forget—especially after reading this book. Maybe it's time for you to say good-bye to the old you and let go of the time you cannot change so that you can give yourself fully to the time you still possess.

## THE PARADOX OF FAILURE

To overcome failure we've been taught to be persistent . . . take initiative . . . be aggressive . . . stick to it, and eventually we will gain the confidence to succeed more often. But the truth is that overcoming failure takes more than mental toughness and fervent initiative. It takes more than an ability to avoid or ignore your setbacks. Overcoming failure takes perspective.

Mistakes are inevitable in every job and every career. I know I made my share. One time I failed to send some important paperwork to a client on time, and she called to let me know of her frustration. I could have stopped at one mistake, but I was on a roll. Instead of apologizing and trying to better the situation, I became defensive. Quickly (and quite understandably, I might add) her frustration boiled over in anger. She told me how awful I was being and threatened to take her business elsewhere. "Go ahead," I told her, "take your business somewhere else." I didn't need her business anyway. She hung up and made good on her threat. But the consequences didn't stop there. In less than a week I received word from four other clients that they would no longer be needing my services. The story had spread, and they didn't like what they heard. In the end, instead of dropping my pride and ego, I lost five clients and a ton of future business.

I don't intend to make light of the ways I have failed, nor of the ways you have failed. Some of our mistakes have been costly, and we squandered years. They may have been painful, too. I understand this. Not that many years ago, I made a poor decision about a business partnership, and it nearly put my company into bankruptcy—that soured everything else in my life. After investing years to move my career upward, I fell close to the bottom in a matter of minutes. The ripples of that mistake took years to subside. But eventually, with some help, I moved on. Since then, there have been other mistakes, but thankfully with less taxing results. What I want you to see is that nobody succeeds without failure. Everybody fails, even the best.

## A More Efficient Perspective

When asked about an unexpected defeat, former tennis great Chris Evert Lloyd said, "If I win several tournaments in a row, I get so confident I'm in a cloud. A loss gets me eager again." She understands that failure has an upside. It's the paradox of failure that many of us need to see.

A person's emotional progression in response to failure goes something like this:

**Anger**

**Frustration**

**Disappointment**

**Self-condemnation**

**Insecurity**

**Fear of failure**

In the beginning of a career, it is easy to maintain a high level of enthusiasm and optimism. For some, this can be maintained for a couple of years, despite setbacks. A go-get-'em attitude can keep us hopeful, even if we are hanging on to our job by a hair. During this time, the lower negative emotions exist (self-condemnation, insecurity, and fear of failure), but enthusiasm and optimism mask them.

Over time the mask tends to come down. After multiple failures, enthusiasm wanes and optimism fades to uncertainty. In short, we begin to feel the full gamut of emotions when we fail. And if we do nothing to improve this situation, the progression of our emotional response often becomes truncated in a subconscious effort to lighten the blow.

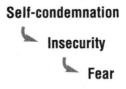

**Self-condemnation**

**Insecurity**

**Fear**

The truth is, however, that the blows of failure only get worse. Each of our three emotions are magnified until we become paralyzed to take any action that risks failure.

**Self-condemnation**

**Insecurity**

**Fear**

**Inaction**

On the other hand, if we have a healthy perspective of failure, we won't let our emotions go beyond disappointment. Once faced with the reality of failure, we adjust our attitude and, with resolve, take the necessary actions to learn from our mistake and move forward with improved action. Ultimately, we end up in a better position than when we started.

Improved action

Anger     Confidence ⌐

 ↘ Frustration   Resolve ⌐

  ↘ Disappointment ⌐

The paradox of failure is that while it's not the most productive path we can take, it is often the most efficient teacher we can have.

## THE EFFICIENCY OF ERRORS

I don't know what your career looked like before you picked up this book, but I have a feeling you've had to face some past failures in the pages that preceded this one. You've probably realized ways that you are being unproductive, and I'm sure that has been frustrating. But in leading you down this path to time freedom, I don't intend to lure you into another trap by showing you your failures and then leaving you to stew in them.

I understand that failure can paralyze us all. And facing the reality of your time failures in this book may have taken a toll on your self-esteem or at least made you feel a little gun-shy about making any changes. If that's true, I'm certain you're not alone. But let me tell you something about failure that is critical: it moves you closer to success. While failures certainly slow us down and if left unattended make us completely unproductive, they can ironically speed us up in the long run if we know how to handle them. This is the correct perspective I mentioned earlier. The truth about failure is that, while it's never the best use of our time, it can often increase our productivity quicker than anything else. If perceived right, failure is the sharpest tool for whittling away our inconsistencies and inefficiencies.

When a client named Dave stopped meeting with his coach, he admitted it was primarily for one reason: the man was prodding him to take steps that he felt were too risky. In the following months after letting his coach go, nothing happened. When I say nothing, I mean nothing different. Dave went about his work the same safe way he always had, long hours and mediocre results. He couldn't understand why he couldn't increase his productivity and free up his days. Then at an event, I told him he was afraid of failure and it was holding him back. It was keeping him from doing the things he needed to do in order to achieve the freedom he desired.

*If perceived right, failure is the sharpest tool for whittling away our inconsistencies and inefficiencies.*

Don't get me wrong; Dave wasn't a sloppy worker. In fact, he was very thorough and reliable. But as many meticulous people are, he wasn't into taking risks. He liked having his ducks in a row and knowing where each duck was headed. He avoided uncertainty. As a result, he had reached his limit of productivity. The only way he would improve was to take some chances. Although it was difficult, he finally did.

The first risk on his agenda was to rehire his coach. The second risk was much more difficult. He was to hire an assistant. For years Dave had been doing everything himself in an effort to avoid failure. What he didn't realize is that he was only prolonging its effects. Dave reluctantly agreed to take the risk. He did a typically thorough job of screening and interviewing people for the job and finally hired someone he felt was a good fit. Then he determined she wasn't. After a month it became clear that he needed to hire someone else. Dave was upset. He had taken a risk, and just like he thought, he got burned. It was difficult, but with some encouragement he tried again. He took new applicants through the interview process and eventually hired a new assistant. This one liked the company he worked for so much she decided to apply for his same position as a salesperson, leaving Dave once again without an assistant. But his coach wouldn't let him quit. He hired another, his third in nearly as many months. And this time there was a perfect fit.

If I ended the story there, the lesson would be simple: don't let the fear of failure keep you down. But remember we're talking about time, and there's an even happier ending to Dave's story. It is true that because Dave followed through with the risk he needed to take—the risk he had to take three times—he overcame his fear of failure. But the greatest testimony to Dave's change in perception is that his increase in free time doubled his productivity and cut his hours on the job by 25 percent. In addition, by the end of his second year with an assistant, his income had exploded by 500 percent.

Obviously, some risks are worth taking.

## THE PRODUCTIVE PERSPECTIVE

Those of us who are brave enough to face our failures understand that to be successful—to continually increase productivity—we have to risk failure. Picking up this book was a risk, and I hope you feel it was worth taking. And I hope that, if you didn't already, you have begun to see that risk is in the very essence of anything worth having. That includes gaining more freedom with your time.

Take a look at the differences between the risk taker and the risk maker and for each description ask yourself, *Does this save or steal time?*

| The Risk Taker | The Risk Maker |
|:---:|:---:|
| Pursues dreams | Pacifies dreams |
| Aspires for greater success | Aspires for greater security |
| Is courageous | Is cautious |

| Thinks about succeeding | Thinks about not failing |
|:---:|:---:|
| Is a pioneer | Is a plodder |
| Is resilient | Is resistant |
| Is tenacious | Is timid |

The differences between the two are many, but the gist of their disparity comes down to their titles. One makes risks by avoiding failure and therefore remains unproductive and prone to regret. The other takes risks with the understanding that it is the only way to increase success, and freedom.

## THREE RISKS WORTH TAKING

The following are what I consider to be the top three risks worth taking in your career. You are not only facing the decision to take them now, you will continue to face these risks after you've made changes to how you work—and I don't want failure to keep you from succeeding with your time.

These risks all carry with them a seed of failure, but with the right perspective, you won't ever go back to the unproductive, swamped person you were.

Risk #1. *Develop an impossible vision.* The writer and poet T. S. Eliot once wrote, "Only those who risk going too far can possibly find out how far one can go."[23] What he was saying is that the only risks worth taking are those that elevate us higher than we are now—those that suggest we will receive something we've never received before. In our case, that means receiving more time and with it, greater success and freedom. To achieve these you must stick your neck out. You must dare to have an impossible vision for your career and life that includes these three parameters:

◆ You can't accomplish it alone.

◆ It breeds fear and excitement simultaneously.

◆ It requires risk.

Take a chance and really dream. Don't sell yourself short. Determine how productive you want to be and how little you would like to work in doing so. Also, consider your life in general and the values you would like your work to promote. Don't see this as permission to be unrealistic. But nonetheless, put yourself out there. How much income is enough? How many hours are too much? What matters when you leave work? How will you ensure these things are protected and promoted? What would you like life to look like? Set goals that are out of reach unless you have some help. Trust me, having a vision like this will only accelerate your success.

**Risk #2.** *Become accountable to others.* In *High Trust Selling* I call this the Law of Leverage because it's a sure way to stretch your potential. There are three forms of leverage available to you:

◆ Personal leverage

◆ Associate leverage

◆ Professional leverage

You need to employ them all in order to maximize your potential. Some may take an investment of your own money, but I have yet to meet someone who invested in this kind of leverage—financially or emotionally—that didn't reap back more than he or she invested.

Let me briefly break down the three forms of leverage so you understand how to use them in your career.

## Personal Leverage

This is merely setting up your own form of discipline that begins when you commit your impossible vision to paper, including the date at which you intend to realize it. A dream with a deadline provides positive pressure. It encourages you to eliminate excuses and take necessary, calculated risks. This is good motivator when we need it; but to get to where we're going, we need more accountability than ourselves.

## Associate Leverage

When you have another person hold you accountable for your vision and the steps required for you to get there, you gain even more leverage. It's one thing to be disciplined; it's another to have someone else in your business. I know this might not be comfortable, but remember that these are risky steps, and you have to take them if you are to ever maximize your time on and off the job.

The easiest way to enlist associate leverage is to ask a close friend or coworker to hold you accountable. Sit this person down and share your impossible vision, including all the details. Then when your friend or coworker is clear on the direction you are heading and has bought into your vision, set up a system by which he or she can hold you accountable. Don't just say, "Okay, so why don't you just ask me every now and then how I'm doing." That isn't effective. Set up something more formal like a monthly dinner meeting or Saturday breakfast and stick to it. Three coworkers named Ed, Kevin, and Don put this form of leverage to use in 1995. At the time they were doing okay but figured the accountability and friendly competition could only help. Six years later they had each more than tripled their incomes and time off.

Regardless of who provides you associate leverage—whether it's your friend or coworker or spouse—the important thing to remember is that it must be someone who takes your goals seriously and finds fulfillment in your fulfillment.

## Professional Leverage

Whenever someone approaches me at an event and shares their goals I always ask them, "When?" because I feel part of my job is to hold them accountable. In many cases, they've spent their own money to come to the event, and I want them to leave with all the tools they need to succeed. This includes professional accountability. I've found that even when a person has associate leverage, there is more to be gained with a coach. I believe coaches can give you a fresh perspective on your career and, if you allow them, your life. Sometimes friends are too close to address a poor habit or attitude in us. Other times, coworkers empathize with our struggles but cannot be as forthcoming as they need to be. A coach can offer an unbiased, candid perspective on your career and help you tweak areas to maximum potential.

To this day, I still meet and talk on a regular basis with a few different men, some friends, some coaches, who hold me accountable for different areas in my business and life. I can say without reservation that if I did not have the leverage they provide, I would not even be close to where I am today. I would be working more than I should, spending less time with my family, and still struggling to succeed. My accountability partners have made a huge difference and so will yours.

**Risk #3.** *Set exceedingly high standards* so that failing to meet them will not have major consequences. This is a simple principle to understand but one that's admittedly difficult to maintain. It takes guts. In order to set your standards so high that falling short isn't a major setback, you have to have the ability to stick to your guns in difficult situations. This summer, I was faced with a difficult situation in my family. It required a lot of my time, which cut dramatically into my ability to be productive at work. I had to reschedule meetings and cancel some commitments I had made. While I hate being inconsistent or having to back out of a commitment, I don't regret the decisions I've made to take care of my family. I cannot make up this time with them—I can always hold a meeting.

This particular risk isn't just about having high integrity; it's about leaving the office every day when you tell your family you will. It's about paying attention to your health despite the work you need to get done. It's about maintaining one face to everyone. It's about saying no even when saying yes is more lucrative. The point is that in your revitalized efforts to be successful, you will most certainly face challenges that don't arise when you are only maintaining mediocrity.

Success presents its own adversaries, and if you're not prepared for them, you are in danger of squandering the time you free up. In fact, this is another time trap we all have to avoid. I call it the Party Trap, and it could be the most perilous of all.

If past failures slow you down, then failure is a trap that steals time from today. But when you recognize that the only time you can do anything about is the moment you are in now, failure takes on a different meaning.

To overcome mistakes we've been taught to be persistent . . . take initiative . . . be aggressive . . . stick to it, and eventually we will gain the confidence to succeed more often. But the truth is that overcoming failure takes more than mental toughness and fervent initiative. It takes more than an ability to avoid or ignore setbacks. Overcoming failure takes perspective.

People with a healthy perspective on failure don't let their emotions go beyond disappointment. Once faced with the reality of a mistake, they adjust their attitude and, with resolve, take the necessary actions to learn from their error and move forward with improved action. Ultimately, such people end up in a better position than when they started. The paradox of failure is that while it's not the most productive path we can take, it is often the most efficient teacher we can have. The most productive people understand this and, as a result, are willing to risk failure to succeed.

All risks carry within them a seed of failure, but with the right perspective, your mistakes will teach you what risks to take. The three most important risks in your career are:

1. Developing an impossible vision

2. Becoming accountable to others

3. Setting exceedingly high standards so that failing to meet them will not have major consequences

When you aren't afraid to take these three risks, you set yourself up for a level of success you may have never thought possible.

Chapter Eight

# The Party Trap
Wasting Time Celebrating Success

*"Success is never final."*

— WINSTON CHURCHILL

*"Try, not to become a man of success, but rather, try to become a man of values."*

— ALBERT EINSTEIN

*"Yet when I surveyed all that my hands had done and what I had toiled to achieve, everything was meaningless, a chasing after the wind; nothing was gained under the sun."*

— KING SOLOMON OF ISRAEL

We all went to Las Vegas to celebrate our success. We were the top-selling 10 percent in our company and we deserved it. Many years later I don't remember a lot from that trip, and most of what I do recall, I wish I could forget. I didn't have personal boundaries then. I knew this but couldn't change it—I was drowning in a cocktail of materialism and narcissism. I was losing control to alcohol and cocaine. Vegas was the last place I should have gone, but I went because it was time to celebrate. After all, I found out I was the top salesperson in my company.

I lost a lot of money in Vegas, but that could be replaced. What couldn't was my time. Not just that weekend, but the years I squandered in the name of success. That wasn't the only trip either—it was just a typical one. There were others, over several years.

One night in Scottsdale, I had enough Kamikazes to last a lifetime. I felt the alcohol for days. I was dressed in a facade of outward pleasure but suffering with inward pain and emptiness. I knew I was hurting myself—but no matter how hard I tried I couldn't change. What began as a little recreation was redefining who I was and erasing who I wanted to become. In essence, my lifestyle was stealing the time my success had created.

## EAT, DRINK, AND BE MERRY, FOR TOMORROW . . .

You know the rest. Tomorrow . . . we die. According to *The New Dictionary of Cultural Literacy*, the saying originated some four thousand years ago when Solomon, king of Israel, penned the following:[24]

> Then I realized that it is good for a man to eat and drink, and to find satisfaction in his toilsome labor under the sun during the few days of life God has given him—for this is his lot.[25]

It's an inspiring passage, as if he's saying, "Go for it—live it up! You only live once, so party hardy!" And many of us live by his proclamation. I certainly did. The problem is, we misunderstand the full meaning of his message.

To understand the significance of Solomon's words you need to get to know him a little better.

Solomon was the firstborn son of King David who was the second king of Israel, a man blessed by God who amassed more victories in battle and riches and fame than any king before him. Solomon's father was the giant slayer, the boy-king immortalized in stone by Michelangelo. It was in his grand stride that Solomon followed. And at first he did very well; he picked up where his father left off and God blessed him even more. It is to Solomon that God says, "Ask for whatever you want me to give you."

Surprisingly, Solomon answers, "I am only a little child and do not know how to carry out my duties . . . So give your servant a discerning heart to govern your people and to distinguish between right and wrong."[26] Because Solomon asked for wisdom instead of wealth or power, God replies, "I will give you a wise and discerning heart, so that there will never have been anyone like you, nor will there ever be. Moreover, I will give you what you have not asked for—both riches and honor—so that in your lifetime you will have no equal among kings."[27]

Not a bad turn of events. Solomon responds to God's offer humbly and he's given the world, literally. "King Solomon was greater in riches and wisdom than all the other kings of the earth. The whole world sought audience with Solomon to hear the wisdom God had put in his heart. Year after year, everyone who came brought a gift—articles of silver and gold, robes, weapons and spices, and horses and mules."[28]

History records that the weight of gold Solomon received as gifts each year was twenty-five tons. All of his goblets and every household article in the palace were formed of pure gold. He amassed fourteen hundred chariots and twelve thousand horses. It is said that silver was considered of little value in his time because it was as common as stones, and imported cedar was as common as the fig trees in the foothills.[29]

If there is one person of whom it can rightly be said, "He had it all," it is Solomon. If anyone should have understood the value of time, the art of making the most of life, it was Solomon.

Or maybe not. In the same passage as his so-called party proclamation, we find these words:

> Yet when I surveyed all that my hands had done and what I had toiled to achieve, everything was meaningless, a chasing after the wind; nothing was gained under the sun.[30]

After devoting more time than any man to the pursuit of wealth and knowledge and pleasure and honor, Solomon concluded that *success isn't what we think it is.* He had everything a person could want—more than anyone in his time—and in the end he said he still "hated life"[31] because his use of time ultimately left him empty, or better said, it left him unfulfilled. "Whoever loves wealth," he warned, "is never satisfied with his income . . . Better one handful with tranquility than two handfuls with toil and chasing after the wind."[32]

Solomon's proclamation to eat, drink, and be merry is not what we've always assumed. In fact, it serves more as a warning. "For tomorrow we die" is not the phrase he chose, but it fits—in the context of Solomon's *complete* message, it reminds us that our free time will be a waste if we don't understand how to truly enjoy life—how to truly be successful.

You see, there is not *more* to success than we realize—there is *less*. And we should understand what that means if we are to ever reach a satisfying conclusion about how we spend (and spent) our time.

## SUCCESS AND TIME

It's frightening how many of us have lived our lives by Solomon's decree and missed the significance of his statement. Solomon was a wise man, yes. But in the end he admitted that his life was meaningless because he used the abundance of his time to pursue things that didn't matter—"a chasing after the wind" is what he called it. "No man has power over the wind to contain it; so no one has power over the day of his death."[33]

I know many successful people who are not yet wise enough to come to this same conclusion, and though they seem to succeed they never cease to squander the freedom their success creates.

There's something we have to understand about all this time stuff that we've been talking about. If we don't know what to do with the time that our success frees up, all that we've learned to this point is, to use Solomon's phrase, "utterly meaningless."[34]

If all you do is take the principles from the previous chapters and use them as a springboard to party harder, you'll end up like Solomon . . . or Howard Hughes . . . or me, a few years ago—chained down and limited by the time that should set you free.

I don't know where I'd be today if my wife, Sheryl, hadn't intervened. She was my fiancé when I was at my worst—during my wasteful Vegas years. And while I didn't have the strength to change, she did.

She came to me one day and told me she was postponing our wedding until we could clean ourselves up. I knew that she, too, was struggling with cocaine and alcohol, but she was wiser and more courageous. She understood that "until death do us part" would be a present reality if we didn't begin investing our success in something more lasting and meaningful. In essence, she understood that our abuse of freedom was devaluing, even diminishing, our time.

Success works hand in hand with time. It should *appreciate* the value of our time; it should give us *more* time to spend on the things that we value outside our job. And if you carry out all that we've discussed thus far, you will reap more time to do just that. But there's one caveat to this kind of success: if you are caught in the Party Trap, success will actually depreciate the value of your time. Unchanged, this pattern will eventually take back the time it once freed up.

If you don't know what I mean, consider the last time you tried to work after partying the night before. How was your productivity?

And that's just the short-term effect. When it becomes a lifestyle, it's a different story.

Over the long term the Party Trap will kill you—not figuratively—literally. Sadly, I've known people of whom this was true, more people than I should.

Success can't be taken lightly. In fact, the way in which you handle success is just as important as how you handle failure.

## THE PARADOX OF SUCCESS

In the last chapter we discussed how failure—though it saps your time initially—can actually shorten your learning curve and boost your productivity if perceived in the right light. In short, the value of your time can increase by failure if you have the right perception of it and reaction to it.

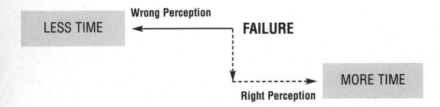

Success works in a similar way.

Your perception of success has the power to enhance or diminish the value of your freedom. By managing your tasks well, you will free up more time on and off the job; this is a reward of success. You probably know what to do with the time you've freed up on the job: most will use it to advance their career and you may do the same. What you do with the time you've freed up off the job is another story—that's where many lose control all over again.

The paradox of success is that if you invest your freed-up time in the wrong things—specifically, in things that don't ultimately promote your highest values—your success can actually take more time from your life than it gives.

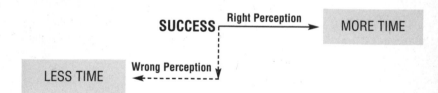

I recently shared this truth with a group of employees of a large national bank and one approached me afterward to tell me about his father. As the story goes, the man always had plenty of money and free time but squandered it for decades. Now, at sixty-five, the age when most men are relaxing and enjoying the fruits of their years of labor, he's living paycheck to paycheck with many regrets for what could have, should have, been.

I'm not saying that retirement is the ultimate reward of success. Nor am I saying it should be the goal. What I'm saying is that because this man's father abused his freedom, his success, for so many years, he's now running out of time to enjoy the life he never had.

## SUCCEEDING WITH SUCCESS

Falling into the Party Trap happens subtly and, for many, somewhat innocently. We achieve a certain level of success and then . . .

- ◆ We lease a new car.
- ◆ We buy a new home.
- ◆ We dine at fancier restaurants.
- ◆ We revamp our wardrobe.

These aren't bad things in moderation, and they are a fair reward for success. Unfortunately, moderation isn't something we Americans are good at—we tend to live above our means or at least in constant juxtaposition with them.

Unfortunately, if we don't slow down and begin investing our freedom more thoughtfully, more purposefully, we will eventually come full scale and end up back where we started or worse, in a place where my client's father still is at sixty-five, wondering when and how life passed us by.

On the other hand, if we decisively invest our freedom in the things we value most, achievement will enhance life. That's what we're after, isn't it? We don't just want to be a productive worker—we want to live a great life. We want to make the most of our life, not just our work time.

If we're speaking from the heart, we probably have to admit that the idea of advancing our careers and simultaneously having more freedom bring with them an anticipation that material comforts and temporary pleasures won't fulfill. If we're honest, many of the things we desire aren't superficial—they are soulful, emotional, heartfelt longings. Things like the desire to spend more time with family, to go on great adventures with friends, to see the world and experience new cultures, to fall in love, to pursue a hobby or a dream you've always had, or to give more time to a cause that you're passionate about. What are you feeling even as I suggest these things?

There's something more we should do with our freedom than merely eat, drink, and be merry.

King Solomon's conclusions about life were simple but profound, and I believe they give us great insight into the six areas in which we must consistently invest our time in order to avoid the laments of the Party Trap—in order to avoid his same regrets.

# THE FIVE MOST IMPORTANT INVESTMENTS OF YOUR FREE TIME

## #1 Health

"Wine is a mocker and beer a brawler," said Solomon. "Whoever is led astray by them is not wise." Something I learned in my bouts with cocaine and alcohol is that nothing steals your time quicker than poor health habits. Just think how much a little cold slows you down. When you add something more invasive, the effects multiply quickly. The four most common dependencies that affect your overall health are:

◆ Alcohol

◆ Nicotine

◆ Food (overeating)

◆ Caffeine

According to the National Health Interview Survey, about 48 percent of adults consume alcohol regularly; 22 percent smoke; 58 percent are overweight (22 percent are obese);[35] and about 30 percent of coffee drinkers claim to need it to function each day.[36] Obviously, each affects our health, which in turn devalues our ability to make the most of our time. How much does it devalue our time? From a daily perspective we can only approximate, but it is fairly obvious that hangovers, smoke breaks, constant snacking, and frequent trips to the coffee maker and bathroom all cut into our productivity during the course of a workday. Where your life is concerned, the short-term effects you experience (in less than a year of use) from these dependencies are ulcers, malnutrition, bad breath, immune deficiency, frequent colds, migraines, dehydration, skin problems, insomnia, anxiety, lack of energy, urinary tract infections, and diarrhea. Generally speaking, the long-term effect of dependence in these areas is a shorter life, with the exception of caffeine. These probably are things you already know, but the correlation I want you to make is that if you don't take care of your body, your time is not maximized. That begins when you get a handle on what you consume. But that's not all. To truly enlarge the value of your time, you must take a proactive approach to health.

Several years ago, I remember looking at a photo of myself standing shirtless and proud in front of a new car I had purchased. I was disgusted at how bad I looked. Caught in the Party Trap, I had not only become an addict, I had put on over forty pounds of fat. The sight of that picture thrust me onto a new path that has kept me full of energy and able to truly live out every one of my days. Here are five simple steps that will help you do the same.

**1.** *Eliminate your intake of nicotine, and moderate your consumption of alcohol.* Some studies indicate that certain forms of alcohol— namely, red wine—are good for your health in moderation and that's fine if you want to go that route. However, it is easiest to eliminate the temptation altogether because moderation leads to indulgence very easily. Where nicotine is concerned, there is no excuse to indulge.

**2.** *Moderate your intake of caffeine to two to three cups of coffee a day.* This is an area heavily researched and thus far most studies indicate that anything more than two to three cups of coffee a day has the potential to decrease your overall well-being and health. This conclusion will likely change over time, but in light of the current uncertainty, I have made a habit of substituting water for coffee when I can. Studies show that two eight-ounce glasses of water in the morning and four to six more throughout the day can do more to increase your energy levels, improve your sleep patterns, and maintain your body's health than anything else, including coffee.

**3. *Begin exercising every day.*** I try to keep things fresh by changing up what I do on a weekly basis, from biking to jogging to swimming to weights. This is important, as one of the biggest deterrents to a disciplined fitness routine is monotony. Don't let yourself get into a rut, but don't put off exercise either.

**4. *Make a list of the foods you will no longer eat.*** Don't go overboard with this—you want it to be something you can easily remember. You know what your vices are. If you want to optimize your energy, eliminate the foods that are dragging you down, and consume more energy-rich foods that are high in protein and fiber.

**5. *Put yourself on a strict sleeping routine.*** I know this sounds old-fashioned, but it really makes a difference. I travel a lot, so one of the things I have to constantly watch out for is jet lag. If I don't keep my body on a regimented sleeping routine, I lack the energy and mental capacity to enjoy my free time. "How long will you lie there?" asked Solomon. "A little sleep, a little slumber . . . and poverty will come on you like a bandit . . ."[37] I'm a firm believer that when you give your body the food and exercise it desires, you will not feel the need to oversleep. And if you're using your time wisely, you will not need to undersleep to stay afloat.

## #2 Financial Fitness

"Go to the ant, you sluggard; consider its ways and be wise! It has no commander, no overseer or ruler, yet it stores its provisions in summer and gathers its food at harvest."[38] The statistics are staggering. According to the Social Security Administration, if you were to follow one hundred people from age twenty-five to sixty-five you would find that:

◆ Nineteen have died.

◆ Fifteen will have incomes exceeding $30,000.

◆ Sixty-six will have incomes less than $30,000.[39]

The statistics reflect the overall neglect of most people with regard to financial fitness. According to the Lincoln Financial Group, three of the top five reasons people suffer from poor financial fitness are:

1. Lack of financial guidance

2. Poor investment choices

3. Procrastination in starting a savings plan[40]

As a child, I learned several money-management principles from my parents, and though I didn't follow them while I was partying my life away, I have kept them as rules since stepping out of that trap and they have eliminated stress from my life and replaced it with security. This keeps my time alone, or with others, at the highest quality.

*Spend only your money, not the bank's.*

1. *Spend less than you make.* Open an account that you only use for your spending budget. Brent and his wife have a separate bank account for this. At the beginning of each month, the money allocated for their personal expenses is deposited in to this separate account, creating a definitive end to what they can spend.

**2. *Don't buy something unless you can afford to pay cash*** (except for a nondepreciating asset like a home). I know it's a temptation to put something on a card when more money is coming, but don't do it. Spend only *your* money, not the bank's.

**3. *Pay off your credit cards in full every month.*** This applies only if you are using your card for monthly expenses in order to obtain travel miles. Otherwise, you shouldn't be using your cards.

**4. *Put at least 10 percent of every dollar you make into an interest-earning savings account.*** The interest will be low, but if you plan to leave it in there, you might as well make a few bucks on it.

**5. *Give at least 10 percent of every dollar you make back to others.*** By this I mean invest your money in the lives of those in need through a church or charity or nonprofit company. This may not be your thing, but I guarantee you that this step will be the best investment you will make with your money.

**6. *Set your own social status.*** Don't get stuck trying to keep up with a certain social status that doesn't fit your budget. Buy the things that you can *afford*—not what you or others think you *deserve*.

These are simple principles, I admit. But few live by them, and as a result many people spend more time than they should stressing and scrambling to make ends meet. There are not many things that make your free time more soothing than financial stability.

## #3 Relationships

"Again I saw something meaningless . . . ," Solomon writes. "There was a man all alone; he had neither son nor brother. There was no end to his toil . . . Two are better than one . . . Though one may be over-powered, two can defend themselves. A chord of three strands is not quickly broken."[41] Solomon is talking about relationships. According to him, a person is to be pitied without someone to share his time with. On the other hand, there is strength, as the saying goes, in numbers. And there is beauty in sharing the best moments of our lives with people we love and enjoy.

Relationships grow more meaningful in proportion to the time we invest in them. "Closeness," says author John Drake, "doesn't happen if our time together occurs only when we get everything else done. Intimacy must be one of the things to be done."[42]

There are four types of relationships we should invest our free time in if we are to reap the full benefits of sharing life:

1. *Modeling relationships.* Who do you respect and admire? Who maintains their standards and a level of integrity that you would like to emulate? Seek out these people and ask them if you can schedule regular meetings (maybe once a month) in order to learn from them. Don't be shy; if these people are as great as you think they are, they should be excited to add value to you.

2. *Mentoring relationships.* There is much to be said about investing in others in order to grow ourselves, but the true test of our knowledge and experience is our ability to pass it on to others. There isn't much that's more fulfilling than pouring your life into another's and seeing that person bloom.

3. *Accountability relationships.* In a previous chapter we discussed the importance of accountability partners in your career, but they are equally valuable outside of work. What is it you desire to accomplish off the job? What do you dream about doing with your free time?

Once you know the answers, ask those people already helping you reach your work goals if they would also hold you accountable for your personal goals and standards. They will already know a lot about you and can likely offer you fresh ideas to help you maintain a schedule that allows you to meet both sets of goals. It is for this reason that Solomon wrote, "Many advisors make victory sure."[43]

**4. *Intimate relationships*.** Where would we be without those we love and those who love us? I won't say much here except that we cannot do without these people in our lives. Without intimate relationships grounded in love, respect, and mutual admiration, our free time is half as joyful and meaningful. "Take away love," Robert Browning wisely wrote, "and our earth is a tomb."[44]

## #4 Knowledge

"Blessed is the man," concludes Solomon, "who finds wisdom, the man who gains understanding, for she is more profitable than silver and yields better returns than gold. She is more precious than rubies; nothing you desire can compare with her. Long life is in her right hand; in her left are riches and honor. Her ways are pleasant ways, and all her paths are peace."[45] There are three ways that we can all invest our time in order to receive the best and most robust return in knowledge.

**1. *Read voraciously*.** "Drink deep of great books," says John Wooden. Nothing furthers your knowledge more than books. A great way for you to invest in your career is to make every other book you read something that helps you professionally. With the other books, I recommend that you do what a friend does. She picks a topic that she's interested in and, for one year, reads everything she can on that topic. She's now well-learned in French history, interior decorating, culinary arts, art history, and architecture. Talk about a great conversationalist.

**2.** *Travel.* Get out more. There's so much more to learn about people, cultures, history, and life in general by spending time in places other than where you live. There are lessons to be learned if you'll get in the car or hop on a plane or train. Brent tells me that he and his wife plan to teach their children history and social studies by traveling to the places and letting them experience them firsthand. I think it's a great idea, and one we should consider for ourselves, let alone our kids.

**3.** *Take up new hobbies.* Do things you wouldn't normally do. Take up hang gliding or running 5Ks or kayaking. Sheryl and I took up scuba diving several years ago, and now one of our favorite events every year is choosing a new place to dive. We read up on where we're going and always end up learning so much from our annual experiences. I have also learned to snowboard and surf alongside my boys. Sheryl is learning to cross-country ski. What are you interested in doing? Try it out this year, and you'll not only learn something more about the topic, you'll learn a great deal about yourself in the process.

## #5 Purpose

This is undoubtedly the single most important investment of your free time. A person who has not sought out his purpose is like a ship without a sail. "The purposes of a man's heart are deep waters," said Solomon, "but a man of understanding draws them out."[46]

In order to make your time matter, you cannot ignore the question: why am I here? It's no coincidence that two books, *The Purpose Driven Life* by Rick Warren and *What Should I Do with My Life?* by Po Bronson, became huge successes in the past two years. The fact that we want to know the answer indicates one thing: we were made for something more than just passing time. I challenge you to invest deeply into this area—"draw out" your purpose—because ultimately it is the root of every motive and desire you have. Read books on the topic of purpose, research what the Bible has to say about it, ask others how they came to know their purpose. Most of all, spend time in solitude and prayer.

Something I do on a regular basis is get away from the hustle and bustle of work and get alone. I go through a series of questions that help me continually focus the pursuits of my days on those few things that constitute my life purpose. At the very least, I recommend that you get alone once a month, away from distractions, to complete the following exercise in order to continually clarify your answer to the *why* question. Below are the questions I ask myself:

- *Do I have confidence in my pursuits?*

- *Are my pursuits making use of my God-given abilities?*

- *Are my pursuits making others' lives better?*

- *Do I have any distractions in my life that are keeping my time from being truly maximized? How can I eliminate them?*

- *Will I be glad of my pursuits a year from now?*

- *Do I have any regrets from last month? How can I avoid those actions in the future?*

- *What is my greater purpose?*

- *Are the pursuits I am choosing to invest my time in each day fulfilling my greater purpose?*

- *How can I better invest my time so that what I desire for my future is possible?*

There's no magic number of questions that you should ask. The point is to get to the heart of your time use—to do your best to understand the gaps between how you are currently spending your time and how you should be investing it. Freedom often gets us way off track if we don't regularly consider these things.

More than that, the goal is to determine what it is you want from your time. That question left unanswered can send you on a lifelong goose chase. I know plenty of very successful people (financially speaking) who are still chasing that ever-elusive bird. They won't ever catch it.

On the other hand, when you know what you want from your time, the best path for your hours and your days becomes much clearer—and much more exhilarating. Once you know what your time is for, the only thing left to do is begin using it to that end.

It's an enchanting place to be—realizing the power you have to change the course of your own history. How will your story read five . . . ten . . . twenty years from now? Have you ever thought about that? It's not a matter of chance.

## Your Most Noble Pursuit

In 1995, a film entitled *First Knight* debuted and went somewhat unnoticed at the box office, due in large part to the huge success of another great film, *Braveheart*. *First Knight*, however, has since become a rental favorite. The film is a wonderful take on the age-old story of King Arthur (played by Sean Connery), Lady Guinevere (played by Julia Ormond), and Sir Lancelot (played by Richard Gere); and it provides a powerful illustration of three characters' journeys to understand and follow the true desires of their hearts.

The story first introduces us to Lancelot, a rogue wanderer who is fearless.

A narrator opens the movie:

. . . And then there was Lancelot, a wanderer who had never dreamed of peace or justice or knighthood. Times were hard. A man made his living any way he could. And Lancelot had always been good with a sword . . .

At face value, we take Lancelot for a man full of passion and adventure—a man who seizes the day. We are drawn to his unbridled, mysterious ways. But we find out there's more to Lancelot than meets the eye. Soon he meets King Arthur, who discerns that he is really masking his pain behind the façade of a tough exterior.

We pick up the story after Lancelot has just beaten the Gauntlet, a medieval obstacle course that had never been bested. Thoroughly impressed, Arthur invites him to the castle to show him the famous Roundtable. As Lancelot leans on the table, he reads the circular inscription.

Lancelot: "In serving each other, we become free."

Arthur: That is the very heart of Camelot. Not these stones, timbers, towers, palaces. Burn them all, and Camelot lives on because it lives in us. It's a belief we hold in our hearts. [*Returns his sword to its sheath and exchanges a brief glance with Lancelot*] Well, no matter. Stay in Camelot; I invite you.

Lancelot: [*Laughing*] Thank you. But I'll be on the road again soon.

Arthur: Oh? What road?

Lancelot: Wherever chance takes me. I have no plans.

Arthur: So you believe that what you do is a matter of chance?

Lancelot: [*Confidently*] Yes.

Arthur: [*Pointing*] Well, at the end of that hallway there are two doors—one to the left and one to the right. How will you decide which door to take?

**Lancelot:** Left or right. Makes no difference. It's all chance.

**Arthur:** Then I hope chance leads you to the left because it's the only way out. [*Lancelot smiles, nods good-bye and turns to leave*]

**Arthur:** Lancelot? [*Lancelot stops and turns to face Arthur as he continues speaking*] Just a thought: a man who fears nothing is a man who loves nothing. And if you love nothing, what joy is there in your life?

They are words that haunt Lancelot despite his efforts to stick to his aimless ways. Words that eventually break through the thick wall suffocating his heart's deepest desires for companionship and a noble purpose. They are words, in fact, that prompt Lancelot to eventually make his time matter for more than chance. In the end, a dying Arthur entrusts the entire kingdom to Lancelot, whose heart has become the embodiment of Camelot.

## Executive Summary

King Solomon's party proclamation to eat, drink, and be merry is not what we've always assumed. In fact, it's not a proclamation so much as it's a warning. "For tomorrow we die" is not the phrase he chose, but it fits—in the context of Solomon's *complete* message it reminds us that our time will be a complete waste if we don't understand how to *truly* enjoy life—how to truly be successful.

After devoting more time than any man to the pursuit of wealth, knowledge, and pleasure, Solomon concluded that success isn't what we think it is. He had everything a person could want—more than anyone in his time—and yet he still "hated life" because his pursuits—his use of time—ultimately left him unfulfilled. "Whoever loves wealth," he confessed, "is never satisfied with his income . . . Better one handful with tranquility than two handfuls with toil and chasing after the wind."

The lesson is simple: there is not *more* to success than we realize—there is *less*. And we must understand what that means if we are to ever come to a satisfying conclusion about how we spend our time.

Success works hand in hand with time. It should *appreciate* the value of your time. It should give you *more* time to spend on the things in your life that you value outside your job. If you carry out all that we've discussed thus far, you should reap more time to do just that. But there's one caveat to freedom: if you're caught in the Party Trap like so many successful professionals, your success can depreciate the value of your time.

Unchanged, this pattern will eventually take back the time it once freed up, leaving you with empty regrets.

To avoid this unenviable plight, begin investing your time in the following six areas:

1. Health
2. Financial fitness
3. Relationships
4. Knowledge
5. Purpose

When you know what you want from your time, the best path for your hours and days becomes much clearer—and much more exhilarating. Once you know what your time is for, the only thing left to do is begin using it to that end.

Chapter Nine

# The Identity Trap

Wasting Time Losing Yourself

*"In a quintessential American way, being busy, being over-worked conveys status and self-worth."*

— AL GINI

*"To say a man holds a job is to mistake the fact. The job holds the man."*

— JAMES GOULD COZZENS

As children we wanted to be some*thing*. A ballplayer, a balle-rina, a doctor, a nurse, a lawyer, a teacher. As teens we wanted to be some*one*. We were all the same something—a student—so what mattered most was acceptance, who we were seen to be. Popularity was more important than our place in the world. But then, sometime after high school our wantings began to merge into a grander vision for our lives. We wanted to be both some*thing* and some*one*. At the heart of that vision was a job.

There's something seductive about our first real job, say authors Barrie Greiff and Preston Hunter. "Young executives experience a high . . . The title, the assistant, lunches with the [bosses], the sense of power, the heady feeling of associating with the affluent—there is something . . . quickly addicting about all of this."[47] For most of us, it is the first time we *welcome* responsibility because with a job comes a sense of control over one's life, and for once, a sense of identity that doesn't have to do with our family or friends. With our first real job, we are given the power to determine who we are and who people see us to be.

It is a legitimate chance to "make something of ourselves," to become recognized by our own accomplishments and to gain status and hopefully prestige. Inherently, there's nothing wrong with all of that. It's part of becoming your own person, part of establishing your place in the world. Unfortunately, too often our job becomes more than *part* of our identity. It becomes *all* of our identity, and we rarely know it has happened. In the pursuit of success and significance, many of us begin selling our souls.

It only takes a year for some—for others, a decade or two—but eventually, instead of finding ourselves in our work, some of us begin to lose ourselves. I'm not talking about a midlife crisis. This is a different crisis that spans the spectrum of age, status, and job position.

A man I've known for almost a decade lives this story.

Sam had a good family for whom he wanted to provide well. He also had close friends who were doing life with him. He was a good man with a great vision and a lot of ambition. He worked hard at his trade and told me he wanted to become the top salesman in his industry.

After a few years, the money started coming in, and it began to look as if his dream was becoming a reality. Then one day I found out he had made it—he was officially listed in the top 1 percent of his industry nationwide, which means he was probably making a seven-figure income. It was quite an accomplishment.

But then I began to hear conflicting reports. When I began asking questions, I discovered that while Sam had managed to become successful by financial and industry standards, he had also become a relational nightmare in the process.

I spoke with some of his coworkers and colleagues. All told a similar story. Sam was a workaholic who had sold his soul to work and in the process had sold out all his friends and family. In his so-called climb, he'd become a backstabber, a crook, a double-talker—anything to advance his career and make himself a name. As it turned out, he made his millions by befriending successful people, borrowing their reputations, and then betraying them when the time was right. I also discovered that his happy marriage had ended in an ugly divorce at his own negligent hand, and many former friends were no longer speaking to him.

Today, I still see Sam at events. I believe he sees them as networking opportunities to further his business. When I notice him walking around, he's well put together and all smiles. But on the inside, he's got to be in shambles. If he were ever in trouble, I don't know if he would have any help or sympathy. I can only hope that as he sits in the audience for what must be his fortieth time, he begins to hear what we're trying to teach.

## WORK SHAPES YOUR IDENTITY . . . FOR BETTER OR WORSE

It was Winston Churchill who said that at first we choose and shape our life's work, and then it shapes us. He meant that in a good way, as if to say, "You choose a line of work and then that work helps you become a better you." It's an encouraging statement with that perspective. Unfortunately, a widespread inclination toward longer hours makes Churchill's statement sound more like a prophetic warning—as if he were saying, "You choose a line of work to become a better you, but then that work changes who you are, oftentimes, for the worse."

In America during Churchill's era, most people assumed a person's work shaped him in positive ways. Although it wasn't yet the American labor movement's slogan, "Eight hours for work; eight hours for rest; eight hours for what we will" was mostly a reality. Today, the notion is a tease. In fact, today we are compelled to ask of a job: Is it shaping a person positively or negatively?

It is true that work can mold us in good ways. We can learn to better relate to people. We can learn to serve. We can learn to value teamwork and perseverance and communication. But as author Al Gini points out, work does much more than that, and it often leads us into a trap.

> Work is at the center of our lives and influences who we are and all that we do . . . work is not just about earning a livelihood. It is not just about getting paid, about gainful employment. Nor is it only about the use of one's mind and body to accomplish a specific task or project. Work is also one of the most significant contributing factors to one's inner life and development.[48]

For most of us, work preoccupies the majority of our time and energy, and that, says Gini, is why our job "not only provides us with an income, it literally names us, identifies us, to both ourselves and others."

We see this truth in our tendency to ask people we've just met, "So, what do you do for a living?" Or "What kind of work do you do?" We ask such questions because, whether we like it or not, our identities are tied up in what we do for a living. How tied up depends on one thing: time.

## TIME DEFINES YOUR IDENTITY

There's nothing wrong with work shaping *some* of our identity. To an extent, that's how it should be. It's great to be known as a hard worker and a successful person. It's healthy and fair to be known for our career accomplishments and, to an extent, the position we hold. I can think of many people in history who are remembered for the work they dedicated themselves to. But what if work is all we are known for? Is that what we really want? Isn't a person's body of work tainted if we learn he sacrificed family and friends or lived a double life of insincerity and ultimate regret in order to advance a career?

"You can't smell the flowers when you're working twelve hours," sang Charlie King.[49] He's right. It's true that you can accomplish much if you give all of your time to a job—or anything for that matter. But at what cost? Has anyone lived such a lopsided life and *not* regretted it in the end?

*The more time you spend working, the more your identity is tied up in your work.*

Howard Hughes was one of the savviest businessmen of his time—the first American billionaire with two presidents in his hip pocket and a stockpile of cash and comforts to last ten lifetimes. He had reason to be proud, right? So it seemed. Hughes died alone in his penthouse with inches-long fingernails and needle marks peppering his arms. And there's something more to his demise than a drug addiction.

Our own experience cannot lie. While work gives us much to be rightly proud of, we want to be identified by more than a job. It's a paradox of sorts. On one hand we esteem work; we hold it in high regard because of what it offers to us: a title, a position, a purpose. On the other hand, we would rather work less if we could. Why do you think people are so drawn to online trading and the lottery and Las Vegas?

While you can always find statistics that show a percentage of people who are completely fulfilled by their jobs—they are always the vast minority. Work for most of us seems, well, like work. A necessity, yes. Enjoyable—it should be. But the embodiment of who we are? Not quite.

If we can find purpose and meaning in our job, that's wonderful; that's the point. But it doesn't have to come by devoting all our time to it. It should come by allowing our work to promote something deeper.

We have sought this depth-of-purpose in the past few decades by working more, but it doesn't seem to be working as we thought. Depression is now the most expensive of all medical costs—70 percent higher than anything else—and stress is next in line.[50] I can't help but think our work habits have something to do with that.

Besides, let's put statistics and arguments aside. What does your heart tell you? Isn't there more you desire for yourself than on-the-job success?

## LIVE TO WORK OR WORK TO LIVE?

Author Joe Robinson tells the story of a salesperson named Dana who was struggling with this identity paradox. According to Robinson, Dana is a single dad torn between his instincts as a "go-to-the-wall" American to do whatever it takes to get his job done and his need to find time for his daughter and life.

As a sales rep for Frito Lay, Dana found himself trapped in the necessity of sixty-plus-hour workweeks. Robinson cites the sales rep's inner turmoil: "There's nobody to take up the slack if there's a family issue that comes up, or if you get sick. You can't wake up in the morning and not feel good. Your work will just pile up . . . everyone wants more time from me . . . I know I'll never make it at this pace to retirement. Maybe the answer is to have a simpler lifestyle, to live out of a tent."[51]

In her insightful book *Married to the Job*, psychotherapist Ilene Philipson shares the following story of one woman who illustrates the extreme of what we're talking about:

When Ingrid entered my office I was struck by this very attractive woman's faultless appearance. She wore an expensive tailored suit; her hair was a perfect brown bob; nothing was creased, askew, or less than understated elegance. As Ingrid spoke she revealed herself to be an extremely intelligent, articulate, thirty-nine-year-old woman, who, it seemed, had annexed her very being to the workplace . . .

Throughout her teens and early twenties she felt comfortable both being productive and having fun . . . She feels her life began to change when she entered an MBA program at one of the nation's leading business schools. The competition was intense, and the requirements of studying and working diminished the time and energy she had for her social life. Upon receiving her master's degree, she was hired by one of the largest, well-established Silicon Valley corporations. Ingrid worked there for four years, steadily moving up the corporate ladder, working long hours and thinking of little else besides her responsibilities, her interactions, her standing at work . . . [Then] Ingrid was lured away from her job by a start-up company that I will call E-Stream . . .

Ingrid worked 110 hours a week. She describes sleeping on the conference-room floor for four hours in her clothes each night, then freshening up in the bathroom . . . She lost weight, never talked to friends or family, and one day found her tropical fish dead because she had neglected to feed them . . . She came to therapy at thirty-nine because she feels her devotion to work has "interfered with my outside life."

To understand the enormity of this statement one must know that Ingrid has no social contact outside work, and no one she can point to as a friend. She has not had sex in eleven years. She typically spends Christmas or New Year's at work, where, she states, "there's always something going on."[52]

The reality is that people like Ingrid, who work seventy-, eighty-, and ninety-plus-hour weeks, *don't have time* to be identified by anything else. They spend very little time at home, so they are not identified by a family role. They have little time to consistently pursue hobbies or interests, so they are not known for what else they might enjoy outside of work. They have little time for friends, so they are not known by their relationships or social graces. In fact, most hard-working people spend any down they possess trying to recuperate from the stress and strain of their schedules. To paraphrase Gini in *The Importance of Being Lazy*:

> Unfortunately, for too many of us our various forms of recreation and play are really about rehabilitation, recuperation, and recovery rather than rapture and the possibility of the rediscovery of self. This is because, for many of us, our play or diversions are really only momentary distractions from the usual pace of life. They are designed to overcome fatigue, numb awareness, or appease a particular appetite so that we can go back to the job to endure and earn more.[53]

Ultimately, when our time is monopolized by our *work*—and/or recovering from work—the only thing that forms our identity is *work*. We become lost in our job. It's an unenviable place that many companies are obliging of late.

It wasn't long ago that having a refrigerator at work was a big deal. Common today are full kitchens, coed gyms, full bathrooms with showers and lockers, child day care, lounges with leather couches and big screen TVs, and even corporate cafés so we don't have to leave the office to get our caffeine fix.

Workplaces have become increasingly domesticated. Philipson notes that Jerry Useem of *Fortune* magazine recently revealed that "46 of the 100 Best Companies [to Work For] offer take-home meals to liberate people from having to cook dinner. Twenty-six of the 100 offer personal

> *Ultimately, when our time is monopolized by our work—and/or recovering from work—the only thing that forms our identity is work.*

concierge services, allowing employees to outsource the time-consuming details of buying flowers and birthday presents, planning bar mitzvahs, or, in the case of one Chicago suitor, organizing an engagement dinner."[54]

Philipson makes her point with the words of one employee interviewed by sociologist Arlie Hochschild who explains: "In America, we don't have family coat of arms anymore, but we have the company logo."[55] In fact, work has permeated so much of our identity in American culture that we now work more hours-per-year than any other country—leapfrogging the notorious workhorse Japan in 2000 by thirty-seven hours a year.[56]

The Center for a New American Dream conducted a survey in partnership with the organizers of Take Back Your Time Day (www.time-day.org), a nationwide initiative held on October 24 to challenge the epidemic of overwork in America. The survey found that "Americans work nine weeks more each year than their colleagues in Western Europe. Put another way, on October 24, if the average U.S. worker and the average Western European worker had worked the same number of days to that point, the European would have the rest of the year off."[57]

With so much time dedicated to working, "when," asks Gini, "will there be time to be human? . . . As Benjamin Kline Hunnicutt so aptly put it, 'Having to go so fast to keep up, we miss stuff—our existence is truncated. Some things simply cannot be done going full speed: love, sex, conversation, food, family, friends, nature. In a whirl, we are less capable of appreciation, enjoyment, sustained concentration, sorrow, memory.'"[58]

## TIME FOR TRUE SUCCESS

While working out one day, I noticed an ad on television. The sound was muted, but I saw two captions during the thirty-second spot and they made the point. The first caption asked,

*Why do we work?*

The second,

*Why are you working?*

The problem with an identity solely founded in work is fairly obvious if we are honest about the things we desire. Sure, we desire success and advancement; you wouldn't be reading this book if that weren't the case. Sure, we desire the boost of self-esteem and the shaping of character that come from having worked hard. These are good things. But we desire so much more, don't we?

You are reading this book to improve your productivity, right? But why *else* are you reading this book? Why *else* are you tired of being swamped? Why *else* are you working so hard?

Now we're getting somewhere.

If you and I were having a lazy lunch on a Sunday afternoon and I asked you to describe your definition of success, what would you say? Think about it. How would you define success for you?

I imagine that at first you might mention things related to work. But the more you thought about it, the sooner you would probably begin to mention things that aren't related to work at all. If you are married, you might relate success to the contentment and satisfaction you receive from your home life. You would likely begin to dream a little and talk about how you want your children to one day be great people. You might talk about spending time with good friends and helping them realize their dreams. Eventually, you might bring up hobbies that you love and have always wanted to give more time to. Reading. Writing. Traveling. Coaching your kids' teams. Learning to play an instrument or fly or paint or take beautiful pictures or snow ski or . . . *you* fill in the blank. Take a moment to describe your definition of success now:

_____

_____

_____

_____

Isn't life about more than work, after all? In the end, if your only identity were work related, wouldn't you be disappointed? If others only remembered you as a successful worker, wouldn't they be missing the whole picture?

## MISTAKEN IDENTITY

The trouble we face with an unbalanced identity is that it is hard to detect if we aren't looking for it. But I've met very few hard-working people who, when faced with the reality of regret, didn't readily admit they were already garnering some of the negative consequences:

- ◆ Guilt
- ◆ Restlessness
- ◆ A growing frustration
- ◆ An urge to justify their schedules
- ◆ Fear of regret
- ◆ Confusion
- ◆ Complexity
- ◆ Anxiety
- ◆ Fatigue

The signs reveal that while you may not have lost yourself completely, an all-work identity doesn't feel right. And it was never meant to. Author

Joe Robinson reminds us of a time when it was easier to identify with other important things:

> Only a couple of decades ago, a vacation was considered a well-deserved break in the action, a time for the family to hit the Great American Highway in search of campgrounds, Tasty Freezes, and the greatest prize of all, the motel swimming pool. The summer vacation was a hallowed ritual in my family. Every year my dad would pile us into the station wagon, pick a direction, and we'd be hugging the asphalt of Southern California to eternity. No air-conditioning, just a windblown horizon of big skies, scenic outlooks, and busted radiators. Going without a vacation would have been unthinkable in the 1960s.

But something happened. We began handing over the keys of our identities to our careers. We began devaluing life in order to earn a better living. Explains Robinson:

> Beginning in the early 1980s something began to snap in the national R&R psyche . . . The much-ballyhooed four-day week turned into a hallucination. The ability to break free of the office and savor downtime disappeared, swallowed up by a vortex of spiraling work hours and a fixation on productivity that has devalued all that is not attached to a task or a paycheck . . . We have euphemized a workplace without end.
>
> But no matter what you call it, it's a habit people would like to break.[59]

I believe he's right. If we are to ever to recapture our true identity and begin maximizing our time, the status quo has to change. And you now have the tools to change it.

## TRAPPED?

There are many real factors that seem to compel us to give more and more time to our jobs: corporate downsizing, advances in technology, greater competition, higher cost of living, and the potential for bigger financial gains, to name the most popular. But in an unfortunate twist of fate, what begins as an honest attempt to stabilize our futures—and quite possibly realize them sooner—ultimately changes our present lives into something that will never produce the futures we desire.

*Not only does an identity wrapped up in work sap our identities, it keeps us from realizing our dreams.*

Not only does an identity wrapped up in work sap our identities, it keeps us from realizing our dreams. In essence, it changes who we are now and who we will become. Take a look at the trade-offs many of us (unthinkingly) make:

| This . . . | for . . . | That? |
|---|---|---|
| Multilateral satisfaction | | Unilateral success |
| Family fitness | | Financial potential |
| Childhood dreams | | Corporate vision |
| Needs | | Wants |
| Pastimes | | Products |
| Personal identity | | Public position |

Not many of us would make the trade-offs if we considered the implications.

I realize that most of us don't want our lives to be defined by work alone, but we often feel our options are very limited. If we work less, we will produce less; we will make less money; we won't complete our jobs; and eventually, we'll be out of a job. The idea of downshifting the amount of hours we work sounds like a slow but certain death. It doesn't seem possible to get more done in less time. But it is. And for many of us, it *has* to be.

## RETHINKING YOUR TIME AND RECAPTURING YOUR TRUE IDENTITY

As I study the people who are enjoying their lives and are *not* swamped by their work, I can trace a point of epiphany where each gained new perspectives on time. As I prodded further, I found that each person came to certain conclusions about time before they were able to make major changes to how they filled their time. There are six conclusions that each had in common. I share these now because they seem to serve as a foundation for any changes you want to make to your use of time:

*How you use your time deeply impacts your identity*

> *Conclusion #1:* Life will never settle down until a choice is made to settle it down.
>
> *Conclusion #2:* Working is not living.
>
> *Conclusion #3:* Time is life first, then money.
>
> *Conclusion #4:* More work usually means less life; less work and more productivity usually mean more life.
>
> *Conclusion #5:* How I use my time deeply impacts my self-esteem, my identity, and my fulfillment.

*Conclusion #6:* I cannot control time, but I can control how I use and respond to time.

When swamped people accept these conclusions, they seem to act as a springboard for redefining their identity and, subsequently, reclaiming the life they desire. I advise you to read them, understand them, and make them your own.

In order to recapture your true identity you must accomplish two things:

1. Stop wasting time on unproductive tasks.
2. Start investing time in productive tasks that produce the life you desire.

Your true identity will be shaped and your path to freedom will become clear as you accomplish the two objectives. This summarizes what we've discussed thus far.

It won't be easy at first, but I've found that when we understand the real implications of being swamped we are much more motivated to make changes in how we use our time, on and off the job. I hope that is your feeling now.

The only thing left to do is determine how we want to spend our freedom.

Take a couple of deep breaths.

Relax. Get comfortable. Don't worry about the time. For just a few more minutes, let nothing be pressing. Now, let's take a little trip.

In quintessential America, working long hours has become the norm, even the expectation. The person who puts in his time to the tune of seventy, eighty, even one hundred hours a week is praised for a job well done. We revere the long-hour laborer. But what is often overlooked are the effects long hours have on one's identity.

Sure, work is good for us. It gives us a sense of purpose and a feeling of accomplishment. But there's a difference between success and satisfaction.

How we invest our time determines who we are and who we will become. That's why our jobs shape our identities for better or worse. The more time we give to them the more we are defined by our work—and the less we are defined by our other values such as being a spouse, a friend, a parent, a fitness enthusiast, a wonderful cook, or a world traveler. You name it. Too much time given to working and who we are becomes solely what we do for a living.

However, if given the choice, most of us want to be known by more than our career and current position. The only way that happens is to balance the time we give to work and the time we give to the other things that make us who we are. There are two steps we must take to make this change: (1) we must determine to stop wasting time on unproductive tasks, and (2) we must start investing time in productive tasks that produce the lives we desire. Both of these are a function of accepting six conclusions about time:

1. Life will never settle down until a choice is made to settle it down.

2. Working is not living.

3. Time is life first, then money.

4. More work usually means less life; less work and more productivity usually mean more life.

5. How I use my time deeply impacts my self-esteem, my identity, and my fulfillment.

6. I cannot control time, but I can control how I use and respond to time.

Chapter Ten

# Freedom
Investing Time in Your Best Life

*"All work contains drudgery; the issue is whether it holds meaning or not."*

— WENDELL BERRY

As I sit on the rugged cliffs perched above the edge of the Pacific, my mind is quiet. The scene before me is still, as though its artist waits for me to take in every last detail of its beauty. Although I'm some twenty feet above the ocean, I think I can feel the touch of the cool tide as it reaches up the sand, then slowly withdraws into the blue.

In moments like these, you have time to think about more than today. I am rewinding the tape of my life and instinctively, I push play. There they are, in Technicolor on the screen of my mind, the memories I cherish most. Those critical moments where I followed my heart, and not necessarily my head. Dinner at a restaurant an hour away, because it was important to a good friend. Midday hooky with my boys at the beach. A plane ride home from a speaking engagement a day early, so I could kiss my wife good night. An all-nighter to finish a writing project. An early breakfast with an event attendee who needed someone to listen. All moments where I wasn't necessarily making a better living, but I was absolutely living my best life.

Before the movie comes to an end, I press pause. I realize I have found my heart. I have found that place where time makes sense. And it's in that place that I long to stay. But time moves on despite me.

The day passes. The vacation ends. The memories still linger, but only like a morning mist now. Back to work, time is moving more quickly than I'd like. Business has re-emerged, urgencies have crept back in, and I long for another magical moment, another hit of something that warms my soul.

I am sitting in my office now. The day has been planned for weeks. The writing of this book is coming to an end. The research is finished, the resources are before me, and the cursor pulses impatiently. I close the office door and attempt to clear my head.

I forgot one thing, however, and that was to turn off my cell phone— it rings. "Hi, honey," my wife, Sheryl, says. "The boys would love to go to IHOP with you this morning. Do you think you can you swing it?"

The moment awaits my decision. *Do I or don't I?* I'd feel guilty if I didn't, but I have work I have to get done. Then from somewhere inside, deep inside, I hear another voice. *What is the value of time? More money or more life?*

My head is telling me I cannot spare a minute—I need to get a lot of writing done today. My heart has a different message. It's reminding me that my boys are more important to me than my work. It's convincing me that even though I will be giving up an hour or more of writing time, one minute with my boys is more valuable. They won't be young for long, and they won't always want to go to IHOP with their dad. A time will come when they will have agendas of their own and their lives won't revolve around their parents' schedule. One day, they will have their own families, and I will long for an opportunity to spend an hour with them chatting and laughing over a big stack of syrup-drenched flapjacks. *Yes, even though I love what I do for a living, this time with my boys, this is what I truly long for. If I really need it, I can make up an hour of writing later, when they're asleep.*

The decision is made, and fifteen minutes later the four of us are sitting at our favorite table in IHOP, laughing like the best of friends, like we always do.

I have found my heart again, and it is full.

## Magical Moments

I'm now on a little island called Nevis in the West Indies. As the day draws to a close, I'm sitting on the beach, staring at the Caribbean, enjoying the salty-sweet breeze and cheering the waves as they lap gently onto the white sand. If I squint toward the horizon, the sea and sky fuse together into one giant sapphire canvas waiting for the sunset to be painted. *It has been a good week*, I think to myself. I have no idea what more is in store.

As I close the weeklong seminar the next morning, an announcement is made to the people in the audience: the following day is my birthday. I am surprised and a little embarrassed at the announcement as I had hoped that detail would slip under the radar. But the secret is out. A cake is rolled on stage, a song is sung (with all the harmony of a flock of crows), and a big smile comes over my face when I realize my wife, Sheryl, is behind it all.

Then a second announcement is given: there is a video to be shown. I think perhaps an anthology of the history of my company, but how shallow of me to go there. The video rolls, and I sit speechless and teary-eyed as I watch a thirteen-minute masterpiece featuring five years of magical moments with my two boys. Sheryl has assembled the video as a birthday wish from my boys who could not make the trip with us. The video is entitled "Welcome to Our Journey of Fun with Daddy."

The song accompanying the video is called "Before You Grow," by Dennis Scott and Timmy Tappan. Its lyrics describe a father confessing to his small boy that he'd like to become the best of friends, to get to know him well before time passes quickly and he's full grown.[60] The words penetrate my heart as the tape continues to roll.

*This is what life is all about.* I watch my small boys dancing and laughing as they run to and from the sparkling ocean waves. I laugh as my youngest son, four years old at the time, sinks a thirty-foot putt on the golf course near our home. I remember the day like it was yesterday. *These are the moments that make me feel alive.*

As the video concludes, I wipe my eyes once more. My heart is full. It feels healthy and strong—the way it should feel—and I want the feeling to last forever.

We all have them: magical moments. Moments where time seems to pass just right. Moments where our hearts are complete and we feel completely alive. Sometimes we're with our families. Other times we're with close friends or just our spouse. And sometimes we're alone in an inspiring, idyllic place. For some of us, the moments only rarely occur. For others, they occur more often. But regardless of the frequency, one thing is for sure: we never want to lose the feeling those moments provide because they remind us that time is invaluable when we know how to use it.

In his book *The Journey of Desire* author John Eldredge explains:

There is a secret set within each of our hearts . . . It is the desire for life as it was meant to be . . . You may not always be aware of your search, and there are times when you seem to have abandoned looking altogether. But again and again it returns to us, this yearning that cries out for the life we prize . . .

The greatest human tragedy is to give up the search. Nothing is of greater importance that the life of our deep heart. To lose heart is to lose everything. And if we are to bring our hearts along in our life's journey, we simply must not, we cannot, abandon this desire . . .

The clue as to who we really are and why we are here comes to us through our heart's desire. But it comes in surprising ways, and often goes unnoticed or is misunderstood. Once in a while life comes together for us in a way that feels good and right and what we've been waiting for. These are the moments in our lives that we wish could go on forever. They aren't necessarily the "Kodak moments," weddings and births and great achievements. More often than not they come in subtler, unexpected ways, as if to sneak up on us.

Think of times in your life that made you wish for all the world that you had the power to make time stand still. Are they not moments of love, moments of joy? Simple moments of rest and quiet when all seems to be well. Something in your heart says, *Finally, it has come. This is what I was made for!* [61]

## WHAT IS PRICELESS?

One of the most memorable ad campaigns of the last decade is the "Priceless" MasterCard ads that always end with the line: "Some things money can't buy. For everything else, there's MasterCard." You've no doubt seen them. The ads usually feature people like you and me spending specific dollar amounts on items like: *Two tickets to a baseball game: $24*; or *Two plane tickets to Paris: $2000*; or *Dinner at your favorite restaurant: $150*. And as each dollar amount is listed and we witness its accompanying scene, we begin to piece together an event that is taking place. Then the ads conclude. It's a scene of a father and son cheering at a baseball game, or a group of friends laughing over dinner, or a couple walking hand-in-hand along a white sand beach—all experiencing a memorable, significant moment in their lives. And then comes the tag line: *Celebrating your 40th birthday with the one you love: Priceless.* We watch, and as soon as that line is spoken, we feel it—that warm feeling deep inside. Maybe we even get a little glassy-eyed. Our hearts are moved because we have experienced similar moments—priceless moments.

What would *your* MasterCard ad look like? What are the magical moments in your life where everything seemed to come together and your heart was full? Where were you? What were you doing? Maybe you were with close friends, trekking all over Europe. Or eating and laughing for hours at your favorite restaurant. Or driving up the coast with the one you love without an agenda, the top down and warm wind in your hair. Maybe you were someplace with your kids . . . enjoying someplace they love, like Disneyland, or a big league baseball game? Maybe you were with your spouse or special someone . . . cuddling on a picnic blanket, staring at a mountain sky full of stars? Maybe the moments weren't planned and they just snuck up and grabbed hold of your heart unexpectedly? As Eldredge points out, they happen quite often that way. It is our hearts' way of saying, *I'm still here! This is what I long for. I'm showing you what makes me alive.*

There are no wrong answers to how or when or why heartfelt moments happen in our lives because only we can know what truly fills our hearts. We know when time has been well spent because our hearts tell us so. And the only difference between those who experience more of such moments and the rest of us is how they deal with the desires of their deepest heart. There are only two options: (1) we either continue to strive after them, arranging for more time to do what we desire, or (2) we grow complacent and resolve to be content spending time on something less than what our hearts desire. Enough of this and our truest desires eventually go dormant.

## We Only Regret Wasted Time

In the national best seller *Tuesdays with Morrie*, author Mitch Albom recounts a discussion between he and his dying mentor on their third Tuesday meeting. The discussion centered on regrets, and it teaches us a powerful lesson about the critical importance of following our true hearts in the time we have now, before it's too late.

The first time I saw Morrie on "Nightline," I wondered what regrets he had once he knew his death was imminent. Did he lament lost friends? Would he have done much differently? Selfishly, I wondered if I were in his shoes, would I be consumed with sad thoughts of all that I had missed? Would I regret the secrets I had kept hidden?

When I mentioned this to Morrie, he nodded. "It's what everyone worries about, isn't it? What if today were my last day on earth?" He studied my face, and perhaps he saw an ambivalence about my own choices. I had this vision of me keeling over at my desk one day, halfway through a story, my editors snatching the copy even as the medics carried my body away.

"Mitch?" Morrie said.

I shook my head and said nothing. But Morrie picked up on my hesitation.

"Mitch," he said, "the culture doesn't encourage you to think about such things until you're about to die. We're so wrapped up with egotistical things, career, having enough money, meeting the mortgage, getting a new car, fixing the radiator when it breaks—we're involved in trillions of little acts just to keep going. So we don't get into the habit of standing back and looking at our lives and saying, *Is this all? Is this all I want? Is something missing?*"[62]

Is there a life that you've been searching for? I'm not asking if you have some happiness in your life, or if you want to be successful, or even if you have more good days than bad—I'm asking if your life is the life you've always wanted.

Or is there still a yearning deep down for something else, something more, something greater? The truth is, we all have the yearning to an extent. It remains in our deepest selves, and though we often cannot put words to it, the longing seems to follow us throughout our days, attempting to guide us to invest our time in certain ways. The question is: will we heed its advice?

*We are designed for something more. Something more fulfilling, more rewarding, more enriching, more exciting.*

We *are* designed for something more. Something more fulfilling, more rewarding, more enriching, more exciting. And often our hearts are crying out for that missing element, that next step to achieve more of the freedom we desire.

"It is only with the heart," asserted Antoine de Saint-Exupery, "that one can see rightly; what is essential is invisible to the eye."[63]

## TIME AND THE SPIRITUAL HEART

Your spiritual heart is the epicenter, the soul of your most desired life. And like your physical heart, if neglected your spiritual heart will eventually stop beating; and your life will seem a dismal existence, an ambivalent passing of time until death. On the outside, you might continue to live a life of quiet desperation—going through the motions—but on the inside you will have expired, having given up your once high hopes of a beautiful life.

The resulting realities of a starving spiritual heart are just as disturbing as that of a starving physical heart. Most common are feelings of confusion, dissatisfaction, sadness, loneliness, anger, and resentment. Eventually, these lead to harsher realities like divorce, bankruptcy, depression, and God forbid, even suicide. The health of your spiritual heart is serious business—more serious than that of your physical heart.

Yet we still continue to suffer from spiritual heart dysfunction every year. Look at the statistics.

The majority of people are dissatisfied with . . .

*Their marriages:* The current divorce rate in the United States is about 60 percent.

*Their jobs:* In a national survey conducted by *Fast Company* magazine, 77 percent of respondents (all professionals) indicated that if money were not an issue, they would either quit their jobs or dramatically reduce their hours.[64]

*Their money:* The same survey conducted by *Fast Company* showed that the vast majority of respondents feel they don't make enough money to live a substantial, purposeful life. When asked to indicate the key factors that would help them achieve satisfaction and balance in their lives, 86 percent identified "making more money" as critical; and 70 percent of respondents said it would take no less than an extra $50,000 a year to achieve satisfaction and allow them to do what they really want to do.

*Their lives:* The *Fast Company* article concluded with these thoughts:

> For the moment—which is all that we can see clearly—most of us are prepared to embrace this precarious blend of wanting and having, of getting and spending, and to call it "balance." We believe that at some point, having "more" of something—more money, more self-knowledge—will change the game in a way that yields a new style of

work, a new way of life, and a new sense of personal freedom. Then at last, we will have it all.

In another national survey conducted by the Barna Research Group, 50 percent of all Americans say they are still searching for meaning and purpose in life, and 60 percent say they are generally skeptical about their lives. In responding to the survey results, founder George Barna said the following:

> The common solution [for a dissatisfied life] is to keep busy and to stimulate ourselves with a variety of new experiences—that way we are not so likely to feel the pain of those fundamental holes in our lives. People have discovered that if they fill the gaps with commitments and excitement, then they're less prone to feel the emptiness of loneliness and aimlessness. Of course, that just prolongs the inner despair that eventually cannot be suppressed any longer.[65]

Unfortunately, like the physical hearts of so many, the spiritual hearts of millions are withering every year. Too many people are dying for tomorrow rather than living for today. In the end, they miss life altogether because they don't make the connection between heart and hope. Hope suggests there is a better tomorrow, while heart instructs you to do something about it today. Hope is backed by faith, and there's nothing wrong with that in-and-of-itself. But heart is backed by action. Heart is the sure voice of hope that conveys to you what must be done with your time now in order to fulfill your truest desires.

*Too many people are dying for tomorrow rather than living for today.*

If we are to reclaim the lives we desire—on the job, off the job—we must not ignore our hearts' attempts to guide our use of time, even if what we are hearing is contrary to what we are hearing in our heads.

## RECLAIMING YOUR HEART
## . . . AND YOUR FREEDOM

What is it that your heart is truly beating for? That's what your time is meant for.

"The heart," said Blaise Pascal, "has reasons which reason cannot understand." Don't be surprised if there are moments when what your heart is saying doesn't seem attainable or even practical. The battle between head and heart is lifelong. But you must learn to trust that it's the heart, as Thomas Carlyle said, "that sees before the head can see." It is only our hearts, in other words, that hold the answers to the life we truly desire. It is our hearts that reveal what makes time matter. It is our hearts that show us the way to freedom.

What new choices do you need to make to how you are using your time? No one can make them for you. You choose to fill the minutes of your days. Those tasks either prohibit or promote the life you desire. Take an honest inventory. Is life a reflection of your uniqueness, your ardent desires—or are you on autopilot, just going through the motions, filling up time? "If your memories of the past are greater than your dreams of the future," my friend Bob Shank says, "you're already dead."

But if a voice deep inside is still telling you there's something more, something better, something worth striving for and fighting for, then there is still time to do something about it. There is still time to fight for, and win, your freedom.

Now is the time to begin. Now is the time to begin living the life you have been too busy to live. Your future is not some far off mystical dream. The look of your future is merely the culmination of your todays. Make today, and every day after, a masterpiece.

## EXECUTIVE SUMMARY

Your spiritual heart is the epicenter, the soul of your most desired life. And like your physical heart, if neglected your spiritual heart will eventually stop beating; your life will seem a dismal existence, an ambivalent passing of time until death. On the outside, you might continue to live a life of quiet desperation—going through the motions—but on the inside you will have expired, having given up your once high hopes of a beautiful life.

Ultimately, too many of us are dying for tomorrow rather than living for today. In the end, we miss life altogether when we don't make the connection between heart and hope. Hope suggests there is a better tomorrow while heart instructs us to do something about it today. Hope is backed by faith, and there's nothing wrong with that in-and-of-itself. But heart is backed by action. Heart is the sure voice of hope that conveys to us what must be done with our time now in order to fulfill our truest desires.

Our hearts show us the way to freedom.

If a voice deep inside is still telling you there's something more, something better, something worth striving for and fighting for, then there is still time to do something about it. There is still time to fight for, and win, your freedom.

# The Quota Trap
## Wasting Time Working Cheap

*"I started selling only what I knew worked, because I couldn't lie anymore—so my managers told me to either close more deals or find another job."*

— MATT COOPER

*"People who've been working for years are earning about the same hourly wage that fresh college graduates make without a day of experience."*

— TODD DUNCAN

I t was Ben Franklin who originally claimed that "time is money," and he understood something that's often lost in today's fast-paced marketplace—but not by everyone.

Visit a lawyer or mechanic and you'll see what I mean. You will exchange money for a service—but that's not all you're paying for.

Spend a few hours with a lawyer and you may receive a few legal documents and some official signatures, but when you get the bill, you will know that you're being charged for more than a few slivers of bark and a couple teaspoons of ink. You will know you are paying for the lawyer's time—more so, in fact, than for anything else.

Take your car to get that whistling sound fixed and you'll be charged for two things: the new parts the mechanic installs and his time. And I'm sure you know, the longer the work takes, the more you will be charged. That's because the mechanic's time is more valuable than the parts he installs. A mechanic understands that without his time, all you have is a whistling car and pile of metal parts. So he charges you according to the value he places on that time.

In essence, the lawyer and the mechanic understand that there is more to a business transaction than exchanging money for a product or service. There is also the exchanging of money for time. It's a truth many marketplace professionals need to be reminded of.

## TRADING TIME

The custom of trading has been around since the beginning of time. In fact, before currency existed it's how individuals obtained what they needed to live. If winter was coming and I needed some warm garments, I might offer you some crops from my field in exchange for a few furs. If you wanted a gift for someone and I was hungry, I might offer you a necklace of beads for a portion of meat. That was then.

Today, we might observe that society rarely trades on an individual level out of necessity. But that's only our observation if we don't consider time as a commodity.

Most of us would readily admit that time has *a* value. The problem is that we never really distill what that value is. Yet, when we look at time as a defined commodity—something that we trade for a negotiated return—we begin to understand the implications of spending it in unproductive or haphazard ways. I've found that many marketplace professionals trade their time for far too cheap a return.

## WHAT'S YOUR GOING RATE?

Have you ever thought about what your time is worth? The truth is that our hourly rate is already determined whether we know it or not.

It's a simple equation. Take the amount of money you've made over the course of the last twelve weeks and divide it by the amount of hours you've worked over that same period of time. The equation looks like this (you can fill in your own numbers here):

$$\frac{\$\underline{\quad} \textit{ (Total income for last 12 weeks)}}{\underline{\quad} \textit{ (Total hours worked for last 12 weeks)}} = \$\underline{\quad} \textbf{ per hour}$$

It does you no good to fudge your numbers. We're trying to maximize the value of your work time and that requires that you be completely honest about *all* the hours you invested in work, including time on the phone and Internet over the weekend and traveling time. It also requires you to be honest about the money you have *already collected*—not the money that *should* come in later.

When most marketplace workers I've trained tally their hourly rate they are surprised at how little they work for—especially when I give them something to compare it to.

Let's say you averaged working 70 hours a week for the last 12 weeks, which means you spent a total of approximately 840 hours working for the quarter. And let's say you made an average of $5,000 a month so that your income for the quarter was $15,000. Not horrible, right? But when you break it down into an hourly wage, it becomes clear that you're not exactly coming out on the good end of the deal.

When you divide your quarterly income ($15,000) by your quarterly hours worked (840 hours), you come up with an hourly rate of only $17.86/hour. To give you a frame of reference, according to CareerPrep.com, if you applied for a marketplace job fresh out of college last year you could expect to earn, on average, about $19.09/hour.[66]

It's unfortunate, but I've found that most swamped marketplace professionals work for somewhere between $10 and $20 an hour—even those who charge more money by the hour. In other words, people who've been working for years, sometimes more than ten years—people not just in their twenties and thirties, but their forties and even fifties—are earning about the same hourly wage that a fresh college graduate can make without a day of professional experience.

What does *your* current workload say about how you've been trading your time?

## Wasting Time Working Cheap

I've found that most marketplace professionals who trade their time too cheaply are doing so for one reason: the quota.

In yesteryear, the traveling salesman was a respected individual. It's what most men my grandfather's and father's age did for a career. There may have been mention of quotas back then—more as goals than requirements—but they weren't necessary. Steady competition, personal dignity, and family responsibility set the standards and inspired such professionals to trade their time for the greatest return.

Nowadays, personal and familial standards are much lower and distractions are aplenty. With competition, greed, and fear of job loss often the only forces compelling us to succeed, quotas can be used like whips on our backs driving us to produce a certain quantity of work but fooling us into ignoring the quality of our time. As a result, work standards hit the dirt, productivity takes on a deficient meaning, and we resort to desperate measures to make our numbers and keep our jobs. This was Matt Cooper's experience.

In a recent *Sales and Marketing Management* article, Erin Strout reveals Cooper's ugly discoveries about today's unrealistic expectations and how it ultimately affects our productivity.

> For Matt Cooper, the cost of earning up to $150,000 per sale was spending every day lying to his customers. It was the promise of huge bonus checks—not his $40,000 base salary—that lured him to join the sales force of a large, well-known Internet company two years ago . . . but what he didn't realize was that dishonesty was the price of admission. The New York-based start-up formed a big-deals team, a group that sold multimillion-dollar advertising campaigns to some of the world's largest companies. The sales force's key strategy? Do whatever it took to close those deals . . . "If you didn't lie you were fired," Cooper says. "It always came down to careful wording and fudging numbers."[67]

Cooper admitted to Strout that he was forced to lie nearly 100 percent of the time. Another rep working with Cooper confessed, "We might have sold all of our telecommunications inventory, but then another company would call to say they wanted to spend $50,000 on a campaign. What would we do? Book it, even through all the space had already been sold. When the numbers didn't come back as high as the customer expected, we'd just chalk it up to a bad campaign. We'd take anybody who was willing to spend a dime."

As a result of his deceitful tactics, Matt Cooper found himself on the receiving end of some serious threats. One customer whom he swindled out of more than $1 million began leaving him increasingly hostile messages. Eventually, the customer threatened his life. "He left a message saying, 'I know you're there. I'm going to find out where you live and blow up your house.'" According to Strout, Cooper never spoke to the customer again and left the sticky situation in the hands of the company. He also admitted that something similar happened a few other times.

Eventually, he couldn't take it anymore. Admitted Cooper to Strout, "I started selling only what I knew worked, because I couldn't lie anymore—so my managers told me to either close more deals or find another job." Essentially, they told him he was wasting company time. Cooper took the high road and moved on, chalking up the experience as a lesson learned.

Not so long ago, Matt Cooper's story would have been rare and disturbing. Today, it's commonplace. In fact, a survey conducted for the article by *SMM* and Equation Research revealed that 47 percent of marketplace managers suspect their employees lie during transactions. Is it merely out of their hunger for money and success that salespeople sink to such shameful tactics? It's easy to assume so, but the managers say no. According to the survey, "Seventy-four percent admitted the drive to achieve [unrealistic] targets encourages their people to lose focus." In other words, we often succumb to substandard strategies when our current practices aren't productive enough to meet our quotas.

## The Quota Quandary

Unfortunately, because quotas tempt us toward speedy (and sometimes seedy) working habits, they often make us counterproductive with our time. For example:

◆ Quotas may increase our pace, but they decrease our focus.

◆ Quotas may increase our exposure (as a business), but they decrease our effectiveness.

◆ Quotas may increase our quantity of completed tasks, but they decrease our quality per task.

◆ Quotas may increase your short-term production, but they decrease your long-term profitability.

Quotas are too often the driving force behind a marketplace professional's time-use strategy. The problem is that it can persuade us into thinking that *quantity* of completed tasks is the most important factor in success. This often compels us to ignore the quality of our work, which significantly decreases the value of our time over the long haul. Let me explain this further.

If a sales professional is motivated to meet a quota, he is often compelled to sell to any and everybody who comes along—whether or not they are a good fit. Like the furniture salesman who strategically shadowed two ladies to the back of the showroom hoping to catch them at the peek of their curiosity. He finally popped his head in at what he thought was an opportune time. He caught them alright—unfortunately, one was breastfeeding her child and the other was asking him if he was an idiot. As a result of continuing such haphazard and hurried selling strategies, this furniture salesman would end up with a majority of customers who never return or refer anyone else to him. Trapped, he would then have to rely on new business—on full-time prospecting—to achieve any degree of success. This will always mean more time spent for less business in return. It's a poor trade-off.

This is just one example from the marketplace. Your situation may be different but the fact remains: if we trade time for too cheap a return, we will remain caught in the trap of having to work more to achieve more success. However, this isn't the only way. When meeting a quota isn't the main motor of productivity, it's an entirely different story.

In her same article, Erin Strout spoke with Brett Villeneuve, the operations manager at Go Daddy Software who says that he purposely hires reps who are less money driven and more relationship oriented. Villeneuve understands that the highest value of a marketplace worker's time is not based on numbers. It is based on the total return for the time invested. For a business model, the equation would look like this:

**True productivity = All business received over time ÷ All time invested**

When we subscribe to this definition of productivity, we've taken the first step toward reaping the most value from our time. Ironically, in doing so, we also tend to decrease the pressure that a quota creates.

## GETTING MORE FOR YOUR TRADE

In the main chapters of the book, we freed up a minimum of four hours a day for you to work on your most productive tasks. It looks like this:

| Time | Monday | Tuesday | Wednesday | Thursday | Friday |
|------|--------|---------|-----------|----------|--------|
| 9:00 | Communication | Communication | Communication | Communication | Communication |
| 9:30 | Paperwork | Paperwork | Paperwork | Paperwork | Paperwork |
| 10:00 | Main Tasks | Main Tasks | Main Tasks | Main Tasks | Main Tasks |
| 10:30 | Main Tasks | Main Tasks | Main Tasks | Main Tasks | Main Tasks |
| 11:00 | Communication | Communication | Communication | Communication | Communication |
| 11:30 | Paperwork | Paperwork | Paperwork | Paperwork | Paperwork |
| 12:00 | Main Tasks | Main Tasks | Main Tasks | Main Tasks | Main Tasks |
| 12:30 | Main Tasks | Main Tasks | Main Tasks | Main Tasks | Main Tasks |
| 1:00 | Communication | Communication | Communication | Communication | Communication |
| 1:30 | Paperwork | Paperwork | Paperwork | Paperwork | Paperwork |
| 2:00 | Main Tasks | Main Tasks | Main Tasks | Main Tasks | Main Tasks |
| 2:30 | Main Tasks | Main Tasks | Main Tasks | Main Tasks | Main Tasks |
| 3:00 | Communication | Communication | Communication | Communication | Communication |
| 3:30 | Paperwork | Paperwork | Paperwork | Paperwork | Paperwork |
| 4:00 | Main Tasks | Main Tasks | Main Tasks | Main Tasks | Main Tasks |
| 4:30 | Main Tasks | Main Tasks | Main Tasks | Main Tasks | Main Tasks |
| 5:00 | | | | | |

We also admitted that having the time to be productive is one thing but *being productive* with that time is another—especially, in this case, when the constant pressure of quotas is involved.

Removing the burden of meeting a quota requires that we produce more in either the same amount of time we are currently working or, ideally, in less time. From an hourly rate perspective, here is what the before and after might look like if you only increased your income but kept working the same amount of hours:

## Before

$15,000 *(Total income for last 3 months)*
$$\frac{\$15{,}000 \text{ (Total income for last 3 months)}}{840 \text{ (Total hours worked for last 3 months)}} = \$17.86/\text{hour (Hourly rate)}$$

## After

$25,000 *(Total income for last 3 months)*
$$\frac{\$25{,}000 \text{ (Total income for last 3 months)}}{840 \text{ (Total hours worked for last 3 months)}} = \$29.76/\text{hour (Hourly rate)}$$

Most "time management" gurus will only show us how to accomplish a greater return from our time by teaching us the art of getting organized and focusing. This only decreases the amount of time we must work to produce the same income. For example, if you worked ten hours less per week over the twelve-week period, the results would look like this:

$$\frac{\$15{,}000 \text{ (Total income for last 3 months)}}{720 \text{ (Total hours worked for last 3 months)}} = \$20.83/\text{hour (Hourly rate)}$$

This is only one step in becoming more productive—one, in fact, that you've already taken in the previous chapters—but it's not the most effective step, nor is it the final step. That's because there's always a limiting factor involved. You. Even if you are the most organized, get-it-done, do-it-now person on the planet, there is still a limit to the amount of work you can complete in a given period of time. In short, your productivity will eventually plateau if all you do is get more focused and better organized. And if meeting a quota requires more than you can do in eight highly organized, strictly focused hours a day, you are still stuck working longer hours under constant pressure to perform. (And let's face it, we all know that most quotas are unrealistic and would be difficult to meet even if we were highly focused and organized.)

To this point, we've gone as far as most "time management" experts will take you—but we must go further to maximize the value of our time trade-offs each day. The only way this can happen is by increasing the value of what we receive for our time, or in other words, trading our time for a higher-valued return.

## GETTING MORE FOR YOUR TRADE

By trading your time for only the highest value returns, you can increase your income while decreasing your work time. It would be impossible and very time-consuming for me to give examples of how this plays out in every particular industry where it would apply. Fortunately, I've learned that when I teach how to accomplish this in the most common marketplace profession—the sales industry—the point still comes across to nearly every professional I've helped. So if you are not in a sales-related industry, don't worry. My suggestion is the same for you as it is for all the professionals I work with in other industries: insert yourself into the examples and advice I offer. For instance, you may be a CPA who doesn't necessarily sell anything in the generic sense of the term, but you still have customers whom you must service. In this case, see yourself as a seller of CPA services who must determine how to trade the time you invest in accounting for a greater return in business and time. Ask: how can I simultaneously earn more income and free up more time? The advice I am about to offer also works if you are an attorney or a physician or a business owner. Find yourself in the advice and alter the following examples to fit your particular profession. I believe it is possible for most every professional to trade his or her time for a greater return on and off the job.

Rich's story is a good example. He is a sales manager who heads a sales force of fifty-eight. For years he overlooked the value of teaching them to only pursue the top customers in their market. His salespeople weren't unskilled or underhanded, but they were taking a haphazard approach to selling, and as a result their investments of time weren't reaping the returns neither he nor they had hoped. Then he implemented a new training program to teach his people to spend the majority of their time prospecting and serving the most valuable customers in the market. In short, he taught them who to—and who not to—pursue. This one change in strategy immediately boosted his team's overall sales. Not only that, his team admitted they suffered far less stress and no longer felt the need to rush their efforts. They knew that the customers they spent time serving would eventually generate a greater return in repeat and referral business. After a few years, the difference was measurable. Sales had risen 300 percent, and no one was working overtime.

You can imagine how that changed the future of Rich's career. But consider how the simple change in strategy brightened the future of every one of his salespeople. Less stress, less pressure, less time at work . . . and *more* productivity. That trade-off is a no-brainer.

To realize the success that Rich's salespeople have, we should follow their same strategy. The steps they took and continue to take today are the keys to maximizing productivity while *minimizing* hours on the job. Here is how Rich's team of salespeople did it.

## TRADING TIME FOR TOP CUSTOMERS

There are four general categories that define all customers, no matter what industry you're in. When I shared these with one client named John, he made immediate changes to whom he prospected and in the following eight weeks received business from thirty-three new, quality customers. In order to begin trading your time for the highest return, you must define your *best* customers. Not everyone is worth your time.

## High maintenance / Low return

Customers who fit this description offer a low return for your time. They are very hard to serve because of unrealistic price and service demands and inefficient business practices. If you are a sales professional, it's obviously in your best interest to avoid trading your time with such people or businesses. Don't waste your time; it's more valuable than that.

## High maintenance / High return

Customers who fit this description have the potential to produce a lot of business but are very difficult to serve because of unrealistic price and service demands, inefficient business practices, and a high need for ego fulfillment. Generally speaking, these customers expect more than you can give them and don't relent until they get what they want. It's like high-end auto customers who want you to woo them for two months because they think they deserve it, then they haggle on price and threaten to take their business elsewhere if you don't comply with their desires. Don't waste your time. Instead invest time in the next two types of customers.

## Low maintenance / Low return

Prospects in this category have the potential to produce a smaller return but are likely to provide a greater return as the relationship grows. Furthermore, these individuals or businesses are easy to serve because of a high level of professionalism, a desire to partner with you, and efficient business practices. These reasons make them a wise invest-ment. My experience is that as you invest little bits of time consistently with these types of customers, the return will grow. They will begin to show their appreciation with return and referral business. A few years ago, my company finalized a seven-figure, multiyear contract with a customer we had been courting for over three years. They had given us a little business over that time, but we knew that once we established ourselves as trustworthy and capable of meeting their expectations, the value of the return would increase significantly—and obviously it did. The goal with low maintenance / low profit customers is to gradually move them into the final category. In a minute, we'll talk about an effective, time-sensitive strategy to accomplish this. First, let's discuss the final and most important category of customers.

## Low maintenance / High return

You should invest the majority of your time in this type of customer. They will trade you the greatest return for the smallest investment. That's because the customers in this category have one overarching commonality. A few years ago I sat next to Ken Blanchard on a plane back to our homes in San Diego, and he explained it this way. He said that the most successful professional relationships have a common "essence." In other words, both understand the purpose of the relationship, agree on the direction of the relationship, and share the same personal and professional values in order to grow the relationship. Relationships of this nature rarely fall into your lap. Most often, customers must be groomed and courted in order to receive their maximum value. But once they have given you business, the idea is to hold on to them for life. That's where your time trade-off is maximize

## GETTING THE FULL VALUE FOR YOUR TIME

Once you understand who is worth your time and then begin to pursue only those types of customers, there are four strategies you need to maintain in order to maximize the value of your working time.[68]

1. *Prequalify prospects before you pursue them.* You may be working from a list of prequalified leads, but you still should determine whether the people you call on are fit for an investment of your time before you call on them. This might mean relying less on your company's list and formulating your own. You have resources you may not realize. To begin your own list of qualified prospects, ask the question: *Who do I know who knows who I need to know?* All prospecting lists should begin with this question. My brother, Jeff, is a successful financial planner. For years he never considered asking me for referrals. Then one day we met and discussed his career. We devised several ways for me to refer him some clients. Within one week, he was doing business with the top salesman at a dealership where I've purchased two cars. You might be surprised at how many prospects you already have access to.

2. *Never call on a prospect unexpectedly.* A coworker named John gave me this piece of advice when I was starting out as a mortgage specialist and it always stuck with me. He told me that I should never call on a prospect that isn't expecting my call or that isn't excited to talk to me. In other words, if my prospects didn't know who I was or why I was calling, I was wasting my time calling them. There are many ways to warm up prospects before calling on them, but in my experience here are the most successful:

◆ Send a value-added approach letter that evokes a sense of curiosity and makes you memorable.

◆ Have a common friend, colleague, or coworker introduce you over the phone or in person.

◆ Have a common friend, colleague, or coworker arrange a meeting.

3. *Cut ties with time-consuming customers*. This includes ceasing to pursue high-maintenance prospects. If you find that you are already investing time in someone that fits that description, you need to cut ties professionally and with integrity. Use a script similar to this:

> Ms. Jones, I have spent some time evaluating my business and I have come to the conclusion that I cannot give you the level of service that you desire. Rather than modify my whole system, I'd like to thank you for your business (or time) and encourage you to find a vendor that can serve you the way you would like to be served.

It's perfectly normal if saying something like this to a customer strikes fear into you. It's not easy to terminate an unproductive relationship because no one likes confrontation. But if you are serious about maximizing your work time, you have to trade time for only the best customers. That will require you to stop trading time with people who take much and give little in return. Former faxaholic, Tim, is able to only work eighty days a year and still make great money because he only invests his time in serving the needs of twelve high-return customers who bring him all the repeat and referral business he wants. He used to serve fifty customers, and it made him very busy but not very productive. Fewer quality relationships are always more valuable and less time-consuming than many mediocre ones.

*Fewer deep relationships are more valuable and less time-consuming than many shallow ones.*

4. *Transition relationships into partnerships*. Most sales professionals I've worked with don't have any idea how much a customer relationship is worth over a long period of time. As a result, they typically

invest more time in new relationships instead of current ones. It's a terrible trade-off. Thomas knows this, and it's why he is one of the best sales professionals I know. He works for Fletcher Jones Motor Cars in Newport Beach. I travel over ninety minutes from where I live and pass six dealerships selling the same cars to give my business to him because he knows the value of a lifetime customer and it keeps me coming back. Here's what Thomas knows.

### His Typical Auto Customer

| | | |
|---|---|---|
| A. | The average commission amount | $1,000 |
| B. | Number of sales per buyer every three years | 1/3 |
| C. | Revenue per year (A x B) | $330 |
| D. | Client life cycle | 20 years |
| E. | Client value over life cycle (C x D) | $6,600 |
| F. | Average client referrals per year | 4 |
| G. | Value of client referrals per year | $1,320 |
| H. | Revenue if first-year referrals close and reach life cycle | $26,400 |

| | |
|---|---|
| **Total Lifetime Value of One Auto Client (E + H)** | **$33,000** |

It doesn't look like much to lose. But what if you missed out on this value with every customer because you were too busy trying to secure new business? Then what would you lose? If you failed to receive the full return from only ten new car customers in one year, you would miss out on $330,000 over the course of twenty years. Or if you failed to go deeper with say two hundred customers over the course of a year, that amounts to $6.6 million lost over twenty years or $330,000 a year. If you want to have more freedom, you don't want to miss out on the full value of business relationships.

The most productive time you can trade as a sales professional is in deepening high-return customer relationships. A few years ago, a sales client named Linda began following this philosophy, and now she has one particular customer who accounts for about $750,000 in business revenue *every month*. Do you think she'd rather spend the time dealing with fifty customers who give her that return? When the right customers are on your side, you don't need many to achieve a high degree of success. This is why Linda only works about thirty-five hours a week.

I'm not suggesting sales professionals should never prospect. What you should see is that prospecting is not the *best* investment of time, and the most successful salespeople—those who spend the least amount of time earning the most amount of money—are the ones who have transitioned from an acquisition-based business to a retention-based business that only invests time in prospecting when

- ◆ Entering a new market
- ◆ Expanding business
- ◆ Replacing customers who have run full cycle or moved on

Once you know your customers well and have built trust with them, transitioning to retention-based partnerships will not be difficult; in most cases customers welcome the change because it represents a greater benefit to them.

That said, there are four sure-fire steps to transition business relationships into lifetime partnerships and begin reaping a greater return in business and time from your time investments.

1. *Take inventory.* Who are your best customers? Who gives you the greatest return for your time? Who are the accompanying players—the customers who give you a good return for your time but not as often or as much as the best customers? And which customers have the potential to give you higher returns with small investments of time over

a longer period? Rank them according to their level of importance in three tiers, with the number of customers in the top level accounting for 60 percent of your business, the number of customers in the second level accounting for 20 percent of your business, and the number of customers in the third level accounting for 20 percent of your business. If you currently have twenty customers, here's what it might look like:

| Client Ranking | % of Your Total Revenue | # of Customers |
|---|---|---|
| VIP Level | 60% | 4 |
| Premier Level | 20% | 6 |
| Standard Level | 20% | 10 |

2. *Determine the amount of time you will invest on a regular basis back into your three levels of customers.* It's important that you are proactive about trading your time with current customers because it will eventually alleviate the need to prospect and free up a lot of your time. The Pareto principle suggests that about 80 percent of your business comes from the top 20 percent of your customers—in this example, that means the top ten customers. Therefore, it makes the most sense for you to invest 80 percent of your time back into these top ten customers and give the remaining 20 percent to the customers in the Standard Level in an effort to raise them to a higher level over time. Using the example above, if we take the four hours a day that we freed up with your dam, the strategy breaks down like this:

| Ranking | % of Revenue | # of Customers | $ Invested Back | % of Time to Invest |
|---|---|---|---|---|
| VIP Level | 60% | 4 | 15% of revenue | 60% (144 mins/day) |
| Premier Level | 20% | 6 | 10% of revenue | 20% (48 mins/day) |
| Standard Level | 20% | 10 | 5% of revenue | 20% (48 mins/day) |

I realize that the allotted time to invest each day may not seem like a lot, but you have to understand that you won't invest time in every customer every day. The idea is to set up a regular contact schedule that tells you who to invest time in each day, week, or month.

3. *Determine your annual contact plan.* Set up your contacts with customers strategically so that you are fostering deeper relationships that will lead to a continual stream of repeat and referral business. This will eventually eliminate much of the up-front legwork. You can create your own schedule based on how much prospecting you need to do and how many customers you currently have, but in general here are my suggested parameters for regular contact with each level (it is best if these meetings are informal and are conducted away from the office):

◆ For VIP Level customers, you should invest a minimum of two hours every month in face-to-face time, shaping and evaluating the goals of your partnership and deepening your relationship.

◆ For Premier Level customers, you should invest two hours every quarter in a face-to-face meeting, and five more thirty-minute meetings (phone or face-to-face) over the course of the year, for a total of nine.

◆ For Standard Level customers, you should invest two hours in a face-to-face meeting once a year to discuss the goals of the partnership, then thirty minutes every quarter in informal meetings over the phone or face-to-face.

The goal of a regular contact schedule is to grow your relationships in each level so that, eventually, you are receiving steady repeat and referral business from each customer. It should be noted that these scheduled time investments do not include necessary calls or meetings for the purpose of discussing referrals and sales—those you should schedule as they arise, letting them replace scheduled prospecting time.

With four hours a day to invest in current customers (and four more hours to use for necessary communication and paperwork), you should have plenty of time to do what you need to do.

Remember that if you still need to spend time prospecting at this point in your career, you should insert prospects into the bottom levels until you have enough customers to occupy all your time. Be careful not to rely on prospecting for too long—there will come a certain point when you have to wean yourself off the prospecting bottle and rely on your system of partnerships for your highest return. Pursuing retention business is a much better and smaller investment of your time than trying to rely on acquisition. The basic weaning formula is to invest your scheduled time each day with current customers and their referrals, and then invest any time left over in prospecting until you are receiving enough business from current customers to occupy all your time.

4. *Finally, cast your vision to your customers.* Obviously, you need your customers on the same page with you for all of this to work. On an individual basis, schedule face-to-face meetings (over meals or coffee is okay), and take the following approach in the meeting:

◆ First, let them know how much you appreciate their business and desire to continue serving their needs by developing a mutually beneficial partnership.

◆ Second, share how you desire to add value to them—with their direction.

◆ Third, ask them to help you determine how the two of you can compose a mutually beneficial partnership based on the specifics of what they will receive from you and what you will receive from them.

Keep in mind that if you've been treating your customers poorly, this may not be well-received initially. If that's the case, instead of trying to force this on your customers, show them your intentions by investing your time in them for two months without asking for anything in return. Then when you've established a better rapport, move forward with a partnership planning meeting.

## A MORE ENJOYABLE RIDE

When Brent, my writing partner, was learning to guide the Klamath River, he told me that initially he didn't enjoy having a full raft. It put more pressure on him and made his mistakes more pronounced. But the more proficient he became and the more confidence he gained, he realized that having a full raft was the best ride of all. More smiles, more laughs, and more satisfied rafters meant more fun and fulfillment for him. Furthermore, when he had the right people in the raft, it was much easier to guide.

I realize that all of this—or a big part—might be entirely new. Don't let yourself get overwhelmed. These steps are easy to implement and easy to maintain once you get the hang of it. Like Brent's experience guiding the Klamath, you may lack confidence at first—and that's normal. But once you get to a place where all your customers (or individuals you service) are on board with you, your ride down the river will take on new meaning and offer a much grander potential. In fact, if you maintain the dam we built in the previous chapters and follow the strategies we've discussed in this chapter, eventually three things are likely to happen.

◆ You will be more productive with your main work tasks.

◆ Your income will either stay the same or increase.

◆ You will work less to maintain the previous two.

When you begin to invest time in the right tasks *and* the right people, you will soon find that eight hours a day is more than enough to maintain a high degree of success on the job and free time off the job. Many clients my company has had the pleasure of serving are living proof. The vast majority are now working an average of thirty to forty hours a week and taking anywhere from six to twenty weeks of vacation a year.

When any of us know *how* to spend our work time and with *whom* to spend it, our careers will no longer flood our days with stress and drown out the other important things in our lives. In fact, with the right strategies, our careers can be the catalyst that helps us create the life we desire. I challenge you to go for it while you still have time.

# Executive Summary

Most marketplace professionals trade their time for far too cheap a return, and it's often a result of that often unreasonable, and almost always inefficient, standard success we call the quota.

Because quotas tempt us toward speedy (and sometimes seedy) working habits, they often make us counterproductive with our time. For example:

◆ Quotas may increase our pace, but they decrease our focus.

◆ Quotas may increase our exposure (for a business), but they decrease our overall effectiveness.

◆ Quotas may increase our quantity of completed tasks, but they decrease our quality per task.

◆ Quotas may increase our short-term production, but they decrease our long-term profitability.

The problem with a working strategy reliant on numbers is that it can persuade us into thinking that *quantity* of work is the most important factor in success. This often compels us to ignore the quality of our work, which significantly increases our work time and, in turn, decreases our freedom. Removing the time-sapping burden of a quota requires that we produce more, in either the same amount of time we are currently working or, ideally, in less time.

Most "time management" gurus will only show us how to accomplish a greater return from our time by teaching the art of getting organized and focusing. By nature, this decreases the amount of time we must work to produce the same return. It is one step, but it's not the most effective step. The better way is to increase the value of what we receive for our time. This will allow us to work less and either sustain our current return or increase it.

# NOTES

1. According to studies conducted by Building Champions™. For more information on the DISC model, visit http://www.discprofile.com/whatisdisc.htm
2. Used with permission from Building Champions © 2003.
3. All figures based on a five-day week and a forty-six-week year.
4. According to productivity expert David Allen in his book *Getting Things Done* (New York: Penguin Books, 2003).
5. Story shared by an anonymous contributor to the Monster.com Web-based archive titled *The Accidental Salesperson*.
6. Joe Robinson. *Work to Live* (New York: The Berkley Publishing Group, 2003), 27–28. Robinson is citing Joan Williams in her book *Unbending Gender: Why Family and Work Conflict and What to Do About It* (New York: Oxford University Press, 2001).
7. I am indebted to my friend Brian Tracy for his research on these two surveys, which are reported in his book *Time Power* (New York: Amacom, 2004), 228–29.
8. For the full report titled "Missing Millions: How Companies Mismanage Their Most Valuable Resource" see www.proudfootconsulting.com/documents/10959-UKMM1002PFV3.pdf
9. I am indebted to Brian Tracy and David Allen for their insight on using similar filing systems.
10. If you don't know how to set an auto-response for your e-mail address, an IT professional in your office or through your Internet service provider can help you do this.

11. My description of the scene is an adaptation of two versions of *The Lord of the Rings: The Return of the King* (2003) screenplay offered by Noora at http://legomirk.com/lotrscript2003/part1.html and a contributor to www.seatofkings.com. The story was originally written in book form by J. R. R. Tolkien in 1938 and adapted for the screen by Peter Jackson, Fran Walsh, and Phillip Boyens.

12. I attribute this phrase to John C. Maxwell in his book *The 17 Indispensable Laws of Teamwork* (Nashville: Thomas Nelson, 2000).

13. Poll commissioned by the Center for a New American Dream and conducted in August 2003 by Widmeyer Research & Polling of Washington, DC. This information is based on a nationally representative telephone study of five hundred American adults. The margin of error for the poll is +/- 4.4%.

14. William Hepworth Dixon, *The Story of Lord Bacon's Life* (London: John Murray, 1862).

15. Paul Andrews, "Saving Time No Longer a Tech Reality," *Seattle Times*, October 20, 2003.

16. Jon Swartz, "Is the Future of E-mail Under Cyberattack?" *USA Today*, June 15, 2004.

17. According to a *WIRED* magazine news report titled, "Viruses Cost Big Bucks," June 18, 1999. This report can be found at www.wired.com/news/technology/.

18. As reported on *Entrepreneur* magazine's Web site, www.entrepreneur.com, in a piece titled, "Viruses Cost Billions," April 23, 2003.

19. Paul Davidson, "Do-not-spam Registry Could Result in More Spam, FTC Says," *USA Today*, June 15, 2004.

20. Michelle Conlin, "Take a Vacation from Your BlackBerry," *BusinessWeek,* December 20, 2004.

21. Brad Stone, "Your Next Computer," *Newsweek*, June 7, 2004.

22. Copyright 2003 Switchfoot. From their Platinum album *The Beautiful Letdown*, Columbia/Red INK, 2003. *Lyrics written by lead singer Jon Foreman.

23. John Cook, ed., *The Book of Positive Quotations* (Minneapolis: Fairview Press, 1997).

24. E. D. Hirsch Jr., Joseph F. Kett, and James Trefil, eds., *The New Dictionary of Cultural Literacy*, 3rd. (Boston: Houghton Mifflin Company, 2002).

25. Ecclesiastes 5:18

26. I Kings 3:5, 7, 9

27. I Kings 3:12–13

28. I Kings 10:23–25

29. All information from the passage in I Kings 10:14–29.

30. Ecclesiastes 2:11

31. Ecclesiastes 2:17

32. Ecclesiastes 5:10; 4:6

33. Ecclesiastes 8:8

34. Ecclesiastes 1:2

35. Survey published by the U.S. Dept. of Health and Human Services, the Centers for Disease Control and Prevention, and the National Center for Health Statistics, Hyattsville, Maryland, July, 2004.

36. Statistic from GlobalChange.com and are excerpted from *The Truth about Drugs*, by Dr. Patrick Dixon. London: Hodder, 1998.

37. Proverbs 6:9a, 10, 11a

38. Proverbs 6:6–8

39. These statistics are as of 2000 and were first reported in my book *Wealth Strategies*.

40. Information is based on an interview conducted in 2000 with Jeff Duncan, a top producer for Lincoln Financial.

41. Ecclesiastes 4:7–8a, 9a, 12

42. John D. Drake, PhD, *Downshifting* (San Francisco: Berrett-Koehler Publishers, Inc., 2000), 100.

43. Proverbs 11:14b

44. John Cook, ed., *The Book of Positive Quotations* (Minneapolis: Fairview Press, 1997).

45. Proverbs 3:13–17

46. Proverbs 20:5

47. Barrie Greiff and Preston Hunter, *Tradeoffs: Executive, Family, and Organizational Life* (New York: New American Library, 1980). As cited by John D. Drake, *Downshifting* (San Francisco: Berrett-Koehler Publishers, Inc., 2000), 9.

48. Al Gini, *My Job My Self: Work and the Creation of the Modern Individual* (New York: Routledge, 2001), 2.

49. "Bring Back the Eight-Hour Day," © Charlie King/Pied ASP Music-BMI. From the album *Inside Out*.

50. To paraphrase Joe Robinson in *Work to Live* (New York: The Berkley Publishing Group, 2003), 25.

51. Joe Robinson, *Work to Live* (New York: The Berkley Publishing Group, 2003), 20–21.

52. Ilene Philipson, *Married to the Job* (New York: The Free Press, 2002), 19–20.

53. Al Gini, *The Importance of Being Lazy* (New York: Routledge, 2003), 32.

54. Ilene Philipson, *Married to the Job* (New York: The Free Press, 2002), 124.

55. On page 125, Philipson is citing from an interview conducted by Arlie Hochschild in her book *The Time Bind: When Work Becomes Home and Home Becomes Work* (New York: Owl Books, 2001).

56. According to statistics provided by authors Jared Brenstein, Heather Boushey, and Lawrence Mishel in *The State of Working America 2002/2003* (New York: Cornell University Press, 2003).

57. Further notes on the survey can be found at http://www.newdream.org/live/time/timepoll.php.

58. Al Gini in *The Importance of Being Lazy* (New York: Routledge, 2003), 5. Gini is citing Benjamin Kline Hunnicutt, "A Fast-Paced Look at the Whirl and Flux of Modern Life," *Chicago Tribune*, September 19, 1999, Books, 8.

59. Joe Robinson, *Work to Live* (New York: The Berkley Publishing Group, 2003), 18–19.

60. "Before You Grow" written by Dennis Scott and Timmy Tappan © 1992 Act IV Music SESAC/Music Match Inc. BMI

61. John Eldredge, *The Journey of Desire* (Nashville: Thomas Nelson, 2001), 1–3.

62. Mitch Albom, *Tuesdays with Morrie* (New York: Doubleday, 1997), 64–65.

63. John Cook, ed., *The Book of Positive Quotations* (Minneapolis: Fairview Press, 1997).

64. From the article entitled "How Much is Enough?" *Fast Company* magazine, July 1999.

65. Provided by the Barna Research Group online at www.barna.org.

66. For the full report see the September 2003 issue of the *Career Choices* newsletter on www.CareerPrep.com.

67. Erin Strout, "To Tell the Truth: Call It What You Like: a Fib, an Untruth, a Fabrication. A new SMM survey reveals that nearly half of all salespeople may lie to clients. Are you creating a culture that promotes deception?" *Sales and Marketing Management*, July, 2002.

68. For a time-effective prospecting strategy, read chapters 9 and 10 in *High Trust Selling*.